A Handbook for Writers of English
Punctuation, common practice and usage

Unprovided with original learning, uninformed in the habits of thinking, unskilled in the arts of composition, I resolved – to write a book.
Edward Gibbon 1737–1794, English Historian,
author of *The Decline and Fall of The Roman Empire*.

A Handbook for Writers of English

Punctuation, common practice and usage

John G. Taylor

INDUS
PUBLISHING COMPANY

A Handbook for Writers of English / John G. Taylor

Indian Edition 2004 published by
INDUS PUBLISHING COMPANY
FS-5, Tagore Garden, New Delhi-110027
Tel.: 25151333, 25935289
mail@indusbooks.com • www.indusbooks.com

Original edition published in English by
How To Books Ltd., UK, under the title of:
A Handbook for Writers of English

Copyright © 2002 John G. Taylor

This edition published by arrangement with
How To Books Ltd., UK

For sale in India, Nepal, Bhutan, Pakistan, Sri Lanka and Bangladesh

ISBN 81-7387-159-0

All rights reserved. No part of this work may be reproduced
or stored in an information retrieval system (other than for
purposes of review) without the express permission of
the publisher in writing.

Note: The material contained in this book is set out in good
faith for general guidance and no liability can be accepted for
loss or expense incurred as a result of relying in particular
circumstances on statements made in the book.

Printed at B.B.N. Printers, Najafgarh Road Indl. Area, New Delhi

Contents

Preface	xi
Acknowledgements	xiii
About the author	xiv

1 INTRODUCTION — 1
- Punctuation – the devil's own rules? — 1
- Article or lecture? — 1

2 THE BASIC ELEMENTS — 3
- The sentence — 4
  - Sentence connectors — 6
  - The fragment — 6
- Paragraphs — 7
- Style — 8
- Spelling — 9
- Terminology — 9
- Layout — 11
- Proof marking — 11
- Postlude — 12

3 PUNCTUATION AND USAGE — 13
- INTRODUCTION — 13
  - Key — 13
- ABBREVIATIONS — 14
  - a. Abbreviations, acronyms and titles — 14
  - b. Abbreviated words — 15
  - c. Common mistakes — 16
  - d. Measures — 16
  - e. Other — 17
- AFFIXES — 17
- AMPERSAND [&] — 17
- APOSTROPHE ['] — 17
  - a. Possession — 18
  - b. Omission — 20
  - c. Other — 20
- ASTERISKS [*] — 21
- BRACKETS [ ] — 22
  - a. Editorial notes — 22
  - b. Secondary level parentheses — 22
- BULLETS AND LISTS — 22

v

CAPITAL LETTERS	23
a. Days, months, periods	24
b. Nationality, language, religion	24
c. Personal titles	25
d. Geography	26
e. Institutions and academia	26
f. Publications	27
g. Other	28
COLON [:] (See also semicolon)	29
a. Lists and examples	29
b. Speech	30
c. Dividing a sentence	30
d. Date and time	31
e. Business salutations	31
f. References	31
g. Other	31
COMMA [,]	31
a. Some general observations	32
b. Lists	32
c. Speech	33
d. General points of clarity	33
e. Separating phrases and clauses	33
f. Interjections	35
g. Dates	36
h. Numbers	36
i. Omissions	36
j. Salutations, etc.	37
k. Other	37
DASH [–]	38
a. Dashes – a typographical note	38
b. The dash	39
c. The spaced dash	40
d. The en rule	41
e. The em rule (M-dash)	42
f. The double em rule	43
DATES	43
a. Current date	43
b. References to dates	43
c. Years	44
d. Periods	45
e. Other	45
DEFINITE ARTICLE, (the)	46
Singular or plural?	46
ELLIPSIS [...]	47
EXCLAMATION MARK [!]	47

a. Following exclamations	47
b. Emphasis	48
EXTRACTS	48
FOOTNOTES AND ENDNOTES	49
FULL POINT (FULL STOP, PERIOD)	49
a. Sentence	50
b. Abbreviations	50
c. Numbers	50
d. Parentheses	51
e. Quotations	51
f. Other	51
HEADINGS AND TITLES	52
Levels of headings	53
HYPERLINKS	54
HYPHENATED AND CONJOINED WORDS	55
a. Hyphenated words and the spell-checker	56
b. Compound words	56
c. Compound modifiers	57
d. Place-names, routes	58
e. Numbers	58
f. Time	58
g. Compass points	58
h. Colloquial and other phrases	58
i. Titles, occupations	59
j. Clarification	59
k. Other	59
HYPHENATION (SOFT)	60
INDEFINITE ARTICLE ('a')	61
INVERTED COMMAS	61
ITALICS	62
a. Emphasis	62
b. Titles	62
c. Names	62
d. Latin and foreign terms	62
MANUSCRIPT: STRUCTURE AND LAYOUT	62
a. Journal articles	62
b. Books	63
MEASUREMENTS	65
NUMBERS	66
a. Numbers generally	66
b. Decimals	67
c. Percentages	68
d. Fractions	69
e. Formulae, E-notation	71
f. Proportions and ratios	71

####### g. Monetary and financial units — 72
####### h. Roman numerals — 72
####### i. Page numbers — 73
####### j. Periods — 73
####### k. Digits or text? — 73
####### l. Ranges — 76
####### m. Other — 76
PAGES — 77
PARENTHESES [( )] — 77
####### a. Explanation — 77
####### b. Clarification — 77
####### c. Style — 78
####### d. Parentheses in lists — 78
####### e. Braces — 79
PLURALS — 79
PREFIXES AND SUFFIXES — 80
####### a. Prefixes — 80
####### b. Suffixes — 82
QUESTION MARKS [?] — 83
####### a. Questions — 83
####### b. Editorial questions — 84
QUOTATIONS — 85
QUOTATION MARKS [" ", ' '] — 85
####### a. General usage, typing — 85
####### b. Quotes within quotes — 86
####### c. Nested quotes — 86
####### d. The single quotes (apostrophes) — 87
####### e. '. or .' – where to place the full point — 87
####### f. Prime and double prime — 88
REFERENCES — 89
ROMAN NUMERALS — 89
SEMICOLON [;] (See also colon) — 90
####### a. Dividing sentences — 90
####### b. Lists — 90
####### c. Clauses — 90
####### d. Expressions — 91
SENTENCE CONNECTORS — 91
SLASH/BACKSLASH [/, \] — 92
####### a. Forward slash — 92
####### b. Backslash — 92
SORTING — 93
SPELLING — 93
####### a. Unrecognised words — 94
####### b. Foreign letters and symbols — 95
####### c. Misspelt words — 95

	SYMBOLS	96
	TENSES	97
	TIME	97
	TYPEFACES AND FONTS	98
	a. Typefaces and PCs	99
	UNDERLINING (Underscoring)	100
4	**REFERENCES AND BIBLIOGRAPHIES**	**101**
	a. Reference lists	101
	b. Books	102
	c. Articles in periodicals	104
	d. Papers etc. in anthologies	105
	e. Chapters in books	105
	f. Papers: numbered series	106
	g. Papers (unnumbered)	106
	h. Institution or organisation etc. as author	106
	i. Acts of parliament	106
	j. Legal cases	107
	k. Other printed material	107
	l. Unpublished material	107
	m. The Internet	107
	n. References in the text	108
	o. Dates	110
	p. References in footnotes and endnotes	111
	q. Sorting your own records	112
5	**CHARACTERS AND SYMBOLS**	**114**
	a. Typographic symbols	114
	b. Pre-programmed symbols	116
	c. Paragraph symbols	120
	d. The Greek alphabet	120
	e. Mathematical symbols and notation	121
	f. Statistical symbols and notation	123
	g. Other symbols	124
6	**TABLES**	**126**
	Table design	127
7	**STATISTICS**	**130**
8	**METRIC CONVERSION**	**133**
9	**COMPOUND GROWTH RATES**	**136**
10	**CURRENCIES AND PRICES**	**138**

11	**ABBREVIATIONS**	**140**
	a. Upper and lower case	140
	b. The full point	140
	c. Single letter abbreviations	141
	MEASURES (Abbreviations)	141
	a. Imperial and other UK measurements	142
	b. Metric measurements	142
	ORGANISATIONS	143
	BRITISH ACADEMIC TITLES	146
	COMMERCIAL ABBREVIATIONS	147
	OTHER ABBREVIATIONS	148
12	**PREFIXES**	**155**
13	**SUFFIXES**	**176**
14	**HYPHENATED AND CONJOINED WORDS**	**182**
15	**UK ENGLISH vs US ENGLISH**	**213**
16	**NATIONS OF THE WORLD**	**216**
	a. Official names	216
	b. CIS (USSR)	219
	c. The USA	220
	d. Other	221
17	**FOREIGN TERMS AND PHRASES**	**222**
18	**PROOF CORRECTION**	**228**
	a. Proof marks	228
19	**INTERNET ADDRESSES**	**231**
	a. International addresses	231
	b. Hyperlinks	232
	c. Information on the Internet	232
20	**REFERENCES**	**234**
	a. Dictionaries and handbooks	235
	b. Electronic dictionaries	237
	c. Encyclopædia	239
	d. Statistics	239
	e. General references	239
	f. British Standards Institution Publications	240
APPENDIX		**241**

Preface

Handbook for Writers*: A guide to punctuation, common practice and usage.* Well, that's exactly what this book is intended to be – a handbook, something to have at hand. Frequently, when translating or proofreading, I am required to check something, possibly a metric conversion, the use of the colon, an abbreviation, hyphenation, the format for an unpublished work (a thesis for example) in a reference list, even the correct name of a country. It appears to me that much of the information for which I have frequent use *is* available, *but* in a number of different handbooks. This publication aims at providing all *essential* information in a single handbook. You will find certain points are repeated in several places. The colon, for example is treated under that section, but also under 'dates and time'. This emphasises the point that a handbook is not intended to be read from cover to cover. Rather, it should be consulted as the need arises. Even then, do not look for rules. Common practice and usage relate to custom. Not all customs die hard: they can change quite quickly in this TV-age. I may possibly have overseen some useful elements and, indeed, you may find grounds for comment,[1] but hopefully there will be a second edition.

This seems the appropriate place to emphasise the fact that this handbook is a guide: it is not a set of hard-and-fast rules for references, layout, or punctuation, and not least, hyphenation. You will certainly find usage not mentioned here, or which may even appear to contradict certain examples. My objective has been to show what is permitted. If you think something else may also be permitted, then I will not argue with you, just as long as you are consistent. That is what your publisher (and the reader) expects you to be.

When asked, authors of best-sellers often claim that the idea for their latest masterpiece came to them in the bath, or on the bus, or while mowing the lawn. In fact, Agatha Christie once said that the best time for planning a book is while you are doing the dishes. I had no such immediate flash of inspiration. Rather, this is the culmination of twenty years' experience as a proofreader and translator. During this time I became increasingly aware of the need for a handbook, not only for the student struggling with his thesis but also for the professional person requiring to write an article, paper, or treatise. Grammar books are found in profusion, as are guides to punctuation aimed at the school pupil or students of English as a foreign language. Hopefully, this publication will also be of interest to these striving souls, but here we are essentially concerned with those of the writer facing the proverbial 'publish and be damned'.

---

1 Contact me on john@jgtaylor.com I will acknowledge all suggestions and possibly include them in the next edition.

Collins Dictionary defines punctuation as 'the use of symbols not belonging to the alphabet of a writing system to indicate aspects of the intonation and meaning not otherwise conveyed in the written language. Chambers Dictionary defines grammar as: 'the science of language, from the points of view of pronunciation, inflexion, syntax and historic development; the art of the right use of language by grammatical rules'. The message portrayed through our writing is determined by syntax – the grammatical structure of a sentence.

As these definitions imply, grammar and syntax change over time following developments in common practice and usage. I have therefore included comments on several elements of writing which fall under the heading of grammar and syntax more so than punctuation, for example, use of the definite and indefinite article, plural forms (group nouns), and more. Finally, the presentation of our argument or thesis will stand or fall on the structure and layout. A brief discussion of headings, footnotes, extracts and references seems appropriate here. I have also added some notes on tables and descriptive statistics. Far too frequently when reading an article, not just a proof, I encounter a paragraph comprising statistics and data which could so conveniently have been wrapped up in a table. And far too frequently these tables lack competent presentation – a layout that catches the eye and draws attention to the *principal* data.

The first notes for this book were originally written using WordPerfect 5.2 (an indication of how long I have been assembling material). There is no doubt about the user-friendliness of this program – several of my clients used it until quite recently. I have deliberately retained some information about WP5.1 and 5.2 as I suspect a number of users of this guide still have files stored away in this format which may need to be recalled and converted.

Acknowledgements

This book is the result of the inspiration of many clients. My work as a proofreader and translator brings me into contact with a wide range of subjects and papers written by an even wider variety of authors.

I am frequently asked by clients to recommend a reference guide to English punctuation. I must confess that I, too, frequently had need for such a guide. Over several years I had accumulated notes with the intention of piecing them together some day into such a book. Not only would these provide a handy reference for myself but also provide opportunity and encouragement for me to scrutinise carefully my own punctuation and grammar.

Special thanks to Bill Mulholland, a fellow-suffering translator, for virtually rewriting an early text and editorial comments; to Andy Evans, a well-known psychologist, whose comments were medicine to the patient; and to Laima, for encouragement and endless cups of coffee. Gratitude is also expressed to the series editor without whose advice I would never have got this far.

About the Author

John Taylor was born in London in 1937. Originally destined for a career in music, he studied piano, timpani and double bass at the Royal Academy of Music. His first degree, a BA at the University of Reading incorporated music and economics. He then became a professional jazz musician, but discovered that economics was more lucrative. He became a teacher of English as a Foreign Language while studying at the London School of Economics. Studies at LSE led to an MSc (Econ.) and involved research, and ultimately a post in Norway. In Norway, he lectured in Local Government and later engaged in further research at Odense University in Denmark. But the mountains beckoned and he returned to take up a position at a county planning office in western Norway. He returned to Oslo to a new teaching post, this time in statistics and computing. His familiarity with economics and local government resulted in commissions for proofreading and translation for government departments, research institutions and local authorities – something which had occupied his spare time from 1973. This became a full-time occupation in 1989, one that enables a seasonal migration of work place to his summer cottage in the forests of eastern Norway. He is also a court interpreter and translator for the Oslo City Justices and the Norwegian Directorate of Immigration. He still turns out an acceptable blues on the piano!

1
Introduction

PUNCTUATION – THE DEVIL'S OWN RULES?

John where James had had had had had had had had had had had the teacher's approval.

Remember this schoolboy 'howler'? With appropriate punctuation this forms a logical sentence. I remember my teacher taunting us with a similar one. Apparently a sign-writer had been employed to paint a sign for 'Smith and Jones Ltd'. Upon completion the boss had one small criticism: *'There's too much space between Smith and and and and and and Jones.'*

I have deliberately not punctuated this and place the ball in your court. However, the footnote provides the solutions.[1] I am sure the point about punctuation will be readily appreciated.

The Archbishop of York once said: 'Intellectually, spelling – English spelling – does not matter.... Intellectually, stops [the period] matter a great deal. If you are getting your commas, semicolons and full-stops wrong, it means that you are not getting your thoughts right, and your mind is muddled.' (*The Observer*, 23 Oct. 1938.) In support of his argument the Archbishop also pointed out that Shakespeare spelt his own name at least four different ways (but he always got his punctuation right!).

Nowhere does the Archbishop, and certainly not Shakespeare, mention the *rules* of punctuation. Neither, to my knowledge, is there to be found a book with such a title. Rather than rules as such, punctuation reflects the traditions of style. But even that is to simplify. Can we talk about a single style of academic writing, or the style of paperback writers? To each his own! Robert Benchley is attributed with saying 'It took me fifteen years to discover I had no talent for writing, but I couldn't give it up by that time as I was too famous.' Most of us can't afford to wait that long to find out.

ARTICLE OR LECTURE?

I have become increasingly aware of the qualities of the different types of articles and papers I am required to read. Some are clearly designed as a lecture, implicitly if not explicitly. There is a difference between the spoken word and the written word. This also implies that when *reading* the text which is to be *spoken*, the punctuation may have to be adjusted accordingly In contrast to the written text, the delivered lecture is history as soon as a statement is proclaimed. The listener is rarely taken up with what *has been* said, rather, with what is *currently* being declared. Tone and emphasis readily replace many punctuation marks, but it is here the reader of literature requires assistance. Consider the following:

> Mr Smith said Mr Jones is a master of English.
> 'Mr Smith,' said Mr Jones, 'is a master of English.'
> Mr Smith said, 'Mr Jones is a Master of English'.

The latter example also emphasises the point that Mr Jones (and not Mr Smith) is an academic, as well. I will not dwell on this point, but the three examples illustrate the need for clear punctuation.

However, punctuation is only a part of the story. The ultimate aim of most authors is not to present a thesis on the English language: it is to present an article which stimulates and retains the interest of the reader in the subject matter. That occasional missing comma, that amusing tie-pin error, will all be overlooked if the article is structured and presented in such a way as to convey a message clearly.

Perhaps my message is that a clear and consistent use of punctuation, spelling (e.g. *-ise, -ize*), text and so forth, is the essential element in preparing a publication. The book has yet to be written which does not contain a dubious sentence. While many sections in this guide contain examples of recognised 'good' and 'bad' usage, there are a few areas where 'specific rules' are hard to find. Look at the section on hyphenated words, for example. I think most will agree that consistency is the key to acceptance.

The title 'common practice and usage' is an indication of the broader content of this guide than punctuation alone. Here are few 'rules' as such. The rule of today is the exception of tomorrow. My examples are drawn from a wide range of texts – books (fiction and non-fiction), articles and magazines. As such they will show a variety of uses and styles. Indeed, what I have considered to be common practice may differ from the experience of others. But this is also the sign of the living language. If you really consider there is a preferred way to punctuate a sentence in order to convey a specific meaning but I have not recommended it, then I would not dispute your judgement. It is indeed the very flexibility of the English language that enables the writer to develop his own style although as a concluding remark we may well heed the words of Sydney Smith (1771–1845), a clergyman and essayist: 'In composing, as a general rule, run your pen through every other word you have written; you have no idea what vigour it will give to your style.'

1 John, where James had had 'had', had had 'had had'. 'Had had' had had the teacher's approval.
'There's too much space between "Smith" and "and" and "and", and "Jones"'.

2
The Basic Elements

When we are writing something, a letter, an article, a thesis, perhaps a note or a description, we are *communicating* something to someone. Even if it is a reminder to ourselves, the message has to be clear and incontrovertible. Three elements of writing help us to achieve this aim: punctuation, grammar and syntax.

Punctuation is more easily understood when the function of the sentence construction is appreciated. The way in which your sentence is constructed and punctuated, the manner by which sentences are grouped into paragraphs and so forth, are some of the elements of style. If the sentence is grammatically correct, the meaning will become clearer. The way in which the words of the sentence relate to each other – the syntax – (in other words, the logical structure of the sentence), is an integral part of grammar.

The first draft of this book included a number of grammatical terms which were questioned by the proof editor. Using the search words 'grammar' and 'glossary', I discovered how much has changed since my A-level English days! The adjectival noun (the 'poor' get poorer) is rarely mentioned as such in the standard texts. But then, I cannot recall learning about phrasal verbs either. A colleague at the University of Sheffield maintained that the development of the language was being accompanied by the development of the grammatical glossary. Witness indeed: comma splice, dangling modifier, fused sentence, trite expression (all from the Internet). I will refer just to the basics – and only where absolutely necessary.

It may be appropriate to emphasise that the material here is not only the result of experience in correcting manuscripts but also the study of the material given in the references. Of course, no two books are the same, not even when issued by the same publishing house. One example is the abbreviation for Reverend. The modern style is to drop the full point after Mr and Dr, for example. So why not Rev? The *Oxford Dictionary for Writers and Editors* gives Revd – no full point. The *Oxford Dictionary of Abbreviations* gives Rev or Rev. (with or without a full point). *Collins Electronic Dictionary* gives Rev. (with a full point) whereas *Collins Abbreviations* (paperback) gives Rev (without). The same applies to *Cambridge International Dictionary* and *Cassells Dictionary*. *Chambers* allows Rev or Rev. When we look at the 'Right Reverend', both *Collins* and *Chambers* give Rt Rev., Cambridge uses Rt. (full point) as does *Cassells*. I haven't even begun on the US dictionaries.

I should add a note here about the use of the term 'full point'. The Oxford English Dictionary, no less, defines a full stop as follows: full stop. The end of a sentence; the single point or dot used to mark this; a period, full point.

We note that alternative terms are 'period' – now mainly US English, and 'full point'. I wonder if Carey (1976) whose book *Mind the Stop* was first published in 1939, would have given it the title *Mind the Full Point* if he had written it today. Roberts (1987) apparently prefers just 'point'. Another term is 'end stop' (Burt, 2000) and which applies to the full stop, exclamation mark and question mark. This omits the full stop used for abbreviations although Phythian (1980) refers to the full stop in connection with abbreviations. The *New Oxford English Dictionary* states 'full point' to be another term for 'full stop' (although it is not given in the *Oxford Dictionary for Writers and Editors*. However, *Hart's Rules for Compositors and Readers at the University Press Oxford* does use this term, also in conjunction with abbreviations. So I am in good company when I choose this term.

If you are intending to have your work published, check the *Guidelines for authors* issued by the publishing house. They will prefer certain uses of punctuation signs and format for references. This book is very largely based on actual examples, even though the text may have been changed. The variety of usage suggests a choice; it also emphasises the need for consistency. Oscar Wilde once said: 'Consistency is the last refuge of the unimaginative', and in the words of the parodist, Horace Smith (1779-1849), 'Inconsistency is the only thing in which men [subst. writers] are consistent'. Most publishers would probably agree with Wilde, while simultaneously nodding their heads resignedly at Smith's comment.

And so! This book will hopefully assist you in certain aspects of preparing your manuscript but you may well profit from an excellent book in the *How To* series: *Improving Your Written English* by Marion Field. If you are a bit 'rusty' on grammar, you will certainly find some gems in the references in this publication.

We can commence by considering some of the basic elements of our manuscript.

THE SENTENCE

The major error made by most authors is a sentence which is too long. Indeed, in one of the books listed in the references, I read that the full point is the only punctuation sign which is not over-used! The occasional short snappy sentence rouses our senses; the abnormally long one dulls our concentration. If your sentence is more than three lines on an A4 manuscript page, look at it and check for punctuation. If it is more than four lines, look at it even more closely and check for punctuation and argument. If it is more than five lines, check for punctuation, argument and logic. More than six lines? Well, you should probably rewrite it.

I could have written the above paragraph as one sentence using commas, semicolons and colons. It is all based on the same subject so that would not have been difficult. But try reading the following:

THE BASIC ELEMENTS

The major error made by most authors is a sentence which is too long: if your sentence is more than three lines, then look at it and check for punctuation; if it is more than four lines, look at it even more closely and check for punctuation and argument; if it is more than five lines, check for logic as well, and if it is more than six lines then you should probably rewrite it.

We have probably just about reached all a reader can absorb in one breath.

I have mentioned the number of lines rather than the number of words. Most texts recommend an *average* of 14 to 18 words per sentence. (This chapter has a mean of 15 words per sentence.) But that does not say much about the length of the longest sentences. Some texts recommend a maximum of thirty words but, as the above example shows, it is erroneous to think that a long sentence may be broken up by the use of a colon. The subject of the sentence may get lost in a myriad of separators. The colon and semicolon, and also the dash, have specific functions and should be used with discretion.

Sometimes a sentence can become too 'wordy'. Frequently the phrase containing 'of' may be rewritten. 'Lots of' may (should) be replaced by 'many', for example. But also other expressions may be written more concisely:

> Considerable doubt has been expressed concerning whether the Minister's series of fiscal actions during the crisis actually had the level of public support that he vociferously maintained to be the case!

– meaning:

> The economic situation raises questions concerning support for the Minister's actions.

We appear to have lost reference to *the level* of support. But that is surely implicit in the rewritten sentence. Thomas Jefferson once said: 'The most valuable of all talents is that of never using two words when one will do.' This does not mean to say we should seek out every phrase or clause and reconstruct it with fewer words. As the author, you should ask yourself whether you feel that you have managed to convey precisely what was intended to be said. Now put yourself in the place of the reader and ask what the written word conveyed to you.

It is not always the length of a sentence but the variation. That long, demanding sentence, the short, sharp witticism, that arresting punctuation mark! This is the stuff of the novel, the drama – and the academic thesis. At least, it ought to be. Here is an extract from Kingsley Amis's[1] book, *The King's English!*

> There is a feeling here and there that the spelling of such words with an X is somehow classier, richer in history, *better* than spelling with CT that everybody

---

1 The 'pronunciation rule' prompts me to write Amis's book rather than Amis' book!

naturally adopts. Pfui! Everybody is often wrong, but not this time. The philological evidence is dubious and no one has yet succeeded in introducing even the ghost of an X into important by-forms like *connecting, connective* and indeed *connect*. Go on writing *connection* and the rest and treating *connexion* and the rest with the tolerant indifference they deserve.

Now, there is no doubt that Amis is a bit long-winded here. But he intends to be. The longer sentences demand concentration. The short sentence or fragment (see below) arouses it. Here are 87 words, 5 sentences; mean 17.4 words. The distribution is 31, 1, 8, 28, 19. The Mean Deviation (an expression of the variation about the mean) is 10.3 words. (See Chapter 7, Statistics.)

It is, of course, hardly necessary to statistically analyse a work in this way. The point is: 'Does the text flow?'. It is the variety of short and long sentences which assists in keeping the reader's mind focused on the content. A mean length of 14 to 18 words per sentence seems to be acceptable, but bear in mind the significance of the short sentence in arresting the reader's attention. If ninety-five per cent of all sentences were in this range for the mean, then the style would be cramped.

Modern word-processors provide a character and word count, and even the mean length of sentence. One or two professional programs give a detailed analysis as above. Rather than analysing the material *post facto*, your reader's interest will be sustained by the considered use of connectors, fragments, and, not least, the terminology.

Sentence connectors

Sentence connectors assist the flow of an argument, but terms such as 'however', 'nevertheless', and others, are frequently overdone. There are quite a number of alternatives to these, which are discussed further under Sentence connectors (see page 81).

The fragment

A fragment is an incomplete sentence. Amis's exclamation, 'Pfui!', is a good example. Used with discretion the fragment is a useful element in style – something to arrest the reader's attention. Overdone, it destroys the essence of style. Even the most 'academic' articles can easily become 'dry' with such phrases as:

> It was hardly surprising that the fifth congress failed once again to reach an agreement on CO^2 gases since the agenda did not explicitly refer to these.

But a fragment can rouse the drooping reader.

> The fifth congress failed once again to reach any decision on CO^2 gases. Hardly surprising! The agenda did not specifically refer to these.

The (very) occasional *pièce de résistance* in French or Latin perhaps, gives a little resuscitation to a tired text. (See Chapter 17, Foreign words and phrases.)

PARAGRAPHS

Whereas the sentence is a statement, the paragraph is a connected train of thought related to a single idea or set of ideas. Normally, the subject of the matter under debate will be mentioned or implied in the first sentence of the paragraph. In other words, the first line should not employ 'he, they' etc., unless it is absolutely clear from the last few lines of the previous paragraph who is being referred to. It is disconcerting for the reader to have to glance back to see who 'it' or 'these' are.

There is no prescribed minimum or maximum number of sentences which may comprise a paragraph. Even if the same theme is under discussion for a page or more, it is often convenient to provide occasional breaks in the text. This improves the visual appearance and enables the reader to consolidate his thoughts and comprehension. The end of the sentence provides space to breath: the paragraph provides a stage where one may collect one's thoughts. Generally, a maximum of 10–12 lines is to be recommended.

The paragraph extending over half a page or more has the psychological effect of warning the reader that he had better have his wits about him to follow the line of argument which will occupy the next few minutes of his time. The occasional short paragraph of three or four lines also provides variety to the layout. Even so, too many short paragraphs can hinder the absorption of an argument and can give the impression of too many ideas being juggled. The reader will have to sort these out in order to establish some order in the train of thought (either the author's or his own). On the other hand, the occasional lengthy paragraph of 15–20 lines provides some 'body' to the text.

It is possible to calculate the mean number of lines per paragraph from the word-count feature. But this is of little importance. Take the psychological approach and look at the visual presentation. Are you satisfied? Then the reader probably is too.

A typographical point. Double line spacing between paragraphs can give the appearance of a disjointed style. Try with the 1.5 line spacing or even set your word-processor to 1.3 line spacing. This gives a pleasing effect. In Microsoft Word this spacing between paragraphs is achieved by using the 'Format' command on the menu bar, and selecting 'Paragraph'. Set 'Spacing before' to 0, and 'Spacing after' to half of the point size used. For example, if you are using Times Roman 12, set the 'Spacing after' to 6. You may set this as the default.

Many printed publications do not use a blank line between paragraphs but require the first word of each paragraph to be indented two spaces (as here). This does not apply to the leading paragraph at the commencement of a chapter which is flush with the left margin. Neither does it apply to the first paragraph under a table or diagram. A table or diagram should preferably be placed at the end of a paragraph and not in the middle unless the page layout really forces this. In other words, a large amount of 'white space' would result because there was not sufficient room on the rest of the page for the placement of the table.

STYLE

Whereas correct punctuation is the key to grammar, the correct use of grammar is the essence of style. By this stage it should be clear that sentence construction is an essential part of style.

When we write an article, a thesis, a book or even a note, we are attempting to communicate – to get our message across. Correct grammar and precise punctuation will greatly assist this mission, but writing a book entitled *The Confessions of a Cabaret Artist,* designed to be purchased at a railway terminal for light reading during travel, will be directed towards an entirely different reader than an article on *Eighteenth Century Musical Instrument Makers in Schleswig-Holstein.*

Style will vary according to whether one is writing a business letter, contract, academic paper, newspaper article, text book, novel etc. Again, the text book may be designed for school pupils or post-graduates. There are nevertheless common elements of style. A useful account of these is contained in Phythian (1998).

Common elements does not mean to say 'rules': there are no 'rules' of style. Of course, if everybody wrote in a similar style, then reading would soon become boring, irrespective of the subject. Vocabulary can be the hallmark of the author, but interpretation and even bending the norms will characterise the author's particular style. But we should not bend the norms so much that the reader becomes confused by a profusion of commas and semicolons. Once he has become distracted by ambiguity his interest will lapse, and so will your chances of being recognised as an outstanding writer within your field!

Style is more than humour, more than a mastery of the language. It is also more than a presentation of ideas and development of an argument. It is a combination of all these and has to grip the reader and retain his interest. If your book has not been accepted for publication, style may be the main culprit. The publishing house will be tolerant towards a few punctuation errors, providing these are not swarming like a plague of locusts; it will even assist in pointing out those few lapses in grammar. But style is your responsibility, and yours alone. It is not something which is learned from a book but rather *acquired* through writing, and reading and absorbing the style of others.

That does not mean to say there are few useful tips on acquiring a style to your writing. Consider the following, for example.

A parliament may be defined as a formal conference or council for the discussion of some matter or matters of general importance. In Britain, it is the highest legislative authority, consisting of the House of Commons (which yields effective power), The House of Lords and the sovereign.

This paragraph builds upon definitions selected from the *Oxford English* and *Collins* dictionaries. Whether we remember this tomorrow morning, or even this evening, is another matter. It lacks style. But consider:

A parliament may be a permanent national convention, or at least so intended, but is more frequently a temporary assemblage of persons eventually succumbing to constitutional delimitation, the frustrations of the electorate, or the impatience of the generals. In fact, a parliament is 'nothing less than a big meeting of more or less idle people!' (Bagehot).

Humorous though this may appear, the latter definition still contains an element of truth. The sequence in the above definition develops and explains the concept, culminating in an outrageous declaration. That's what I call style.

SPELLING

Frequent surprises will be revealed by the spell-checker.[2] First, the spell-checker is not without its faults. Even so, think twice before dropping the unusual word straight into the waste bin. But beware! The spell-checker will detect that *airmailletter* was misspelt (should be *airmail letter*), but will fail to detect *air mail letter, air-mail letter,* and *airmail-letter* as being erroneous. Neither will it detect that *air-ship* should be *airship*, nor that *air strip* should be *airstrip* and *air conditioning* should be *air-conditioning* (see Chapter 14).

Hyphenated words can be a headache (or should that be head-ache?), and a discussion of these is given in Chapter 3, Hyphenated and conjoined words. There are a number of electronic dictionaries available (see Chapter 20) which are useful aids. We can state here that the use of the hyphen will vary from one dictionary to another, but at least you will have a guide to consistency.

TERMINOLOGY

When proofreading I do encounter some strange terms. Of course, every subject has its own jargon, but my rule of thumb is that if it is not found in the *Oxford English Dictionary* or *Encarta*, it probably does not exist! At least, not at that point in time nor in normal usage.

---

2 In English we would carry out a spell check. It is correct to write spell checker in UK English, but I have found that the US form spell-checker is also encountered in English.

But language is a living science and new words are being born by the day and by the hour. We may all find ourselves playing the role of a *neologist*. Recently I encountered a phrase expounding the *attractivity* of something or other. Naturally, I though the author meant *attraction*, or even *attractiveness*. Could the sentence be turned around to make the subject *an attraction*? There was something or other which appealed in the term, and I realised that as soon as the author had defined or justified the use of the word, it was very appropriate *in that context*. (After all, we do have *perceptivity* in the language!) A similar situation arose when one of my clients referred to *multiculturality*! Somehow this was more appropriate in the given context than *multiculturalism*! The suffice –ity, means 'a state of', whereas –ism relates to a doctrine or practice.

New words may be invented; others may be given new, flexible definitions. Flexibility is indeed an element of style. You may be surprised at what has already found its way into print. Take a glance at *The Oxford Dictionary of New Words* (1998). But it is your responsibility to ensure the reader understands your definition of a word. At the end of the day you are the author, and you take the final responsibility for your product. The proofreader will assist you in the general presentation, grammar, punctuation and style, even layout, typefaces, fonts and compilation of a table of contents and an index – the latter often being a matter of familiarity with the word-processing[3] program. The aim of the following is to assist you in presenting your material in a lucid and logical manner such that the audience readily appreciates and understands your message and, however 'heavy' the subject matter, enjoys your approach. Remember that you, yourself, know the subject matter of what you are writing or talking about. Your readers and listeners may not. You have to convey it to them.

In assembling material for this book I have also looked at what others have assembled. The list of references contains many of these (see Chapter 20). Somewhere along the way I realised that the books which were most enlightening were those written by practising authors, possibly more so than those by practising teachers. But, to be fair, the latter were catering for a different market. I have previously mentioned *The King's English* by Kingsley Amis. Amis has written a couple of dozen best-seller novels and a dozen or so non-fiction works. While *The King's English* is neither a grammar book nor a guide to punctuation, there is so much to learn from the sheer joy of reading this text.

Possibly the ultimate guide to punctuation is Eric Partridge's *You have a point there*. First published in 1953, we can note that customs and habits have changed. But the twenty-eight pages (no less) devoted to the comma alone, and thirteen to the semicolon contain many words of wisdom and not a few words of caution.

---

3 Originally two words. Now mostly hyphenated, but even found conjoined.

These texts are at the top end of the scale – even for the doctoral candidate in the history of the English language. But all of the books mentioned have pointed to one thing: Punctuation is not fixed, rigid and inflexible. Punctuation is what makes the text clear, lucid, intelligible – and stimulating. Nobody should insist absolutely that a comma and nothing else is correct. *You* are the writer – it is your book – you know what you want to say. Well say it, and make sure you say what you mean. If someone comes back to you and says 'well, I was sure that what you meant was...', and it wasn't, then you had better look at your punctuation too. If you are in doubt about the punctuation, then hopefully the present book will help.

A final comment might be to cite the immortal words of Lewis Carrol. 'When I use a word, it means what I choose it to mean – neither more nor less'.

LAYOUT

It may be surprising to some to know that as much time can be used for formatting and layout as on the actual proofreading. Changing typefaces/fonts, adjusting tables, ensuring all titles and sub-titles are correctly labelled in order to generate the index, are time-consuming exercises. Avoiding split tables may necessitate moving these to another place in the text, tabs may have to be reset, fonts changed, and so forth. Generating and checking the Table of Contents demands a thorough check that headings and subheadings have been correctly formatted throughout the text.

PROOF MARKING

Correcting a proof for the typesetter used to be a demanding exercise. The PC has changed all that and we are now largely responsible for our own manuscript and the wise man will always seek the advice of a colleague. But beware! Asking a colleague to 'just glance through this will you, when you get a moment', is a rather vague request. He may be an expert in the subject area but not necessarily an experienced writer. I frequently receive manuscripts which have been 'checked' (by a colleague) – but for what I do not know. Foot-and-mouth disease perhaps. Better to engage a professional who, while not being familiar with the subject content, is an expert in the language and who has no reservations about pointing out the many bloomers! It should nevertheless be remembered that the professional proofreader should correct the grammar, but this does not mean that an illogical sentence (which the proofreader does not understand) suddenly acquires clarity and meaning. Perfect grammar and syntax does not mean a publisher will welcome your work with open arms.

Many will have seen the standard proofing marks used by editors. These are rather daunting. My experience is that one can suffice with a selection of these as summarised in Chapter 18.

It may be appropriate to conclude this section with a few comments about publishing – more precisely about having your work rejected. Now, if it is rejected a frequently stated reason is that 'the material does not fit into our publishing programme'. Nonsense! 'Where there's muck, there's money' – as the adage goes. But your manuscript was probably so mucky that it was politely rejected. Of course, a few comments with the appendage 'Resubmit' is considerably more positive. But when this is conditioned by 'text needs to be tightened up', or similar, this means something more than 'reduce the number of words'. Thus, rather than cutting out chunks of text, it really means 'say what you mean in fewer words; come straight to the point'. And if the point is not made having been given this lifeline, you may well be advised: 'Having re-read your manuscript, we feel it is not appropriate to this journal. We wish you luck in bla, bla, bla!'

Your proofreader should be sufficiently versed in the language, editing procedures, the language of editors, the skills of 'tightening up', and so forth, that he can assist in getting your manuscript published. But remember, you are the master (or mistress) of the house, you know the subject matter, you know the jargon. So does the editor in all probability. The proofreader does not. You do your job, and he will do his. I would like to say that the final responsibility is with the author, but in reality it is a joint effort. You can even sell wool to a sheep if it has been properly carded!

POSTLUDE

postlude [music]: a final or concluding piece or movement.

I often wonder whether the authors of many of the manuscripts I read really have read their own material as a 'normal reader'. Who is a normal reader? Probably anyone who buys the book! Criticism is always hard to take – self-criticism even harder. But the normal reader is not a critic of the grammer, punctuation or the occasional spelling mistake. He may be expected to be a strong critic of the content, its meaning and clarity. When comunication is established between the written word and the reader's mind, it is like listening music. The occasional wrong note might even be amusing. Were *you* really irritated – in fact did you even notice – that 'grammar' and 'communication' in the previous lines were misspelt?. Did you react to the full point following the question mark? Did I forget the preposition 'listening *to* music'? Like Kingsley Amis, you might say 'pfui!'.

You will find some mistakes in this book, although no more *deliberate* ones. The intention of the following is to help us set our libretto to music. I trust the occasional wrong note will do no more than change the chord and not result in a discord.

3
Punctuation and Usage

'If you want a silver medal, you should not write to the head of the country on such a piece of paper and with mistakes.' Nicolai Sych, head of education in the region of Vologda, reacting to a Russian schoolgirl's letter to President Putin in which she failed to capitalize one letter and missed an exclamation mark. [Quoted in *Newsweek, 3.7.2000.*]

(The major mistake, apparently – reported elsewhere – was to omit the exclamation mark: 'Dear President Putin!')

INTRODUCTION

Punctuation is quite explicitly defined in most dictionaries, as for example:

> ***marks used to organize writing:*** *the standardized non-alphabetical symbols or marks that are used to organize writing into clauses, phrases, and sentences, and in this way make its meaning clear* (Encarta Dictionary).

Hardly to be disputed. But there are many more conventions – usage – which, when incorrectly applied, may fail to make the meaning clear at best, or result in ambiguity or obscurity at worst. It is with this thought in mind that I have included *usage* in this section with the aim of including all those points which the writer may encounter in presenting his book, thesis, article or paper. All the examples shown as correct usage are based on actual extracts (although the editor of this series pointed out that several were, in fact, incorrect. They have either been removed or pointed out as erroneous). Reference has been made to a number of dictionaries: Cambridge International, Cassells, Collins, Chambers, Longmans, Penguin, New Oxford English Dictionary (NODE), and others. Several US dictionaries were also consulted.

KEY

▶ A new point! I have found that this symbol is preferable to numbering each point a), b), or i), ii)...etc.

In the examples, the **preferred** use is indicated as follows:

✓ The dash – although infrequently used – is a useful substitute for parentheses.

Examples of the **misuse** of punctuation symbols are indicated:

✗ The dash should not follow:- a colon before a list, after 'e.g.', a comma or full point.

Other illustrative examples are given in Arial typeface.

13

ABBREVIATIONS

Chapter 11 contains a summary of the most frequently encountered abbreviations.

Generally, it appears that the full point is considered superfluous in many instances. Times are also changing. In general, the full point is far less used today than previously in abbreviations. The *Concise Oxford Dictionary* (4th edn, 1954) gives T.T. for teetotaller (and tuberculin tested). In the 7th edition (1982), TT (no full points) is given for both as is also the case in the *Oxford Dictionary for Writers and Editors* (2000). *Collins Abbreviations* does not use the full point at all. I do not think that many editors would accept this.

While the context will normally clear any confusion, it is important to retain the full point to distinguish between certain abbreviations such as I.B.M. (Intercontinental Ballistic Missile) and IBM (the computer company, International Business Machines Corporation).

Important components to the I.B.M. were manufactured by IBM.

IBM is also an abbreviation for 'The International Brotherhood of Magicians', who are not particularly known for their involvement in missile production.

▶ A common error with abbreviations is to use a full point where it is not required, or to omit one. As a general rule a full point is used where the final letter of the abbreviation differs from that of the whole word, for example Rd (Road), Ave (Avenue), Sq. (Square), Str. (Street). But this is an area where there is an increasing trend to omit the full point altogether.

A. Abbreviations, acronyms and titles

▶ Abbreviations for institutions, organisations and other bodies do not normally use full points: UN, EFTA, EEC, IBM. An acronym is a word derived from the initial letters of the words incorporated, and pronounced as spelt! Example: NATO, BAMMO (Battered and Maltreated Mistresses Organisation).

▶ Titles no longer employ full points although this was common previously: Mr., Mrs., etc. This actually broke with the 'rule' that abbreviations concluding with the final letter of the unabbreviated form do not need a full point. These have nevertheless gone today and appears logical when we encounter Revd (for Reverend), and also Rev. But we will also encounter Rev (without a full point), likewise Rt Rev and Rt. Rev. (with full points).

It is now quite common for honours such as OBE, DSO, etc. not to use full points.

The full point may be found on more formal documents: Ph.D., M.Sc.(Econ.) etc., but PhD, MSc etc. are widely used. The full point is normally retained in names: J. G. Taylor. But even here the practice is less widespread than previously (J G Taylor).

French used to require M. (for monsieur) but here also we encounter M, Mme and so forth, again without the full point.

▶ Organisations and bodies such as the EU, NATO (also Nato) do not use full points.

▶ All correct.

✓ O.K., o.k., or OK

✗ Neither Ok nor 'ok' are o.k.

'okay' is not accepted by *The Authors' and Printers' Dictionary* (OUP), but is okay by *NODE*, *The Cambridge International Dictionary* and US dictionaries.

B. Abbreviated Words

▶ A full point is not used for:
  – cardinal points (S, NE)
  – elements (Al, Mg)
  – metric measurements (km, m) (see C below)
  – mass in scientific use (oz, lb)
  – currencies (DM, p)
  – plurals do not normally use a full point: hrs, mins and so forth. The journey takes 2 hrs 3 mins, arriving at 4.30 p.m.

▶ Upper case M is sometimes preferred for million to distinguish from m (metres). However, note that M is also the Roman figure for 1000.

▶ References to nationality, when abbreviated, are not obliged to use a full point:

The participants included M. leClerc (Fra), Herr Staffenbaum (Ger) and Sir Snoddley-Scratchit (Eng).

▶ Latin words tend to retain the full point: et al., et seq., etc. Note that cf. is derived from the Latin 'to confer'; cf (without a full point) means 'cost and freight', while c/f is an auditing term meaning 'carried forward'. However, eg is now also encountered as well as e.g., although your spell-checker may still react. The same applies to ie (and i.e.). I prefer to stick to the points.

We may note here that Latin terms and abbreviations do not require italics where they are in everyday use: ibid., op. cit., but *ipso facto* (by virtue of the fact), *loc. cit.* (at the place cited) and *sic*[1] are less frequently encountered, and therefore normally italicised.

---

1 Nearly always placed in square parentheses [*sic*].

▶ Abbreviated phrases tend to use the full point, c.i.f. (cost, insurance, freight), but this is also less common than previously and cif will be encountered. Similarly, we find both f.o.b. and fob (free on board), plc (public limited company), etc. *R.S.V.P.* is frequently encountered as RSVP (*répondez s'il vous plaît*). AKA (also known as) was previously written as an abbreviation [a.k.a], but now appears to be an accepted word as in 'Jones AKA "Jones the Bones" was found guilty', and is pronounced as spelt. The lower case version is also found: Reg Green, aka 'veg'.

▶ Words, other than those relating to measurement, reduced to a single letter normally use a full point: b. (born), d. (died), f. (female), m. (male, married, month). (See Chapter 11, Abbreviations – measures.)

▶ Generally, the plural of an abbreviated word does not require the full point: (ed., eds), but eds. with a full point is certainly not uncommon. Note that ch. (chapter) has chs as the plural form. The abbreviation for typescript is TS, plural TSS (no full point).

C. Common mistakes

▶ Some abbreviated words have become everyday expressions and do not use a full point when used colloquially:

✓ We will put an advert (ad) in the paper. She is having her op on Thursday.

▶ e.g. (*exempli gratia*) should be interpreted as 'including' or 'such as' or 'for example'. The correct use is before a list:

✓ Serif typefaces are required, e.g. Times Roman, Century Schoolbook, Garamond.

Do not use 'e.g.' as in the following:

✗ It was claimed for e.g. that the bank statement had been falsified!

I do not like the following, but I do encounter this quite often:

The theory was questionable (see e.g. Jones (1998)).

Preferably write in full: 'See, for example, Jones....'

▶ E.g. should not be followed by a colon, dash, etc.

✗ There are at least a hundred group names, e.g.: herd, flock, flight, pack.

D. Measures

▶ Metric measurements do not use the full point; English measurements, with few exceptions, normally do (see Chapter 11 D). However, a number of scientific journals tend not to use the full point. A comprehensive conversion table is given in Chapter 8.

E. Other

Do we use U.K. or UK, similarly U.S.A. or USA? Older dictionaries give only the former versions. Indeed, the full points have been generally dropped and the forms UK and USA are now given in *Oxford Dictionary for Writers and Editors*. Interesting to note that the *Oxford Dictionary of Abbreviations* (1998) also gives USA for United States Army.

American dictionaries vary. *Random House* prefers U.K. to UK but USA to U.S.A. – the latter given as the abbreviation for United States Army. The Princeton Language Institute gives only U.S.A. for United States of America (the army isn't mentioned).

Conclusion: Consistency!

AFFIXES

See also Prefixes and Suffixes; Chapter 12, Prefixes; Chapter 13, Suffixes.

An affix is attached to the beginning (e.g. as in–, mis–, non–), or the end of a word (e.g. –al, –ly,) in order to modify or change the meaning. An affix may also comprise a word which is either prefixed (e.g. over-), or suffixed (e.g. -out). Affixed words may be conjoined (overjoyed, lockout), or hyphenated (over-excite, line-out). Where neither conjoined or hyphenated, they may form an adjectival phrase or phrasal verb, for example. We encounter differences in meaning for hyphenated, conjoined and separate word forms (a backup or substitute, a back-up file, to back up the hard-disk). These are discussed in more detail in the references above.

AMPERSAND [&]

▶ Normally only used in firms' names: Smith, Brown & Brown (Solicitors).

These should be used in literature lists where the ampersand is included in the publisher's trade name: A&C Black, Oliver & Boyd. Do not replace the 'and' with the ampersand if it is not part of the publisher's trade name: Thames and Hudson Ltd. There is an increasing tendency for the ampersand to be used in references in the text: but this is not recommended.

✗ (Johnson & Wright, 1996:85)

See References.

APOSTROPHE [']

This is sometimes referred to as the single quotation mark (inverted comma) where used as an alternative to double quotations (see Quotation marks).

A. Possession

▶ An apostrophe is used to indicate ownership, possession, or as a connection between a subject and an object. In a sentence we may distinguish between the subject (singular/plural) and the object (singular/plural). For example: The girl's friend; the girl's friends; the girls' friend; the girls' friends.

The general rule is that the placement of the apostrophe is determined by the nature of the subject.

Subject	Object	Apos.	Example
Singular	Singular	's	The sailor's hat.
Singular	Plural	's	The girl's hats.
Plural	Singular	s'	The members' bar.
Plural	Plural	s'	The members' badges.

Collective nouns. These refer to a collection of articles, groups of persons, animals, etc. Examples are herd, flock, women. They are normally treated as singular, but see Definite article, Plurals.

✓ Women's organisations [organisations to which women belong, e.g. Women's Christian Association]

Note: The woman's organisations [refers to organisations to which one woman belongs].

✓ Women's Lib; The Women's Guild

✗ The Womens' Club. [Should be Women's: s' is not used with the group term].

▶ Where the plural changes spelling (apart from adding *s*), we use *s'*:

✓ the baby's mother, the babies' mother, The Ladies' Golf Association

We would also write:

✓ in one year's time...(singular), and in two years' time...(plural)

An apostrophe is used for age groups:

✓ the under two's; the over thirty's; the under 5's.

Note the singular form in the text (not the plural form).

✗ the over thirties.

The apostrophe is only required for the last subject in a list or sequence:

✓ Immigrants and refugees' applications were handled urgently.

It should not be assumed that all terms ending in 's' indicate possession. A distinction must be made with plural nouns such as The United Nations Association, The Boy Scouts Association. I recently encountered The Women

PUNCTUATION AND USAGE

Priests Movement. Instinct suggests an apostrophe 's' (Priest's). However, this was not an organisation to which women priests belonged. In fact, it was a body supporting the ordination of women as priests. In this case the apostrophe 's' could have been misleading. The plural and the possessive are also illustrated in the following:

- ✓ The PCs of today are more powerful than many mainframes of the '70s. The PC's power is more than a byte.

▶ A further distinction between the individual and a group is also made by the placement of the apostrophe:

- ✗ The Worker's Educational Association; National Cyclist's Union
- ✓ The Workers' Educational Association; National Cyclists' Union

It has to be said that even though these are the correct terms (as used by these bodies), one may question why the apostrophe is used at all when it is not used in 'The Boy Scouts Association'.

▶ Some words ending in *s* have the same form in the plural, e.g. series, means.

The series' monthly cover for 1997 will be red.

Rewriting seems to be the best solution.

The covers of the monthly series *Society Today* will be red in 1997.

The last two points raise the issue of 'possession'. The Boy Scouts Association is not necessarily one which the scouts actually own. Rather, it is an organisation *for* the management of scouts' activities and interests. To some extent the same could apply to the publication series and the s' could well be dropped here, as it would if we were referring to the series author.

Names ending with *s*, e.g. Jones.

Do we say 'Jones' house', or 'Jones's house'? Well, how would *you* say it? Whether we use *Jones'* or *Jones's* depends largely, but not solely, on the pronunciation (the 'pronunciation rule' – we would not say Smithses!).

One may encounter both Jones' and Jones's. However, if we are referring to one person, it is normal to use Jones's dog (i.e. the dog is owned by one person called Jones).

If we are referring to several persons named Jones (all members of a family), then Jones' might be considered to give a better indication of the entire family rather than an individual. although Jones's would not be incorrect.

- ✓ The Jones' house is located at the end of the street.

But, of course, if the family's name is Harris, we would almost certainly say Harris's house – whether we are referring just to Mr Harris or the whole family. The 's is generally used with two-syllable names e.g. Morris's shop. But while I have also seen Morrises shop, I have not seen any objection to this style in any punctuation book. (But I have not read them all!)

Note:

✓ Jesus' disciples

Kingsley Amis points out that foreign words ending with a silent 's' use the genitive s:

✓ Louis's book

Plural subject requires s' as in the following:

✓ Smith and Thomsons' investigation verified this.

Names in references. Where a reference is made in the text in the following manner, it is a matter of preference whether the date should divide the subject and the object:

Smith's (1995) study was strongly criticised.

Personally, I prefer: Smith's study (1995) was...

Place names involving possession normally use 's: Land's End, Shepherd's Bush. There are several apparent irregularities in the use of 's. It is place names where we find many inconsistencies. For example, many visitors to London have walked in St. James's Park and probably even strolled along St. James Walk, around St. Giles Circus, or Blackfriars church (the church in the district of Blackfriars in east London and which happens to be in Black Friars Lane).

Similarly, we also find St. Bees Head (in Cumbria) with no apostrophe, but the island of St. Mary's (in the Scilly Isles) apparently possessing nothing. Finally, the capital of Guernsey, one of the Channel Islands, avoids all possible confusion by dropping both an apostrophe and the genitive 's', – St. Peter Port.

These irregularities appear to be at the whim of the local town planning office. My advice is to check in an atlas or gazetteer. The above examples were from the *Greater London Street Atlas* (Nicholsen) and *Philips Atlas*.

B. Omission

▶ Particularly in colloquial language, letters may be dropped and are indicated by the apostrophe: isn't; it's; 'scuse me! – 'e's not at 'ome.

C. Other

▶ The apostrophe is used in abbreviated dates:

✓ In the gold rush of '95 ...

An apostrophe in the following is not recommended although is encountered in US English:

✗ The music of the 70's showed the direction in which it had turned.

(See Dates.)

▶ We may encounter: 'I went to the doctor's the other day.' Clearly what is meant is 'doctor's surgery'. This is acceptable in colloquial form but it is more correct to say 'I went to the doctor the other day.' One publisher rejected my use of the apostrophe in one week's salary, and two months' vacation. I would argue that the link between the adjective and the noun suggests that the apostrophe is (strictly) correct as, for example 'Today's train is cancelled'. But there again styles are changing and the modern argument seems to be 'if it's in doubt, it's probably superfluous – and if it's superfluous, drop it'.

▶ A common error is to use an apostrophe where it is not needed and has no significance:

✗ I found this. Is it your's?

▶ Another similar error is to use it's instead of its. The former is an abbreviation of it is.

Typographical note

Sometimes the single and double apostrophe may appear as [' "] instead of [' '] and [" "]. Under 'Tools' and 'Autocorrect' in Microsoft Word, select 'Autoformat' and tick 'Replace straight quotes with smart quotes'.

ASTERISKS [*]

▶ These may be used to avoid publishing an offensive word:

✓ He told him to go to ****!

A more usual form in today's permissive society is:

✓ He told him to go to h...!

Typographical note:

Disconcertingly, three consecutive asterisks or more followed by 'Return' place a stippled line across the page. If you wish to place three asterisks in the middle of the page, enter 'Return' twice, than move back one line using the up-arrow. Type the three asterisks and 'centre'. If you enter 'Return' the stippled line will reappear. Instead, used the down arrow to go to the blank line below (created by the second 'Return').

***

Three 'minus' signs will produce a line across the page – can be useful. Three 'equals' signs produce a double line. I have not found any reference to this in my 'Bible' but other readers may be more familiar with this feature. But follow the above step by step and your genius will emerge!

BRACKETS [ ]

See also Parentheses.

These are normally referred to as 'square brackets', and are used as follows.

A. Editorial notes

▶ The square bracket is used to indicate editorial notes within a text or a quoted passage:

✓ Jones maintained that Smith had confirmed that he [Jones] had not signed the cheque.

✓ Smith maintains that 'the commune [i.e. municipality], and not the state, is the true representative of the people' (ibid.).

B. Secondary level parentheses

See 'Parentheses'.

▶ The square bracket is used as parentheses within parentheses (except bibliographic dates). They are occasionally used to house an explanatory note.

✓ A hypothesis has no validity until tested (see, for example, Smith, A. R. (1958)). [This book discusses the relationship between a theory, a hypothesis and models.]

BULLETS AND LISTS

▶ Bullets are a useful tool for clarification. They serve to improve layout and make the text clear. However, they do have a tendency to give a text something of a 'schoolbook' character, i.e. lists of terms to be memorised.

A full point is not used for:
- cardinal points (S, NE)
- elements (Al, Mg)
- metric measures (km, m)
- mass (kg, lb)
- US Postal abbreviations (NY, CA)

- currencies (DM, p).

Note that the full point occurs *only* at the end of the list. An exception is where each item comprises a longer phrase, a sentence (or even several sentences). In this case each item will conclude with a full point or appropriate punctuation sign. Secondary level (sub-lists) may use a dash. Again, check the publisher's preferences for primary and secondary level bullets.

> The following issues will be taken up at the meeting:
> - Salaries. A bonus scheme will be presented.
> - Holidays:
>   – Longer working hours in exchange for an extra week's holiday?
>   – Extension of Easter holiday.
> - New safety regulations; compulsory helmets.

▶ Bullets may be numbered: 1., 1), i, I; alphabetic: a., a), A; or as symbols. In this text I have found the following to be useful (✓ ✗) in many examples.

▶ Numbered bullets are best avoided where listed items also contain brackets.

✗ The following were stolen: 1) Radios (3); 2) TVs (3); 3) videos (2); 4) cameras (5).

Compare this with the visual impression of the following:

✓ The following were stolen: a. Radios (3); b. TVs (3); c. videos (2); d. cameras (5).

Numbers should be used if the list is headed: 'The following five points should be noted...', for example. But ask yourself 'do I really need numbered bullets at all?'.

CAPITAL LETTERS

These are used more frequently in English than in some languages. However, times are changing. A useful guideline is 'capitalise the specific, but not the general'.

✓ The Board will meet on Tuesday.

✓ A new board of directors will be elected on Wednesday.

But either The Board of Directors disagreed or The board of directors resigned is acceptable. My inclination is that a specific action requires the specific rule:

> The Board of Directors has proposed a dividend of 28 p.

A. Days, months, periods

▶ These employ capitals in English. Many languages use lower case.

- ✓ It was a Monday in late June that I first met her.
- ▶ Lower case is used for the seasons in English:
- ✓ It is said that the worst gales of winter usually come in the autumn. But: The May Bank Holiday is often called the Spring Holiday. What a pity Christmas is in the winter.
- ▶ Periods in history are capitalised:

Iron Age men were of iron, but men from the Middle Ages were fairly 'middling'. As for those from the Dark Ages, we can only guess!

B. Nationality, language, religion

Capitals are required in English when referring to nationality:

- ✓ The manuscript was written in French, but the author was a German with a taste for Italian wine!

Note the following:

- ✓ He was Russian, but his wife came from Byelorussia.

(This may be encountered as Byelo-russia, but is incorrect.)

- ✓ He was a non-Russian immigrant.
- ▶ A capital is used for Anglo-Irish, Franco-Russian, Afro-Asian, etc. It is also required for Franconian (a group of dialects), and Francophile (person admiring the French and French culture).
- ▶ Derived words should retain the capital such as in: Germanic, Londonese (the cockney dialect), Liverpudlian, Brummie (from Birmingham).

Many foreign languages are less demanding as, for example, the French *quartier latin* – the Latin Quarter of Paris.

- ▶ If the product is related to a specific town or city, the capital is retained: Edam (cheese), plaster of Paris. Where a product relates to a specific region, capitals should be used, e.g. Cornish cream, Yorkshire pudding, Jersey cow, Cheddar cheese, Scotch whisky, Welsh dresser, Russian roulette, etc. Even if the product is widely produced, the capital should still be retained as in Brussels sprouts, French fries, Swiss roll, Indian ink, Roman numerals, Pekinese dog, but surprisingly, not gum arabic.
- ▶ Where the product has taken on the name of a region or country but is universally made or drawn into the language as a general term, the capital is no longer required as in champagne, china, swede (vegetable), jersey and guernsey (sweaters) an oxford (low-heeled laced shoe), a berlin (or berline) (chauffer-driven car of particular design originally from Berlin), mongol (now a taboo expression for a person with Down's syndrome).

PUNCTUATION AND USAGE

We find both béarnaise and Béarnaise sauce. You may find that your spell-checker capitalises most of these even where the capital is not required.

▶ Religions are capitalised, but the *abstract* noun is not required to be capitalised:

✓ In general terms we might state that Christians and Christianity are fundamentals of *christianisation* where the deity is a spiritual god, but when specifically referring to the Jews (the Jewry) and Judaism it may then be stated that the Deity is the true God. Further, many Muslims will maintain that Mohammed is the Prophet of Love and Peace. Not even the Greek god of war was revered as the prophet of peace – and certainly not by *atheists* whose views were more *catholic*.

▶ Ethnic groups are always capitalised.

✓ The Red Indians (now referred to as Native Americans) and the Aborigines have survived as indigenous peoples.

▶ Specific references to groups of countries, movements, etc., use capitals:

✓ While the former Communist bloc is now considered capitalist, the Third World has yet to benefit from the New Order.

But where referred to in general terms these do not require capitals:

✓ Members of the white race in third world countries are no longer regarded as colonialists. Indeed, communism here has taken on another meaning.

This is yet again an area where the house style should be checked.

C. Personal titles

▶ If the title refers to a specific person, capitals are used.

✓ Crown Prince Charles. The Minister of Finance. It was stated by Professor Smart...

They are not used when talking in general terms.

✓ The doctor, minister and the professor all agreed.

▶ Capitals are used for both words in a title, and also in a hyphenated title:

✓ The Deputy Director, The Vice-Chairman.

▶ We would not capitalise names such as d'Almeida, even where this commences a sentence.

✓ de la Mare has long been a favourite poet of children in all ages.

▶ Curiously, some continental languages do not use capitals where English does.

✓ The Marshallian experience, The Marxist-Leninist doctrine, The Churchillean temperament...

Having said that, we do find caesarean operation, although many dictionaries do capitalise this. (May also be spelt 'cesarean' or 'cesarian'.)
Note also, Smith Junior, but Smith jr. (Smith Jr. may be encountered.)

D. Geography

▶ The points of the compass use lower case unless incorporated in a place-name:

✓ His cottage was situated to the south of London, on the South Downs near a station on the (pre-British Railways) Southern Railway, approached from an easterly direction coming from west Brighton.

There is no place called West Brighton. Therefore, west Brighton refers to the western end of the town of Brighton. The Southern Railway served the south of England prior to nationalisation in 1948. The inversion Brighton West is a form used for administrative and electoral districts.

▶ Where referring to geographical regions, cultures, etc., we capitalise Western, Oriental. But in general terms the lower case is used:

✓ The modern jazz style known as West Coast jazz was essentially related to a number of musicians playing in the Western states. On the other hand East Coast jazz seemed to apply to any the music of any state east of California. The eastern and western styles are quite distinctive.

✓ The gemstone known as Oriental emerald is neither a gemstone nor oriental.

Some dictionaries use oriental ruby (no capital), etc.

✓ The film on TV tonight is a western.

Similarly, a distinction must be made between north west and North-West. The former is a general term; the latter a specific region. It employs both the hyphen and capitals.

✓ The industrial area lies to the north west of the town.

✓ The opening up of the North-West was to await the arrival of the railroad.

▶ Cardinal points use capitals: N, SW, SSE, but S.W. London (district)

E. Institutions and academia

▶ It is the practice in many languages to capitalise only the initial letter of an institution name: The Norwegian school of librarianship, The Institute of political science. These are capitalised in English: London School of Economics, The Institute of Sociology. Translations should also be capitalised:

The Norwegian School of Librarianship.

Only those words forming part of the title are capitalised: the city of Vilnius; the Andes mountains; the UNO, but The International Court of Justice; City of London; Luton Town F.C.

▶ Academic subjects used to be capitalised: Among the new studies were Sociology, Maritime Law and Phrenology. This is generally not practised today:

✓ She was the first professor of physics at Oxford.

✓ Students had a choice of anthropology or primeval history as a subsidiary subject.

('Primeval' may also be spelt 'primaeval'.)

An academic title is normally capitalised:

✓ He was appointed Emeritus Professor of Sociology. The Director of Education was dismissed.

▶ Institutions are often abbreviated and capitalised, e.g. FAO, UNO, WFP. These should be referred to as the FAO..., the UNO..., etc. The *pronunciation* will determine the nature of the indefinite article.

✓ A United Nations official was expedited to the region.

✓ An FAO grant ensured that the risk of famine was reduced.

Note that we use capitals for The Soviet Union, but the soviet was re-elected. (A soviet is a council and thus we have the verb *to sovietize*.)

▶ Capitals should apply to all names in an institution or body.

✓ Rutland County Council, The Trades Union Congress, Arsenal Football Club.

These may be dropped for council bodies when referring to them generally:

✓ Islington social services were praised by the minister. The borough council voted to increase the transport subsidy.

Capitals should be retained in a formal document:

✓ The Court sentenced him to thirty days.

But again times are changing and many would not capitalise 'court'. In a newspaper report, lower case would be normal.

F. Publications

▶ The title of a manuscript may use capitals or be entirely upper case:

Regional Economic Growth or REGIONAL ECONOMIC GROWTH.

▶ Upper case is sometimes preferred with lower case capitalised for subtitle:

A HANDBOOK FOR WRITERS OF ENGLISH

REGIONAL ECONOMICS: An Introduction.

▶ Capitals are optional for chapter titles:

✓ Chapter 1. Regional economic growth in perspective.

or –

✓ Chapter 1. Regional Economic Growth in Perspective.

Note that a capital normally follows the colon in titles:

✓ Chapter 2. Regional government: An institution in decline?

▶ References to numbered volumes, chapters, divisions or sections, tables, diagrams and figures should be in capitals:

✓ Further information is given in Chapter 6. See also Table 3.1 and Figure 5a.

▶ References to paragraphs, lines, sections, items, formulae, do not use capitals.

Avoid abbreviations for chapter etc. in the text:

✗ See Chap. 6. As shown in Fig. 3... This was mentioned in para. 2.

G. Other

▶ In advertisements a 'telegraphic' form may be used where two contrasting statements, or similar, are employed. Each statement may begin with a capital letter:

✓ Change of government – Change of policy

▶ Brand names use capitals such as Hoover Inc. Products now in general use and taking the name of the original manufacturer use lower case. The hoover was a revolution for the housewife. The spell-checker may react to some.

▶ Acts of Parliament, laws, statutes and so forth, are capitalised:

✓ The Transport Act; The Green Paper on Recirculation; The Bill of Rights; The Bye-Law relating to Parking, The Rio Convention.

While general terms are not capitalised, Act is always capitalised.

✓ The council considered a number of new bye-laws. A parliamentary Act was also under preparation.

▶ The definite article is capitalised only when part of the title:

✓ It was mentioned in the *Local Government Chronicle*, but not in *The Illustrated London News*.

▶ I encountered a rather special use of the capital letter in a crime book where 'the perpetrator went into his Other state of mind prior to executing the dastardly deed!' This reminds me that members of the House of Commons refer to the House of Lords as 'The Other Place'. *NODE* does not capitalise this, but I feel this to be wrong.

▶ Capitals are often used for many abbreviations even though the full text is not capitalised; e.g. the PC, the WC.

COLON [:]

See also Semicolon.

▶ The colon appears to be used relatively infrequently. Glancing through five or six academic texts I found several chapters without a single colon. But like the semicolon, it can be used to improve the structure, and thereby the clarity of a sentence. It may introduce an explanation or elaboration of that which has preceded the colon.

The Rio treaty was soon forgotten by the delegates: Rio was remembered only for its beaches.

It may also be a contrasting or contradictory statement. Note that a colon does not have to be followed by a complete sentence (see Comma, I).

✓ Two's company: three, an orgy.

A. Lists and examples

▶ The colon is used prior to a list. The list is normally contained within the sentence.

✓ The following issues have been included for discussion: the economy, employment, exports and party membership.

▶ If the subject matter is discussed issue by issue within the following paragraph(s), the colon is best replaced by a full point.

✓ There were three points in his argument. The first was the validity of the evidence; in his view the true rate of inflation was much lower than originally projected. Secondly, unemployment was expected to continue to fall; substantial new investments had been made by foreign investors: national investment was non-existent. Thirdly, the rate of interest had remained stable; the reason believed to be the low rate of inflation as mentioned above.

Note the use of the semicolon, here used to separate the subsidiary information on each issue (see Semicolon).

▶ A colon should not normally be used following 'such as' or 'including'.

✗ The menu included a variety of exotic foods such as: quail, snail, donkey-tail soup, poached zebra kidneys and more.

▶ The colon should not be used following 'e.g.' in lists:

✗   Many clues were found, e.g.: footprints, fingerprints, and a questionable lady's item.

Rewrite using 'for example' or 'including' and exclude the colon.

B. Speech

▶ A colon is used before a quotation or a question contained in inverted commas:

✓   As Cindy Adams once said: 'Success has made failures of many men.'

✓   The trade union leader wanted an explanation: 'If Rome was built in a day, who was in charge of that job?'

A colon is incorrect in the following:

✗   His answer was that: 'the price has already been adjusted.'

In fact, we do not even need the inverted commas here at all as this is indirect speech. But we could write:

✓   His answer was: 'The price has already been adjusted.'

C. Dividing a sentence

▶ A colon may be used to divide a sentence where the second part is a dividing clause, for example, and where this is contrary to or negates the main clause:

✓   The Labour Party voted for reduced state control: this was, however, a contradiction of their election manifesto.

▶ The colon is used relatively infrequently in many European languages. Where used, it is often the norm to follow the colon with a capital letter. This is *not* the case in UK English where a capital will only apply to speech and proper nouns.

✗   He repeated the question: She still refused to answer.

A capital may occur where a question follows the colon and which is not direct speech.

✓   One repeats the inevitable question: Why did the driver proceed as he did?

▶ Avoid more than one colon in a sentence:

✗   Note: Committee meetings will be held as follows: Monday and Thursday mornings.

The first colon (following 'Note') should be replaced with a full point or exclamation mark.

✓   Note. Committee meetings will be held as follows: Monday and Thursday mornings.

PUNCTUATION AND USAGE

D. Date and time

▶ The colon is occasionally used in dates and times, especially where resulting from a computer output. 02:10:94; 01:30.

It is preferable to reserve the colon for hours, minutes, and seconds:

✓ 12.10.98; 10:23:07.

See Dates.

E. Business salutations

▶ The colon was previously used in business letters but is not used today:

✗ Dear Sir or Madam:

F. References

See References. References in the text use the form Jones (1994: 15) – space after the colon. This does not apply to biblical references: Galatians 11:6.

G. Other

▶ Where lower case is used for chapter titles, lower case *normally* follows the colon although exceptions will be found.

The immediate post-war years: a new era dawns

(No full point at the end of a title.)

▶ If the word following a break is *however, indeed* or *nevertheless*, a semicolon is preferable to a colon (see Semicolon).

✓ The pre-war period was one of prolonged scepticism: it was one of growing fear. The post-war period was eventful; however, it scarcely constituted a new era.

▶ A complete sentence is normally required following a semicolon. This does not apply to the colon.

✓ The election was democratic: the voters, Republican! The results were proclaimed; they were also disclaimed.

▶ A colon is used in ratios such as 1:3, meaning one out of every four (see Numbers, F).

COMMA [,]

▶ The comma is probably the most used and misused punctuation character in English. Used properly it is the key to clarification. An important point to be remembered with the comma is that 'quick reading' is becoming common practice (quick reading courses are widely offered – and not only in academic institutions). The comma will assist in clarification, but an overdose will have the opposite effect.

A. Some general observations

The comma is the natural break in speech and in the written text. However, we read more quickly than we can speak aloud and fewer commas *may* be needed in the written text. English tolerates longer sentences than is the case in several European languages requiring more commas. Indeed, one important use of the comma (or indeed, its omission) is to introduce clarity into a text, to clarify the meaning where appropriate. But excessive use of commas is a common disease. I recently read:

✗ Universities have strong cultures, following from the interaction of the actual disciplines.

My guess is that the author was not really sure about the point he/she was making, and so included a comma as if to assure the reader that this was all good solid stuff.

▶ Do not use the comma to join two sentences which are clearly not connected. For example, the following mistake is not uncommon:

✗ Bush was elected, he had been sure of his father's influence.

In this case the comma may be replaced by a semicolon.

There are still a number of traditions regarding use of the comma, some of which are fading. A good example is the comma after salutations in letters (see Salutations below). This is not used in modern English, although old traditions die hard. Generally, we do not seem to be bound by many of the 'rules' of yesteryear. A comma in addresses is now almost taboo:

✗ 16, London Road

✗ Dear Mr. Smith,

B. Lists

▶ Commas are required in lists of adjectives or nouns:

✓ Rarely had there been voiced such vociferous, compelling, overbearing and clear, yet unsubstantiated evidence against a minister.

▶ US English tends to place a comma before the 'and', more so than in English although this is also the norm for some UK publishers. It is certainly required where the last item is qualified or where clarification is necessary. The uninitiated might just believe that there was a single football club called Fulham and Chelsea. Careful punctuation will erase any doubt.

Arsenal, Bolton, Fulham and Chelsea, the leader just a month ago, all face relegation.

✓ Arsenal, Bolton, Fulham, and Chelsea (the leader just a month ago), all face relegation.

C. Speech

▶ As seen above (Colon, B), speech, particularly the shorter comment, should be introduced by a colon. Tom emphasised the point: 'The offer is refused.'

The comma is occasionally a better choice than the colon with regard to the flow of the text:

Tom thought carefully before saying, 'No, the offer is too low.'

In a divided sentence, the comma should be used.

✓ 'Yes,' he answered, 'but only with a discount.'

▶ Note the comma *inside* the inverted commas: 'Yes,' ...

D. General points of clarity

▶ A comma is clearly required in the following:

Dickens and Jones and Barkers are popular London stores for tourists.

Do we mean Dickens and Jones, and Barkers, or Dickens, and Jones and Barkers? (Actually, we mean the former.)

▶ Commas should not be used to separate adverbs where they serve no purpose. Even so, the comma may serve to emphasise the suspense of a situation:

✓ Anxiously, they awaited the return of the jury.

One author 'corrected' my translation of his article to read: They anxiously awaited the return of the jury. To my mind, this was a change of style and lacked the 'drama' of my original.

E. Separating phrases and clauses

▶ There is a rule which states that a comma is used following an adverbial clause when this precedes the main clause.

The transfer had been made, even though it had clearly been delayed.

This is surely another rule in decay. The following seems absolutely o.k. to me.

The transfer had been made even though it had clearly been delayed.

We will not concern ourselves too much with grammatical rules but should, perhaps, emphasise the importance of style. Inverting a sentence is one way of introducing style into a text as well as removing superfluous commas:

✓ When the letter arrives, please post it on.

as an alternative to:

Please post the letter on when it arrives.

▶ A useful rule (principle) is to avoid unnecessary commas.

✗ It was stated, on the other hand, that the rules could be bent.

Re-ordering gives a better flow:

✓ On the other hand, it was stated that the rules could be bent.

As the above suggests, rewriting such as to reduce the number of commas often improves the 'readability'.

▶ Subsidiary clauses were formerly required to be separated by commas:

The committee, which had just been re-elected, now included three women.

Some writers consider that this interrupts the flow for the quick reader, especially where the clause is concise and the sentence not unreasonably long, and prefer:

The committee which had just been re-elected now included three women.

While some may disapprove, if you do select to drop the commas, drop both. This does point to the subtlety of punctuating the written word and that which has to be spoken.

▶ A comma is not used in conjunction with 'and' where the same subject applies or the two clauses are clearly related.

✗ The proposal was made, and the resolution was formally adopted.

✓ The proposal was made and the resolution was formally adopted.

▶ A common mistake is to place the comma before *and* instead of after when isolating a clause or phrase:

✗ The proposal was re-drafted, and in spite of some further objections, was then approved.

✓ The proposal was re-drafted and, in spite of some further objections, was then approved.

This error can occur with several prepositions and conjunctions:

✗ The regional plan was debated, but in spite of several attempts, was not put to the vote.

✓ The regional plan was debated but, in spite of several attempts, was not put to the vote.

▶ Hint: Read the sentence without the intervening phrase or clause.

F. Interjections

▶ An interjection may be a single word, salutation or address, or a phrase. A pair of commas is required:

✓ At the present time, no, although we are expecting new supplies.

▶ Commas, in pairs, are required when addressing a person or a group:

✓ Believe me, Sir, you have not heard the last of this.

✓ As I informed you, Minister, the workers are revolting.

▶ Formerly, it was a rule that commas were required in pairs where a phrase or clause is placed in the middle of sentence.

The court rose early, about three-thirty, with instructions to convene at nine the next day.

As the intervening phrase qualifies 'early', the logic of the punctuation is clear, but not in the following:

✗ The secretary, who had recorded the statement, was asked for a verbatim report.

The following is correct:

✓ The secretary who had recorded the statement was asked for a verbatim report.

The following provide examples of the use the comma which fails to clarify a situation. Who actually recorded the statement? And who wants the transcript?

The secretary to the Director who had recorded the statement asked for the transcript.

The secretary to the Director, who had recorded the statement, asked for the transcript.

Here is a good argument for alternative punctuation, or re-writing the sentence:

The secretary to the Director (who had recorded the statement) asked for the transcript.

The Director's secretary, who had recorded the statement, asked for the transcript.

Indeed, this illustrates the point that, rather than rules, commas should be placed where appropriate in order to facilitate understanding, and to 'lubricate' the flow of the written word. If it doesn't, ask yourself if re-writing the sentence or using alternative punctuation is not better?

G. Dates

▶ Originally, the comma was used to separate dates (the adverbial phrase):

> By 1992, the government had been in power for thirteen years. In 1993, new electoral boundary reforms were proposed.

Many appear not to consider this necessary today. By 1992 the government had been in power for thirteen years. It should nevertheless be retained to separate a subordinate clause:

✓ In 1992, by which time the government had been in power for thirteen years, there was considerable need for new legislation on the homeless.

▶ A comma should also be retained to separate dates and numbers:

✓ In the debate held in March 1993, 256 members voted against the proposal.

This would also be used where the written form is given as this is, in effect, a reversal of the sentence structure:

✓ In the debate of March 1994, six members abstained.

See Dates for a further discussion of the comma in months and dates.

H. Numbers

See also Numbers, Roman numbers.

▶ Figures exceeding 4 digits.

✓ 9999; 10,000; 100,000.

Continental convention is to employ a full point here (and a comma in place of a decimal point):

> There were 100.000 at the match. The temperature was 15,5 centigrade.

▶ The decimal comma may be encountered in some international scientific journals.

I. Omissions

The comma can indicate an omission as in the following:

✓ The manager wanted the issue postponed; the delegation, an immediate discussion.

derived from:

> The manager wanted the issue postponed: the delegation [wanted] an immediate debate.

PUNCTUATION AND USAGE

J. Salutations, etc.

▶ Previously, salutations in letters employed the comma:

✗ Dear Sir, ... Yours faithfully,

✗ Dear Mr. Jones,

▶ Modern business practice is not to use the commas although a few text books still suggest it. The full point after Mr is gone – and was never really necessary.

✓ Dear Mr Jones ... Yours faithfully

See under Colon for formal business letters.

K. Other

▶ As indicated above, there used to be a number of rules (and possibly still are) about commas and phrases, but the modern trend seems to be *logic*! Is that comma really necessary? For example, the use of a comma with 'that':

It was decided that, if the motion was defeated, the committee would resign.

This conditional clause, '*if...*', does not strictly require to be distinguished by the presence of commas. On the other hand, we might want to draw attention to an exceptional state of affairs:

✓ It was thought that, in spite of the vote, the Chairman would continue.

Some would argue that the structure of the sentence leaves something to be desired, but it is those occasional quirks in style which draw attention to the subject matter.

▶ A comma may serve to emphasise a point. Consider the following:

The question was: 'Did he or didn't he?'

Was the painting genuine or was it a clever fake?

The inclusion of a comma can draw particular attention to a phrase:

The question was: 'Did he, or didn't he?'

Was the painting genuine, or was it a clever fake?

The dash (–) may be even more appropriate:

✓ The question was: 'Did he – or didn't he?'

▶ The dash is occasionally preferable to the comma, especially where a sentence can contain many commas:

✗ It was stated on the other hand, that in spite of objections by the board of management, itself comprising minority shareholders, the rejection of the proposal would have several short-term consequences, some of which, in spite of government support, would have long-term, if not permanent consequences for the company, and quite probably, the board.

The above sentence, while grammatically correct, contains no less than nine commas. We can isolate a particular phrase with the use of a dash, and thereby facilitate reading. We might also examine the possibility of reducing the use of commas:

✓ It was stated on the other hand, that in spite of objections by the board of management – itself comprising minority shareholders – the rejection of the proposal would have several short-term consequences, some of which (in spite of government support) would have long-term, if not permanent consequences for the company – and quite probably, the board.

(See Dash.)

▶ Finally, we could remind ourselves of the two quick fixes for removing commas:

1. Invert the sentence (with the possible loss of style):

   Nevertheless, it was decided... → It was nevertheless decided...

2. Replace the comma with 'and' or another conjunction – or even divide the sentence:

   The Socialists opposed the motion, the Centre abstained, the right wing was unanimous in its support, the others were just confused!

   → While the Socialists opposed the motion and the Centre abstained, the right wing was unanimous in its vote. The others were just confused!

DASH [–]

Typographically, there are a number of different forms of dash. The restrictions of the typewriter led us into bad habits where many use the 'minus' sign [-] both as a hyphen and a dash [–]. Indeed, negative values should be preceded by the dash. (Example –32, not -32.) How to achieve the dash on your word-processor is discussed below.

The **hyphen** is used in compound words and is not discussed here. (See Hyphenated and conjoined words). We include it, however, within the discussion of the typography in order to distinguish it from the normal dash, the en rule and the em rule. (The term 'rule' here means 'dash'.)

A. Dashes – a typographical note

The typewriter gave little choice in distinguishing between a hyphen, a dash and an en or em rule. The hyphen frequently sufficed for all these except the longer em rule where a double hyphen [--] was used. The modern word-

PUNCTUATION AND USAGE

processor contains a number of dashes, all obtainable under the 'Insert > Symbol' feature, or on the keyboard. The basic dashes, distinguished by their length, may be obtained with the use of short-cut keys. The normal dash and the en rule may be identical in appearance. The important distinction between the dash and the en rule is that the latter is 'spaced', i.e. has spaces on either side. The en rule and em rule are sometimes referred to as the N-rule and M-rule, respectively.

Type	Symbol	WordPerfect 5.1[1]	Corel Word-Perfect	Microsoft Word v.7 and later
Hyphen	-	'Minus' key	'Minus' key Charmap 0,45	'Minus' key
Dash; En rule	–	Ctrl+V, 1,4 or Ctrl+V, 4,33	Charmap 3,50	Ctrl+numerical 'minus' key[2]
Em rule	—	Ctrl + V, 4,34	Charmap 3,8	Ctrl+Alt+numerical 'minus' key[3]

1. The modern printer will reproduce the three dash forms although some fonts may be restricted.
2. Microsoft Word contains an 'automatic' en rule. Where a hyphen sign is typed with a space on either side, this symbol automatically converts to a dash as soon as the following word is completed. For example, typing 'Democrats - Republicans' becomes 'Democrats – Republicans'. Alternatively, hold down the Ctrl key while hitting the numerical 'minus' (hyphen) key once.
3. Microsoft Word also contains an automatic em rule. If two consecutive hyphens are typed *without a space between two words*, this automatically converts to an em rule [—]. Alternatively, hold down the Ctrl key while hitting the numerical 'minus' (hyphen) key twice.

B. The dash

See also Hyphen.

The dash is distinguished from the en rule in that it is not bounded by spaces. It is used as a 'joiner' as in the following. (Do not use the 'minus' sign.)

✓   The Baltic states: Estonia–Latvia–Lithuania.

Thus, the following would be incorrect:

✗   Radio – television communication channels

For events, treaties, etc., the dash is used as follows:

✓   The G7–Soviet Agreement. The Lib.–Lab. Alliance, The Sino–Japanese war.

▶   The dash is also the correct sign for negative values. [A typesetter will normally use a sign which is longer than a hyphen but shorter than an en rule.]

✓ Absolute zero is −273.15° c.

✓ 3 + (−4) = −1

The spaced dash should be used where this symbol means 'subtract':

✓ −2 − 4 = +2

▶ A dash is used to repeat a suffix which is not normally hyphenated:

✓ Courses in both macro− and microeconomics were introduced.

▶ The hyphen (sometimes referred to as a floating hyphen) and not the dash should be used in the following:

Two- and three-room apartments were available on short- and long-term lease.

▶ The dash is normally used for time periods involving hours: Closed 12.30–13.30.

▶ The dash may be used in dates and bibliographic references, although many publishers prefer the spaced dash (see below).

C. The spaced dash

In the preceding section, the dash was described as a 'joiner'. Where the dash, by implication, means 'to', many publishers (but not all) prefer the spaced dash (similar to the en rule). The spaced dash is used in the following:

Dates

✓ Mozart 1756 – 1791. The 1939 – 45 War.

– but not where it signifies 'between' :

✗ She was managing director 1995 – 1998.

✓ She was managing director between 1995 and 1998.

The unspaced dash will certainly be encountered for dates, but may yet require spacing for clarity:

✓ J. S. Bach (1685–1750); Augustus 63 BC – AD 14; Inhabited AD 763 – ca. 831.

Ranges

✓ In the range £2000 – £3000. Salary $60,000 – 75,000.

Bibliographic references

✓ See pp. 40 – 54.

✓ Vols II – IV cover the post-war period.

As mentioned, you may encounter 1939–45; $10–$20; pp. 4–7. The hyphen *is* encountered, but rarely, and most publishers would regard it as incorrect: pp. 47-53.

▶ As mentioned above, the spaced dash indicates 'subtract' in mathematics:

✓ $6 - 4 = 2$

D. The en rule

Typographically, the en rule and the dash are identical, except that the en rule is always spaced. Whereas the dash meant 'to', then en rule is a useful substitute for other punctuation symbols and may replace the comma, semicolon, colon or, when used in pairs, parentheses.

✓ The major powers were present – England, France, Germany and the USA.

✓ The motion was passed – in spite of the intense opposition – and enacted the following day.

It is observed that the en rule is stronger than the comma and, as the latter example shows, draws attention to a particular point to be emphasised. The use of the en rule should not be overdone but will bring clarity to a long sentence already containing many commas.

▶ The en rule may also be used to indicate a break in the train of thought or continuity:

✓ The governor declared that he had been elected – but this was a little premature it seemed.

– or an afterthought:

✓ The Chairman stated that he had resigned – he was, in fact, dismissed.

▶ One useful application is as an alternative to parentheses:

✓ The TV – not the PC – will probably be the two-way communication means of the future.

▶ Sometimes, a comma would appear more natural than a colon, but for reasons of clarity the en rule is the most appropriate punctuation. In one manuscript I encountered the following:

Caffeine binds to the adenosine receptors, but creates effects which are quite the opposite – energising, stimulating and anxiogenic.

Clearly, neither a comma nor a colon would be appropriate here. Why? The reason is that we do not have a list of objects; rather, these are adjectives describing the various qualities. This example goes to show that common sense rather than hard-and-fast rules should be the essential guideline for punctuation.

▶ The en rule may be used in lists in place of a colon:

✓ The economy is expanding in several directions – employment, trade, exports, and not least in business confidence.

Formerly, it was not uncommon to find the colon and the dash used before a list:

✗ The attic was full to the rafters:– shoes, picture frames, chests, books, and even – of all things – a harp!

This is not used today – and neither should the dash be preceded by a semicolon.

▶ The en rule is also preferred by some publishers in references to citations meaning 'quote from':

✗ 'Woman was God's second mistake.' – Nietzsche (1844–1900).

E. The em rule

The em rule is attached to a word (or syllable, etc.) or comma to indicate omission of text. It may also precede a full point. The em rule is most frequently encountered as an affix, following a letter or preceding a punctuation symbol. It is not 'spaced' at both ends and is longer than the en rule.

✓ She told him to p— off. He did, and ended up in —.

▶ The em rule is frequently used in novels in place of the en rule, particularly in US publications where we might find, for example:

Smithers—now desperate—made a final bid to escape her clutches.

▶ The em rule may also be used to indicate a change of speaker and where inverted commas are not used. This seems to be popular with some crime writers in accounting trials:

—But I put it to you, Smith, the proof is there.

—I still say that the evidence was planted.

—I am talking about hard proof, not figments of the imagination.

or even separating question and answer with the em rule:

Well, did you agree to that?—Not in so many words.

How many words then?—I am not given to verbosity.

This style was popular in a series *Notable British Trials* published in the 1930s by Hodge & Co. Ltd., London, and is still occasionally encountered.

PUNCTUATION AND USAGE

F. The double em rule

▶ Some publishing houses use a double em rule in references to indicate the same author. While not available on the PC, these are usually about 3 ems in length. Sometimes two double ems may be encountered. However, this practice is normally frowned upon as the em rule means ibid. – i.e. *exactly* the same author as the preceding reference.

Swan, Michael (1991). Practical English Usage. OUP. 639 pp.

— (1992). Oxford Pocket Basic English Usage. OUP. 288 pp.

Norway. Ministry of Local Government (1990). Local elections. Oslo. 2 pp.

— — (1992). Local Government Finances. Oslo. 13 pp.

— Ministry of Transport (1991). Local transport subsidies. Oslo. 22 pp.

DATES

See also Times.

A common format for dates is 8th May 1995, alternatively 08.05.1995 (DD.MM.YYYY), or 08.05.95 (DD.MM.YY). This is the ISO standard as used in the EU and EEA. However, national customs do not always adhere to these conventions.

A. Current date

▶ The UK norm for dates is day-month-year (d-m-y) whereas the US norm is m-d-y. Thus. 08.05.1995 indicates the 8th of May 1995 in UK English, but August 5th 1995 in US English. Some European countries follow the UK standard, others the US standard. Your word-processor should allow you to select the appropriate style as default.

The international system for all-numeric dates uses y-m-d. This is also convenient for sorting, encountered as *2000:04:20* (reflecting the sort keys), but colons are best left to hours and minutes, for example *2000-04-20 19:25*.

▶ A tip here is that it is preferable to use the full date, *2000-04-20* rather than *00-04-20*. Curious things can happen when a zero occurs at the beginning of a number which is to be subjected to a PC sorting routine.

B. References to dates

As indicated above, the full version is normally required.

✓ He was born on 8 May 1910.

▶ A full point after the date is not normally used (8. May 1910), but a comma may be used following the month, 8th May, 1910. A full point is

43

used, however, in many foreign languages – which may not capitalise the month: 8. juni 1910.

▶ A full point should not follow '5th' as in the following.

✗ May 5th. was finally determined as the date for the election.

▶ Most modern word-processors automatically superscript ordinals such as 1st, 2nd, 3rd and 4th. This feature may be turned off. He died on May 5th is preferred by many to He died on May 5th. In literary works, text is appropriate: He was married on June the third – and repented on the fourth. (See Numbers.)

C. Years

Originally, A.D. (*Anno Domini*) and B.C. (Before Christ) were used. Many dictionaries now use AD and BC. Note SMALL CAPS. Incidentally, a.d. (*ante diem*) means 'before the day'. BC follows the date; AD precedes it:

✓ 600 BC and AD 2000

We may nevertheless encounter the following, but which is incorrect

✗ We all know what happened in 79 AD.

▶ A number of versions of reference to decades exist. Some are no longer recommended, others are taboo.

The present norm is a single *s* following the date: In the 1990s ... In the '90s ...

✓ In the 1890s, the music hall reached its prime: by the 1990s, barely a half-dozen theatres remained.

The plural form –ies must be used in the following:

✓ In the Nineties, the music hall reached its prime.

✗ In the forty's and fifty's....

▶ If the number is shortened then the apostrophe should be used:

✓ The gold rush of the '80s became a stampede in the '90s.

The following use of the apostrophe may be encountered, particularly in US English, but is not recommended.

In the 90's, the music hall reached its prime.

The apostrophe is encountered, however, in the adjectival form:

The 1950's style was not to my taste.

Nevertheless, the preferred adjectival form is s' – both for singular and plural.

✓ The 1980s' music style was dominated by heavy metal.

✓ The 1990s' styles were considered tasteless by many.

But do not use:

✗ In the 90ies, the music hall reached its prime.

✗ The '90's styles were cheap – and nasty.

D. Periods

▶ Avoid the hyphen (minus sign) for periods:

✗ 1914-1918.

The dash should be used. Many publishers use a spaced dash, particularly where the full year is used.

✓ 1914–1918; 1939 – 1945; AD 763 – ca. 831.

The second date in a period may be abbreviated: 1939–45. The spaced dash should not be used here:

✗ 1939 – 45.

▶ Practically every punctuation book points out the error of (mis)using the hyphenated date, indicating how frequently this error is encountered:

✗ The war lasted from 1939–1945 (instead of from 1939 to 1945).

Many European languages use a text form which when translated directly becomes 'in recent decades'. The nearest translation would be: 'in the last twenty to thirty years... (thirty to forty years)', etc. It is possible to write 'during the last decade' but this may be misunderstood. Webster's New World Dictionary gives the following definition:

> DECADE: a period of ten years; esp., in the Gregorian calendar
> *a*) officially, a ten-year period beginning with the year 1, as 1921–1930, 1931–1940, etc. *b*) in common usage, a ten-year period beginning with a year 0, as 1920–1929, 1930–1939, etc.

E. Other

It is immaterial whether you write 'It was announced in 1990 that the law would be changed', or 'In 1990, it was announced that the law would be changed.'
(The comma after the date is no longer considered necessary by some.)
The apostrophe was previously used in: I will arrive in 3 days' time. My wife is taking 2 weeks' holiday in Brazil. The modern trend is to drop these. Note nevertheless: It is a two-hour journey and not It is a two hours journey.

A HANDBOOK FOR WRITERS OF ENGLISH

DEFINITE ARTICLE, (THE)

This is used more frequently in certain continental languages than in English. A common mistake made by foreigners writing in English is to use the definite form where this is not required.

▶ Avoid repetitive use of the definite article. The following is heavy reading.

Check the use of the capital letter in the titles.

At the other extreme is the command:

Check use of capital letters in titles!

It is recommended that the definite article is used to stress the main subject(s) of the sentence.

Check use of the capital letters in titles.

▶ The definite article is italicised when part of the name of a publication:

✓ The report appeared in both *The Times* and the *Daily Mail*.

The correct titles of the newspapers are: *The Times* and *Daily Mail*.

Singular or plural?

'The family is coming to dinner on Sunday' or 'The family are coming to dinner on Sunday'?

This problem is commonly encountered. Another example might be 'The Committee was in agreement...' or 'The Committee were in agreement...'. The norm here is whether the family or committee, or whatever, is regarded as an entity or as a group of individuals. If you consider the family to comprise Aunt Jane, Cousin Bill, Grandma and your sister's children, they could be considered as a group of individuals. Individuals are plural! So, they *are* coming to dinner.

If, on the other hand, your visitors are your parents, brother and sister and their respective partner and children, you will probably consider them as an entity. An entity is singular: the family *is* coming to dinner.

The same applies to the Committee. If the Committee members voted differently, you could write: The committee were divided in their opinion. Alternatively: The Committee was unanimous in its decision. But it would not be wrong if you wrote: The Committee was divided...the Committee were unanimous in their decision. It really depends upon where you wish to place the emphasis.

Incidentally, I am informed that US English is far more focussed on the collective noun in the singular.

Some words are slightly ambiguous: The minutes of the meeting are available in the library. But we could say: The minutes of the board is one of several sources of information; the annual reports are another. Strictly speaking 'minutes' is plural, but again we are thinking of these as a document or a record of the proceedings.

ELLIPSIS [...]

Several consecutive full points are known as an ellipsis. This may be used to indicate missing text, especially where the text is familiar:
- ✓ The story commenced as normal: 'Once upon a time ...'
- ✓ The chart showed each planet in detail: Mars, Jupiter ... Pluto, and the new discoveries.

Similarly, the ellipsis may indicate food for thought:
- ✓ Like another previous tyrant, the PM thought she would last a thousand years...

There are no fixed rules about the number of full points in an ellipsis but is normally three. Observe that the spacing between the points is narrower than normal [...]. This will be achieved automatically where a proportional typeface is used. If a non-proportional typeface is used, such as Brougham, the spacing will be broader [. . .]. The problem of spacing is solved with most word-processors in that the ellipsis will probably be found as a symbol.

The ellipsis functions as a full point and requires no further punctuation at the end of the sentence.

EM RULE; EN RULE (SEE UNDER DASH)

EXCLAMATION MARK [!]

The exclamation mark takes the place of a full point unless included in quoted speech.

A. Following exclamations

Short exclamations of shock or surprise are followed by an exclamation mark.
- ✓ 'Stop that!'

Strictly speaking, the exclamation mark serves as a terminator and a final full point is not required.
- ✗ She shouted, he stopped, and she availed herself of the situation!.

Note the following:
- ✓ He shouted 'Stop!' at the top of his voice, but to no avail.

B. Emphasis

Where attention is intended to be drawn to a remark or a deliberate misquote, the exclamation mark is appropriate:

✓ His high-jump record was considered quite a feet!

It may occasionally appear in the middle of the sentence:

✓ Having hopped the whole twelve inches was considered quite a feet(!) for a flea.

A double exclamation mark is rarely encountered, but makes a point:

✓ He married on the fifth – and repented on the sixth! So did she!!

EXTRACTS

▶ The term 'citation' was previously used to denote a quotation from or reference to a book, paper, or author, especially in a scholarly work (*New Oxford English Dictionary*); a passage quoted from a book or other work: 'the quoting of a book or author in support of a fact' (*Collins Dictionary*), normally about 50 words in length. The term 'quotation' rather than 'citation' seems to be preferred today.

The term 'quotation' may be reserved for a smaller passage which is retained in the text and contained within quotation marks (see Quotations). An 'extract' usually refers to a longer passage of several lines. These are often presented as an indented paragraph, sometimes using a smaller typeface and single line spacing, even if the main text employs broader line spacing.

> The student of the behavioural sciences soon grows accustomed to using familiar words in initially unfamiliar ways... He knows that the scientific denotation of the term 'personality' has little or nothing to do with the teenager's meaning. (Siegel 1956: 1)

▶ Many publishers do not place a final full point after the reference to the extract (as in the above example). Others place it following the final closing parentheses, but omitting the full point at the end of the quoted text: ...teenager's meaning (Siegel 1956: 1).

▶ It is permissible to omit the author's name at the end of the extract if this *immediately* precedes the citation.

✓ This apparent anomaly is explained by Siegel (1956: 1):

> The student of the behavioural sciences soon grows accustomed to using familiar words in initially unfamiliar ways... He knows that the scientific denotation of the term 'personality' has little or nothing to do with the teenager's meaning.

(See Parentheses, Quotations, References.)

FONTS (SEE TYPEFACES AND FONTS)

FOOTNOTES AND ENDNOTES

Somewhere, with reference to footnotes, I read 'avoid them!'. Indeed, even where more convenient than endnotes they may nevertheless be tiresome interruptions. Their main function is to provide useful *supplementary* information. The golden rule has to be: 'if it is important, retain it in the text'. A ten-line footnote seems to indicate something important that you forgot to put in the main body of the text. Keep 'em short – to the point. But neither make the point so short that it is meaningless.

▶ Placement of the footnote reference is important. If possible, and where there is no ambiguity, placement at the end of the sentence is preferable (readability).

✓ It was suggested that a logit analysis would reveal the relationship.[6]

Otherwise, the footnote references should be unambiguous. Note that they are placed after the punctuation sign. (Some older texts place the number before the *comma*, but this practice has changed.)

✓ The methods used included ANOVA,[4] multiple regression and guestimates.[6]

▶ Do not use footnotes in a title or sub-title. This may be tempting when adding an acknowledgement (This book was inspired by... Thanks to...).

✗ Foot-and-mouth: Better to cull the minister[1]

Even though this is a 'Thanks to John Brown for comments' footnote, it looks like you are having to explain what the title means.

▶ Endnotes are an alternative to footnotes; they get everything 'out of the way'. But if we are honest, few can be bothered to flick to the end of the book. But whatever, do *not* use footnotes *and* endnotes. Only once did I encounter both in a scientific article where formulae were found in footnotes; all other supplementary information in endnotes. Naturally, these employed different numbering styles for the references in the text.

FULL POINT (FULL STOP, PERIOD)

The term 'full point' is used in many books on copy-editing, while 'full stop' seems to prevail in a number of punctuation handbooks. The American term is 'period' (also used by Shakespeare). I have preferred to use 'full point' throughout.

A. Sentence

The full point concludes a sentence. This means that a full point cannot appear at the commencement of a line.[2]

B. Abbreviations

See Chapter 15, Abbreviations.

The general rule is that if the abbreviation concludes with the same letter as the full word, then it does not require a full point (but does not apply to measurements). Further, if the singular version employed a full point, then one was applied after the plural 's'. Thus we had ed. (editor) and eds. (editors). But there were some anomalies, as for example ch. (chapter) and chs (chapters). Generally, the plural does not employ a full point after the s.

Full points were previously used in degrees – and still are:

✓ Ph.D., M.Sc.,(Econ.), B.Sc.

but times change and it is now common to find:

✓ BA, Dlitt, PhD

In forms of address the norm has definitely changed:

✗ Dear Mr. and Mrs. Jones. This style is now considered out-of-date. The modern usage is:

✓ Mr, Mrs, Mss, Dr, etc.

You may find Rev or Rev. (largely US), and also Revd – no full point.

▶ Time should be lower case with full points. 4 a.m., 6 p.m. (not am, pm. See Time, also Abbreviations).

▶ More common, perhaps, OK or even O.K. Note that o.k. is OK, but *not* ok! Or use 'okay'.

C. Numbers

The decimal point is used in British and American English. The continental norm is the reverse use of points and commas in figures.

US, UK: $135,725.50 e.g. Norwegian: NOK 135.725,50

The decimal character required may be selected on the modern spreadsheet, if required.

---

2 This is useful for editing some texts on the word-processor. For example, placing a full point at the beginning of every line before a heading enables one quickly to locate headings using a command such as the following: [Find <Return>.]. When the editing is completed all the periods located at the beginning of the line can be deleted using the Find-Replace command.

PUNCTUATION AND USAGE

D. Parentheses

▶ The full point is placed inside the parentheses if the entire sentence is contained within them:

✓ (His innocence was proved at a later date.)

Otherwise, outside:

✓ He had served his time (his innocence was proved at a later date).

This principle also applies where the text concludes with an abbreviation:

✓ (This has been referred to by Isaksen et al.)

✓ He was re-elected for a new term. (He was eighty years old at the time.)

▶ A closing full point is not required for references such as:

✓ 'Thank you for your e-mail. This Internet of yours is a wonderful invention.'
                                            (George Bush, quoted in Newsweek)

E. Quotations

▶ The full point remains inside the quotation marks where it concludes a sentence:

✓ On being asked which language he preferred, Abdul commented: 'English is Greek to me! I prefer French.'

▶ The full point will lie outside a quotation which is a phrase or term forming part of a sentence:

✓ I may have been mistaken but I didn't hear Prescott say 'sorry'.

If the entire sentence above is speech, it will be punctuated as follows:

✓ He retorted angrily: 'I may have been mistaken but *I* didn't hear Prescott say "sorry".'

▶ In the *Instructions to Authors* issued by one publisher. I read the following:

Punctuation should follow the British style, e.g. 'quotes precede punctuation'.

I also noticed that this publisher did not include a final full point as in the example above:

...much comment (particularly by Isaksen et. al.)

Times may be changing!

F. Other

▶ Full points are not used in titles, chapter headings, subheadings, etc. They may (rarely) be omitted at the end of a sentence if it creates confusion.

A HANDBOOK FOR WRITERS OF ENGLISH

The full point is a vital element of the email address and entering *www.hotmail.uk*. (with a final full point) would result in an error message.

My former e-mail address was jgtaylor@online.no It is now ...@c2i.net

Better to use square brackets:

✓ ... address is [jgtaylor@online.no]. It is now [...@c2i.net].

It is important to use the full point when referring to types of computer programs:

✓ His .exe files malfunctioned but the .com files were fine, so he established a 'dot com' company.

▶ Full points are not use in bulleted and similar lists of short items, with the exception of the final item. Neither are commas required at the end of the each line.

✓ The following comprised the main elements of the party's new policy:
  - lower taxes
  - a minimum wage
  - smaller class sizes
  - cheaper whiskey.

▶ A full point is not used for cardinal points (S, NE), elements (Al, Mg), metric measurements (l, km, m), mass (kg, lb), currencies (DM, p). Plurals do not use a full point: hrs, mins, and so forth (see Chapter 11).

HEADINGS AND TITLES

See also Typefaces, Fonts.

Headings provide a structure to the text. There may be several levels of headings to consider and which may be distinguished by the font size and typeface. Chapter headings may be in upper case, capitalised (each word) or lower case:

1. GOVERNMENT EXPENDITURE AND THE RATE OF INFLATION
2. Government Expenditure and the Rate of Inflation
3. Government expenditure and the rate of inflation

Previously, US publishers largely preferred the second example, UK publishers the third. Today, both of the latter forms are widely used in both the US and the UK.

▶ Headings and titles do not end with a full point. Neither should they contain abbreviations:

✗ Govt. Income and Expenditure Following Devaluation.

▶ If possible, avoid floating hyphens in titles:

✗ Short- and long-term investment strategy – an analyst's approach

✓ Short-term and long-term investment strategy – an analyst's approach

The title may comprise two fragments. These should normally be separated by a colon:

✗ The Multinationals: IBM, GEC and Ford

As indicated, abbreviations and acronyms (IBM etc.) are permitted in titles where familiar. A full point may be necessary where a colon is already in use:

> The Multinationals: IBM, GEC and Ford. A critique

Normally, the text following the full point is the sub-title unless a dash is used.

> Handbook for writers – a guide to punctuation, common practice and usage
>
> Handbook for writers: a guide to punctuation, common practice and usage

A capital letter *may* follow a colon in a title. The article following a colon in a title is normally lower case.

Levels of headings

It is advantageous to consider the number of levels of headings before commencing to write. At the same time the typeface and font for each level should be determined. These can be changed later and extra levels added if necessary.

One consideration is whether numbered levels are required. These are useful in technical and legal texts, and also in certain academic texts where clarity in the structure is helpful to the student. This structure can become somewhat diffuse if too many levels are used. A maximum of four is normally sufficient. Remember also that the font size will assist in clarification. It is not necessary to include all levels in the table of contents (TOC), and indeed, the layout of the TOC will be helpful in portraying the contents of the book. Even a TOC containing the chapter subheadings is often preferable to the practice of using a page or so of the introduction of each chapter to state the aim of the ensuing discussion.

▶ Even though your text may use 1.5 line spacing, keep long titles to single line spacing. The TOC should be single line spacing, but give an extra half line above and below the chapter heading.

▶ As far as possible, determine the number of levels required and the typeface and font for each level *before* you begin. It might not be necessary to number the lowest level. The following example contains six levels (five numbered), and is excessive, not least visually. Four levels (three numbered) is often sufficient.

Chapter 1.   LOCAL GOVERNMENT

1.1   The County Council
...
...

1.2   The Town Council
1.2.1   THE MAYOR
1.2.2   COUNCIL MEMBERS
1.2.3   THE COUNCIL'S FUNCTIONS
1.2.3.1   Budget and finance
1.2.3.1.1   Local financial income
1.2.3.1.2   Government grants
               Block grants
               Ear-marked grants
1.2.4.1   Town planning
1.2.4   COUNCIL ELECTIONS
...

In any case, three levels will be sufficient for the Table of Contents and which, for the above, can appear:

Chapter 1.   Levels of government

1.1   Central Government
1.2   The County Council
1.3   The Town Council
1.3.1   The Mayor
1.3.2   Council Members
1.3.3   The Council's functions
1.3.4   Council elections
1.4   District councils
1.5   The Parish Council

You may well consider that section numbering is not necessary throughout the text at all. Congress and seminar reports which will be taken up in group discussions may nevertheless also benefit from section – even paragraph numbering. It is probably advantageous to remove these when preparing for publication in the *Congress Papers*, for example.

HYPERLINKS

In this technological age your manuscript may well refer to email addresses, web pages, etc. When you type these, it is normal that your manuscript will recognise this as a hyperlink. The address will change colour, normally blue, and be underlined.

http://www.askjeeves.com or john@jgtaylor.com

If you are connected to the web, just clicking either of these in your text will connect you to that site.

PUNCTUATION AND USAGE

▶ A hyperlink may be removed while retaining the text of the email address or web site. Use the help menu on your word-processor to look up *Hyperlink, Remove*. In Microsoft Word this is done by placing the cursor on the address and clicking the RIGHT-hand mouse. Select *Remove Hyperlink* or uncheck the *Activate Hyperlink* box. The colour of the address should now be the default (black), and the cursor is normal. At least you will no longer risk activating the link while editing your manuscript.

HYPHENATED AND CONJOINED WORDS

See Hyphenation (soft); Affixes; Prefixes and suffixes.

Soft hyphenation (see next section) is the division of words as appropriate at the end of a line. In this section we are concerned with 'hard' hyphenation, i.e. joining two or more words to make a new word, sometimes called a **compound** word (e.g. *cross-section*). We also consider a number of prefixes such as *co-, non-*. It should be emphasised that in the following much of the discussion refers to generalisations. There will be exceptions to almost every and any point made. Further, customs are changing. You will be penalised if you write 'mini-series' instead of 'miniseries'. This is a handbook for consulting and not a text covering the rules of the game (even if I do use the term 'rule' occasionally).

In addition to hyphenated words the term 'compound word' is also used for non-hyphenated, **conjoined** words (e.g. *crossroads*) and occasionally to a constructed term, e.g. *smog* = *smoke* + *fog*, and one I like, *guess* + *estimate* = *guestimate* (NODE).

Certain terms used in combination without a hyphen, strictly speaking, are also compound terms (e.g. *cross action, through ticket*). Where a compound or conjoined word forms an adjective or occasionally an adverb, it is called a compound modifier (e.g. *double-glazed [window], undercover [agent]*).

Many compound words were not originally hyphenated. Some became hyphenated and finally merged. Thus, one may encounter *oil field, oil-field*, or *oilfield*, and similarly *data base, data-base, database* (the latter is now normal). Indeed, we find both *wordprocessor and word-processor*.

▶ US English tends to favour a compound word without a hyphen. This applies particularly to nouns (US *crankshaft*, UK *crank-shaft*). Previously, the distinction seemed to relate to single syllable words. US English more readily adopted multi-syllable conjoined terms than did UK English (US *underprivileged*, UK *under-privileged*) although there is an increasing tendency to conjoin multi-syllable words in UK English as well: *over development* may now be encountered as *overdevelopment*.

This distinction does not apply to verbs which are very largely separate words in both US and UK English. Of course, there are many conjoined verbs as well: *to crosscheck, to overthrow, to undertake*, etc.

A. Hyphenated words and the spell-checker

There are at least 18,000 hyphenated terms and conjoined words in the major dictionaries, and probably about 2000 or so in daily use, essentially nouns and adjectives. There are no concrete rules about hyphenation, or even when words should be conjoined. For example, we may encounter *oak leaf* and *oakleaf* in different dictionaries. A problem arises when we hyphenate a word that should not be hyphenated, i.e. it should either comprise two separate words or a conjoined word. Thus, *post-master* will not be recognised as an error for *postmaster* by the spell-checker. Of course, conjoined words will be recognised when they are incorrect, e.g. *bridgebuilder*. The word-processor will probably suggest *bridge builder*, but will not react to *bridge-builder*. Indeed, the hyphenated version may be given in another dictionary!

It is clear that differences may be discerned between, for example, *down town* and *down-town* or *downtown*. The former is an adverbial phrase (*I thought that we could go down town this evening*). The hyphenated form is frequently used as an adjective (*There's a down-town café which has excellent kebab*). The conjoined term is also encountered as an adjective or noun (*The café is located in the downtown. After she became a punk, I feel that she has become very downtown!*). For some terms, the hyphen may indicate quite a different meaning, e.g. *air force* and *air-force* (both nouns).

This problem may be further expounded using 'air'. We have an *air bag*, an *airport*, and an *air-brake*. We also have an *air lieutenant*, an *airman* and an *air-hostess*. We may travel by *air taxi*, an *airship* or an *air-bus*. So where and what are the rules? Better to call these generalisations!

B. Compound words

▶ Compound nouns may comprise an adjective + noun (long-line, shortfall); two nouns (picture-postcard, tablecloth); adverb + noun (up-train, upkeep), and which may be hyphenated or conjoined. There are also many terms which are not hyphenated e.g. a chicken run. Others, particularly those with a prefix, are hyphenated (a mini-skirt), but there is a growing trend towards compound nouns (minicab, minicruise).

▶ Compound verbs comprising an adverb plus a verb are normally are either hyphenated (to over-excite) or conjoined (to undercut). Where a verb has a noun form, the latter is often hyphenated (to pay off – a pay-off: to hand out – a hand-out).

- ▶ There is a 'double-consonant rule' which states that when two words are conjoined resulting in a double consonant, a hyphen should be used. But the trend even here is to drop the hyphen. Thus we find book-keeper and bookkeeper, also under-run and underrun. We will encounter over-regulate (conforming to the rule), but overrule, override, underrate (apparently contradicting it).

- ▶ The 'double-consonant rule' does not apply to prefixes (to misspell). However, it will normally apply where the prefix ends in a vowel (to re-elect), but we find both to re-enter and to reenter (mainly US).

The spell-checker may or may not react to these. As indicated above, it will not show that baby sitter (two words) or over-ride are incorrect! Worse, it will not detect pre-amble (preamble); in-sufficient (insufficient) or any other mis-hyphenated term, regarding these as 'soft' hyphens as encountered at the end of a line.

C. Compound modifiers

Where compound words preface a noun or a verb, they are called compound modifiers. Examples are: an *upper-class* family, a *newly-decorated* room, *ground-to-air* missile. There are no rules concerning hyphenation but the following may be noted:

- ▶ When an adjective is formed from a noun phrase, a hyphen is normally used:
- ✓ In the long term shares will recover. Some must be regarded as a long-term investment.

- ▶ Where the present continuous '-ing' form is used to form an adjective, the term is nearly always hyphenated, fast-talking salesman, the measures were far-reaching. (This does not apply to nouns, e.g. a shortcoming),

- ▶ Occasionally three words or more words may be hyphenated into a compound word:

    The natural-gas-based industries. She used a carmen-rose-colour-base make-up!

I think that I can just about accept the last example, not knowing which hyphen to drop!

Clearly, there is no general rule. We may find farm-hand and fish-farm-hand but also oyster-farm and pearl-oyster farm. Rather, consideration should be given to the meaning. Technical articles in particular will require careful use of the hyphen. The placement of the hyphens in terms such as cast iron wheel flange machine tools may need some thought.

D. Place-names, routes

A distinction should be made between names which are hyphened:

✓ Take the tube to London-Heathrow

and routes where a spaced dash means 'to':

✓ The flight route is London-Heathrow – Paris-Orly.

E. Numbers

Written numbers between twenty-one and ninety-nine.

Values of 100 and above normally use numbers, but text may be more appropriate in a title. Hyphenation might also be appropriate:

✓ Six-hundred freqwently misspellt words

✓ One-hundred-and-one Dalmatians

Special measurements use numbers and are hyphenated:

✓ It was made of 18-carat gold. It filled a 2-gallon barrel.

F. Time

When text is used, time is hyphenated:

✓ The train departs at seven-thirty; the connecting bus leaves at four-fifteen.

G. Compass points

Most compass points are hyphenated:

✓ north-west, east-north-east, south-west-by-south.

Note the following, (but don't ask the logic of this):

east-by-north, east-by-south, west-by-north, west-by-south, BUT north by east, north by west, south by east, south by west.

H. Colloquial and other phrases

Many of these comprise three or more words and are largely, but not exclusively, hyphenated.

Once upon a time there was a man, a real man-about-town, although he lived in no-man's-land. He had a get-rich-quick attitude and was a right so-and-so. Life had its ups-and-downs for his mother-in-law, largely on account of his devil-may-care attitude. He was hard of hearing, but always first past the post at opening time.

We may encounter some phrases which certain dictionaries choose not to hyphenate, for example, over-and-out and over and out. Generally, if the term takes an adjectival function it is hyphenated, e.g. down-and-out, a step-by-step approach.

▶ The adverbial form is not generally hyphenated: We will go through this step by step.

I. Titles, occupations

Titles are mostly hyphenated such as air-vice-marshal, Attorney-General, as are many occupations: ballet-dancer, office-boy, delivery-man, lady-in-waiting. But there are also not a few exceptions: car mechanic, steel worker, bank manager, office cleaner. Occupations ending in 'man', 'lady', 'master' are frequently conjoined: milkman, charlady, postmaster (exception station-master). Curiously, we have the music mistress, but the postmistress.

J. Clarification

▶ A hyphen is clearly required when used to distinguish between two different meanings. Observe the difference between the following:

The jacket was made of a light brown material... It was a lightweight, brown material

The jacket was made of a light-brown material... It was light-brown in colour

▶ A hyphen is used to separate a prefix where necessary to distinguish between two forms of a word. The following are examples where the hyphenated prefix changes the meaning of the word, e.g. recount (re-count), recollect (re-collect), recover (re-cover), recreation (re-creation), reform (re-form), refund (re-fund), resign (re-sign), predominate (pre-dominate), pretension (pre-tension).

K. Other

Many other words are used in compound form where hyphenation may also clarify the text as in:

The project was now regarded as being less important in the revised budget.

– as opposed to:

There were more less-important projects for which money was then available. (I actually read this in a report. I found it acceptable in the context.)

▶ A 'suspended hyphen' is used to avoid repetition (see Dash).

✓ Two-, three-, and four-room apartments were available

A hyphen may be used to create a compound word where this serves to clarify a point:

✓ There were only two kilo packets available. (Just two packets of one kilo each.)

✓ There were only two-kilo packets available. (Only packets weighing two kilos were available.)

A common mistake is can-not for cannot. It may nevertheless be noted that a point may be emphasised by keeping the two words separate: 'I told you,' John said emphatically, 'I can not do that – so don't ask me again. Well, not before Saturday!'

Book titles: both words in a hyphenated term retain the upper case where the upper case is used throughout the title.

✓ *Counter-Revolution: Inter-Regional and Urban-Rural Conflict in Indonesia*

HYPHENATION (SOFT)

By soft hyphenation we mean the division of words, usually into syllables, at the end of a line – a process sometimes referred to as *syllabification*. The word-processor has a hyphenation function which may be turned off, enabling manual hyphenation to be undertaken if desired.

A useful definition of a syllable is given in *Collins English Dictionary*:

syllable:
– a combination or set of one or more units of sound in a language that must consist of a sonorous element (a sonant or a vowel) and may or may not contain less sonorous elements (consonants or semivowels) flanking it on either side or both sides: for example 'paper' has two syllables.

– or in brief 'a word, or component of a word, perceived as a single sound unit.'

Most publishing houses include several options for hyphenation and most word-processors contain a hyphenation option although this may not necessarily comply with the requirements of the publishing house. There are a number of basic phonetic rules:

1. Short words. Words of five letters or fewer should not be divided. Exceptions are prefixed words. Division may take place after the second or third letters where this does not create confusion. For example, re-creation (to make new) and recreation (leisure activity) are two different words. These may be hyphenated respectively: re-cre-ation, recre-ation.

2. Hyphenated words. (e.g. under under-ripe) Use the natural hyphen or hyphenate following the prefix or before a suffix.

3. Long words such as re-embellishment *may* be hyphenated re-embellishment or re-embellish-ment.

4. Initial letter. Somewhere I read 'Do not divide after the first letter of a word. An exception may be permitted where the remainder of the word forms a variant of the whole'. Example: evaluation, e-valuation. But why would you want to do that anyway?

5. Avoid hyphenation where this may result in two separate words: carpet > car-pet; therapist > the-rapist; anaesthetic > an aesthetic. Not always easy – ontogenesis > onto-genesis(?).

The word *station* should be hyphenated sta-tion (and not stat-ion). Generally, the final syllable following the hyphen will commence with a consonant, e.g. industrious-ly. However, it is quite permissible to hyphenate the word between two vowels where these belong to two separate syllables: industri-ous; (as well as in-dustrious). Another possibility: indus-trious (but not indust-rious). By way of further example we have nec·es·sary and un·nec·e·sary (where · illustrates the optional hyphenation points).

When in doubt, follow the phonetics of a word. If the first syllable is not accentuated, then divide before the accented syllable: manipu-*la*tion rather than mani-pulation or manip-ulation!

Collins English Spelling Dictionary provides all options for 150,000 UK and US words. This handy reference shows, for example, evalu-ation. However, when a prefix ending in a vowel is affixed to a word commencing with a vowel, hyphenation (other than after the affix) is not recommended: re-evaluation. But there are considerable differences between the publishing houses as well as word-processors.

INDEFINITE ARTICLE ('A')

▶ Generally, 'a' is used before consonants and 'an' before vowels. But it is the pronunciation which determines the nature of the article. Thus, we have a hair, a hierarchy, etc., but an honest man, an heir to the throne, and so forth. A hotel and an hotel are both acceptable. Words beginning with 'u' may also take on 'a' or 'an' – dependent upon pronunciation: a unit, an understanding.

▶ The indefinite article preceding an abbreviation is dependent upon the pronunciation of the initial letter: a PhD, an MA.

▶ The indefinite article may be dropped in 'telegram style' as used in advertisements. This is also a captivating style for chapter headings:

✓ Change of government – change of direction.

INVERTED COMMAS

See Quotation marks.

ITALICS

A. Emphasis

✓ Italics are used to *emphasise* a word.

B. Titles

Book and journal titles should be italicised in the text.

✓ More in information is found in Partridge's book *Usage and Abusage*.

▶ There are particular rules to follow for references in the literature list. (See Chapter 4, References and bibliographies)

C. Names

Ships, trains etc. should be italicised, but not buildings.

✓ The most famous train in those days was *The Orient Express*. It was as popular as the Tower of London among tourists.

D. Latin and foreign terms

✓ As a politician his speeches could continue *ad infinitum*.

▶ Latin abbreviations in common use do not employ italics: op. cit., ibid., et al. Others, less familiar, will do so, *ipso facto*.

✓ He maintained that it was his rite [*sic*] to get drunk on a Saturday night.

▶ Many foreign words such as café and bistro (French slang) have become anglicised and do not employ italics. But, again, check with the publisher.

▶ Where a foreign title is in italics the translation should use the normal typeface:

✓ His best seller was *La femme fatale* (The fatal sex).

MANUSCRIPT: STRUCTURE AND LAYOUT

A. Journal articles

An article in a journal will normally require an abstract followed by the main text and references.

Abstract
The abstract should not exceed more than twenty lines, preferably ten or twelve. Remember who the target group (the potential readers) are. Are they specialists who are already very familiar with the field? Are they students or

persons interested in the field without specialist background knowledge?

The abstract may well be the first contact that the (potential) reader has with the subject. It should present the subject matter and argument in a straightforward manner, but should also contain sufficient information to indicate the level of background knowledge required in order that the content may be comprehended and will be informative, either for the general public or the specialist.

The main text
Although an article will not contain a table of contents, subheadings add clarity to the structure. It is often sufficient with one level, occasionally two. The first section, *Introduction*, should contain a comprehensive account of the content, the hypothesis to be tested and the methods used in the analysis. The nature and source of the data should be sufficiently described. Naturally, the content of this section will depend on the nature of the subject to be treated, but all too often I read articles which assume that the reader is already familiar with the content and where the introduction offers little enlightenment on the subject to be discussed.

The *Summary and conclusions* are the vital ingredient. Even if the argument in the main text has been difficult to follow, the summary and conclusions should clarify the results of the discussion. It may be that the argument has been difficult to follow, but this final section should serve to clarify the preceding discussion enabling, if necessary, the article to be re-read with a better understanding.

B. Books

If your book is to be printed by a publishing house, then the publisher will take care of most of the layout. But even if this is a research report to be photocopied and distributed in just a few dozen copies, a professional approach to layout and structure will be appreciated by the reader. The following summarises the main elements of the layout although many are not necessarily obligatory. You may find more detailed information in a number of publications in the *How To* series on writing a dissertation, an assignment, a textbook, a report, and more.

Pagination
Pagination commences with the first right-hand page of the book (often the title page): all right-hand pages are therefore odd numbers. Each new section in the introductory section, known as the *prelims* (discussed below) normally begins on the next right-hand page. New chapters sometimes begin on the next right hand page. The page number is not shown on blank left-hand pages.

Page numbering may be top or bottom outside (i.e. towards the margins). Where this is located at the top-outside and the publisher requires the chapter title page to be numbered, this will exceptionally be placed at the bottom.

The introductory sections referred to as the *prelims* (discussed below) are normally numbered in lower case Roman (i, ii etc.). However, I notice that several publishers now use normal (Arabic) numbers throughout. As the page number does not appear on the first page of each section, and neither on blank pages, plus that fact that many of the prelims are just one page, the first page in the prelims where the page number is shown may be viii, x, (8 or 10 if Arabic number are used), or even higher.

Where the publisher chooses to commence each new chapter on the next right-hand (odd-numbered) page, where the facing left-hand page is blank this will mean that the page number is not given on either of these pages. Some publishers therefore number the first page of each chapter where this commences on a right-hand page.

The Prelims

The *prelims* contain general information about the book.

- First page of each section not numbered.
- Each section commences on next right-hand page except where stated.

Dedication
- Often first right-hand page of the book. Text frequently italics: *To my wife...*

Title page
- Title, author, position or title.
- Next right-hand page.

Table of Contents (TOC)
- Next right-hand page.

The TOC may be generated automatically by most word-processors, and incorporate several levels of headings.

The following lists may appear on consecutive pages. They do not have to commence on a new right-hand page.

List of illustrations

List of tables

List of contributors
- Used where several authors are involved. May follow Preface (see below) or be included in the final section 'About the Authors'.

Foreword

Acknowledgements
- Advisors, consultants, typists, etc. Usually included at the end of the Preface but may comprise a separate section.
- Commences on right-hand page.

Abbreviations
- Abbreviations (institutions, organisations etc.), Notation (mathematical symbols) where required.

Glossary
- A glossary may be included here or at the end of the book. It contains a list of specialist terms which may need to be explained.

MAIN BODY OF THE TEXT

Chapters
Each chapter should begin on the first available right-hand page, but may begin on the next new page even if this is a left-hand page. If the book is an anthology with different authors for each chapter, then a new chapter should begin on the next right-hand page.

Chapter title pages are normally not numbered. A blank (left-hand) page at the end of a chapter is not numbered.

Bibliography
Usually commences on next page (after final chapter). Where literature lists are included in each chapter these may follow on after the text or preferably commence on the next page.

Appendixes
Often numbered I, II, III etc, alternatively A, B, C...
The term 'annex' is now used by some publishers.

Index
This may be generated with any modern word-processor.

About the author(s)
A short autobiographical note. Commences on next available page. The *List of Contributors* may also be included here. This section may also be located at the beginning of the prelims.

MEASUREMENTS

See also Chapter 11, abbreviations, measures.

NUMBERS

A. Numbers generally

Originally there was a clear distinction between UK and US values of a billion and more.

The *original* UK scale relates to powers of a million.

A million = 10^6 = 1000^2 = 1 million.
A billion = 10^{12} = 1 million^2 = 1,000,000,000,000 = a million million.
A trillion = 10^{18} = 1 million^3 = a million billion (or a million million million).
A quadrillion is 10^{24} (UK).

France and Germany previously used the same scales as the UK, but these countries later adopted the US system and which is also gaining popularity in the UK, particularly in scientific journals. Confusion may be avoided by ignoring the terms million, billion and trillion, and referring to powers of 10. (The power indicates the number of zeros following the 1.) The most commonly encountered term where confusion arises is 'billion' – also called a milliard – (a million million UK; a thousand million US). As stated, times are changing, but add a footnote if you think that there is any doubt.

Value	UK	US	
million	10^6	10^6	
billion	10^{12}	10^9	(UK = 1,000,000,000,000; US = 1,000,000,000)
trillion	10^{18}	10^{12}	
quadrillion	10^{24}	10^{15}	
quintillion	10^{30}	10^{18}	
sextillion	10^{36}	10^{21}	
septillion	10^{42}	10^{24}	
octillion	10^{48}	10^{27}	
nonillion	10^{54}	10^{30}	
decillion	10^{60}	10^{33}	(Originally, a billion billion UK)
milliard	10^9	(now obsolete) = (US) 1 billion	
zillion	10^∞	10^∞	(an infinitely large number).
			There are a zillion stars in the universe.

A nano is a billionth part or 10^{-9}.

The abbreviation for a million can be confusing. Personally, I previously used mill. (which only seems to appear in the *Random House (US) Dictionary*). This is interesting as *mill* (no full point) signifies one-tenth of a US cent. The following is a summary of several dictionaries:

PUNCTUATION AND USAGE

Dictionary	1 million
Cambridge Internat. Dictionary of English	m or M
Chamber's Dictionary	m, m., M, M.
Collins Authors' and Printers' Dictionary	m.
Collins Dictionary	M or M.
New Oxford English Dictionary	m
Oxford Concise Dictionary	m.
Oxford Dictionary for Writers and Editors	m.
Oxford Dictionary of Abbreviations	m
The Longman Dictionary	m
The Penguin Dictionary	m
The American Heritage Dictionary	-
Encarta Dictionary	m
Random House Dictionary	mill.
Merriam Webster	-

The symbol m seems to be favoured, but the choice is yours. Just stick to it.

▶ Most dictionaries quote M as being the Roman symbol for 1000, but we also encounter m. (for mille = 1000). Once again, the publishing house might have views on this, but as long as you are consistent your preference will probably be accepted.

▶ Continental countries generally indicate a negative value using what the English refer to as the division sign: ÷2 rather than –2. Whereas the English would write 8÷4 = 2, the continental (and scientific) method would be 8/4 = 2.

For astronomical (lit.) values, light years or parsecs may be used. (A parsec is the distance from which the Earth's distance from the Sun would subtend one second of arc, approximately 3.26 light years).

▶ US English uses the symbol # to mean 'number', for example, Apartment #34.

B. Decimals

▶ Note that English and American use commas and full points in opposite fashion to continental use.

US/UK: $12,345,678.90   Continental: NOK 12.345.678,90

▶ For four-digit amounts the comma is usually omitted: $1,234.50 = $1234.50

A recent practice has been to replace the separators with a space, although this can create problems when using right-margin justification. It will also be found that some scientific journals have adopted the continental style of a comma separator for the decimals: $12 345 678,90. Remember that your word-processor uses spaces for line breaks! Further, right-hand justification may put awkward spaces between the number groups.

▶ Generally, do not commence a sentence with figures. However, it is my impression that this may be permissible in technical and medical journals. The publisher may also accept commencing a sentence with a decimal figure when this relates to millions, billions, etc.:

> 2.6 million refugees left in just three weeks.

Prefacing this with 'Some 2.6...' is a satisfactory solution, but only if we are referring to a general amount. Neither should sentences commence with a decimal point, and preferably not with a number at all:

✗ .37 kilograms of sodium was added to the mixture.

Rewrite commencing with a zero: 0.37 kg..., or preferably rewrite the sentence:

✓ The amount of 0.37 kilograms was added to the mixture.

A leading zero should be used in the middle of a sentence, 0.37 rather than .37, as this gives clarity.

▶ Long decimals values are normally written without punctuation:

✓ Napier's constant, $e = (1 + 1/n)^n = 2.71821828459045......$

but grouping into fives increases legibility:

✓ pi = 3.14159 26535 89793 23846 26433 83279 50288 41971 69399 37510...

C. Percentages

As a percentage is a specific amount, numbers are often preferred:

> Unemployment fell by twenty-six per cent during the period March 1996 – June 1998.

✓ Vacancies rose by 23%, unemployment fell by 7% in the period.

▶ Avoid commencing a sentence with a percentage given in numbers. Rewrite.

✗ 26% of total production was lost.

✓ Of the total amount produced, 26% was lost.

▶ The verb should correspond with the subject. In the above we were concerned with *an* amount. In the example below, the amount is considered as a plural.

✓ Of all units imported, 26 per cent were damaged in transport.

PUNCTUATION AND USAGE

▶ (Note UK per cent, but percentage; US percent.) A recent trend noted in the UK press is to use the abbreviation pc. Demand fell by 40 pc in October.

▶ The percentage symbol [%] is preferable with decimals: 2.1%, 6.785%, rather than 2.1 per cent, etc.

The continental style frequently places a space before the % character (e.g. 2.6 %). This is not done in English or American.

Further, avoid the following:

✗ The %-age declined steadily in the period.

▶ Percentages can be confusing when used relatively as with:

✗ Whereas unemployment was 6% in 1987, it had increased to 10% in 1990, a 60% increase in four years.

Not only are we referring to absolute and relative amounts in the same sentence, such statements also require to be qualified, perhaps with a reference to the absolute numbers.

▶ For very small amounts it is convenient to use per mill (or per mil), or ‰ (= per thousand) rather than using a percentage. The level was determined to be less than 2‰. If decimals are involved, it may be better to use text: The level was under 1.5 parts per thousand.

'Per mill' (per mil) – from the Latin 'per mille' – does not use a full point. Observe that 'per mill.' (with a full point) means per million.

▶ Consideration should be given to using proportions rather than percentages in certain circumstances. 'Almost 63% of customers lived within a mile of the shop.' Surely more informative to write 'About 5 of every 8 customers...'

D. Fractions

▶ Generally, use the text form for fractions less than 1 unless a very precise amount is to be stated. Use numbers for values incorporating fractions which exceed 1 (e.g. 1½).

✓ The test tube was half full; the normal amount was at least five-eighths. Wastage was five-sixteenths.

✓ There were between 2¼ and 2½ lbs in each box. Normally there were approximately 3 lbs.

Abbreviations for mass etc. may be used when numbers are employed.

Most word-processors will automatically convert the quarters and halves: 1/2 becomes ½, 3/4 becomes ¾, for example. Fractions in eighths (⅛, ⅝ etc.) will probably have to be inserted from the 'Symbols' table (using 'Insert'). To type 1½ (for example), a space has to follow the initial '1' before typing 1/2 to give 1 ½. If this is not done the result will be 11/2. The space must

A HANDBOOK FOR WRITERS OF ENGLISH

then be removed, giving 1½. For other fractions, rather than 3/5 for example, another method is to superscript the numerator and subscript the denominator giving $^3/_5$. This will naturally apply to values exceeding 1 and where the numerical form is preferred to text, e.g. $1^5/_9$.

Converting fractions to decimal equivalents

Conversions from fractions to decimals is simply the numerator divided by the denominator: $^7/_{16} = 0.4375$.

Converting decimals to fractions (proportions)

This conversion is more problematic than the other way around, but the occasion might arise where such a conversion serves a purpose. Occasionally it is more convenient to state a proportion (or fraction) rather than a decimal or a percentage. For example: 'About 2 in every 7 of those released were apprehended in less than twelve months'. Much better than 'about 28 percent...'.

The table shows the corresponding numerator (N) and denominator (D) for all decimal values greater or equal to 1/20 and less or equal to 19/20. These are approximate in that certain inconvenient denominators are excluded (elevenths, thirteenths, seventeenths, etc.).

Dec.	N	D	Dec.	N	D	Dec.	N	D	Dec.	N	D
.04	1	20	.27	3	11	.51	1	2	.75	3	4
.05	1	20	.28	2	7	.52	8	15	.76	3	4
.06	1	16	.29	2	7	.53	8	15	.77	7	9
.07	1	15	.30	3	10	.54	6	11	.78	7	9
.08	1	12	.31	5	16	.55	11	20	.79	4	5
.09	1	11	.32	5	16	.56	9	16	.80	4	5
.10	1	10	.33	1	3	.57	4	7	.81	13	16
.11	1	9	.34	1	3	.58	7	12	.82	9	11
.12	1	8	.35	7	20	.59	7	12	.83	5	6
.13	2	15	.36	4	11	.60	4	5	.84	5	6
.14	1	7	.37	3	8	.61	4	5	.85	17	20
.15	3	20	.38	3	8	.62	5	8	.86	6	7
.16	1	6	.39	2	5	.63	5	8	.87	13	15
.17	1	6	.40	2	5	.64	7	11	.88	7	8
.18	2	11	.41	5	12	.65	13	20	.89	8	9
.19	3	16	.42	5	12	.66	2	3	.90	9	10
.20	1	5	.43	3	7	.67	2	3	.91	10	11
.21	1	5	.44	7	16	.68	11	16	.92	11	12
.22	2	9	.45	9	20	.69	11	16	.93	14	15
.23	2	9	.46	5	11	.70	7	10	.94	15	16
.24	1	4	.47	7	15	.71	5	7	.95	19	20
.25	1	4	.48	7	15	.72	5	7	.96	19	20
.26	4	15	.49	1	2	.73	8	11	.97	19	20
			.50	1	2	.74	11	15	.98	19	20

E. Formulae, E-notation

Very often formulae in technical articles are difficult to read because of poor spacing. There are no rules here, but compare:

$e = 1+1+(1/2!)+(1/3!)+(1/4!)+(1/5!)...(1/n!)$

$\text{Logit}(p) = \beta_0+\beta_1 PA+\beta_2 R+\beta_3 L+\beta_4 T$

with:

✓ $e = 1 + 1 + (1/2!) + (1/3!) + (1/4!) + (1/5!)...(1/n!)$

✓ $\text{Logit}(p) = \beta_0 + \beta_1 PA + \beta_2 R + \beta_3 L + \beta_4 T$

▶ Another problem of clarity arises with exponentials – largely because writers either do not know what they represent, or assume everyone else does! The difficulty arises with output from statistical programs giving, for example:

The results of the analysis showed a = 2E4, while b = 1.7E-3

This E-notation should be converted to normal notation. $E2 = 10^2$; $E-3 = 1/10^3$ etc.

In the above: $a = 2 E 4 = 2 \times 10^4 = 20000$ (or 2 followed by 4 zeros). (The '2' has been moved 4 places to the *left*). By the same argument, we move the decimal point the other way for $b = 1.7E-3$. That is, $b = 1.7 \times 10^{-3}$ or $1.7 \times 1/(10^3) = 0.0017$. (The '1' has been moved 3 places to the *right*.)

I recently read in a book about the Universe by Azimov: 'An ordinary galaxy will emit about ten thousand trillion trillion (10,000,000,000,000,000, 000,000,000,000) kilowatts of energy in the form of microwaves.' I would have been just as vague if he had said 10E27, but a little more impressed if he had written 10^{27}.

F. Proportions and ratios

Proportions are normally easily comprehended.

✓ One in five objected: one in ten abstained.

But do not mix proportions and percentages:

✗ Whereas two-fifths agreed, 27 per cent abstained.

✗ Almost a half were opposed while more than two-fifths abstained.

The mind boggles at calculating the proportion who actually agreed in the latter example! In fact, it was probably about one ninth. Try converting these to proportions based on the same unit (here, ninths would probably suffice). Remember that some readers have difficulty with numbers above 100, proportions other than quarters, and percentages of any amount! Try explaining to someone the logic of the following: Output more than doubled, from 400 to 900 units – an increase of 125 per cent.

▶ It is sometimes a mistake to convert absolute numbers to a percentage unreservedly. Absolute values keep the volume in perspective. Of the 355,000 tons produced, 175,000 (49%) were exported.

▶ Ratios are sometimes misunderstood. A ratio of one to three is given as 1:3. Note that this implies 'one in four'. ('The ratio of men to women was 1:3' meaning that of every four persons, three were women.) Ratios should be expressed as numbers.

G. Monetary and financial units

It is immaterial whether one writes The budget exceeded 13 million USD, or The budget exceeded $13 million. However, with amounts under 10 units either: The budget was under $3 million, or The budget was under three million USD.

That brings us to the question: $3 million was budgeted, or $3 million were budgeted.

Instinctively, if the whole amount was budgeted for one purpose, then '$3 million was budgeted for defence'. If this amount was to be apportioned to several purposes, then '$3 million were budgeted for schools, hospitals and the police'. This is one of those grey areas where the more conservative would maintain that $3 million is a plural amount. See note under Plurals.

▶ The ECU symbol [€] now appears on the keyboard and is available with Windows 98 and later. It is achieved using Alt Gr + E. The above paragraph referring to USD also applies to ECU.

▶ In finance, the expression 'the market rose by 25 points' refers to decimal points, here, a quarter of one percent.

Abbreviations for the main monetary units are given in Chapter 10.

H. Roman numerals

See also section on Roman numerals.

Roman numerals are used for volumes (occasionally chapters):

✓ This is discussed in Paine, R., *Coast Lapp Society* vol. II.

✓ Described in Chapter III.

While Henry Vth is acceptable, the following is not. Incidentally, you will have to superscript Vth yourself.

✗ A full description is given in the Vth chapter!

▶ Lower case Roman numbers are used for the introductory pages (prelims) in a book.

PUNCTUATION AND USAGE

▶ Copyright date uses Roman numbers.
✓ © MCMLXXXIX

I. Page numbers

References are given as p. 5.

▶ The dash (–) and not the minus sign (-) is used to mean 'up to and including'. Most publishers used an unspaced dash. There should be a space after 'p.' or 'pp.'.

✗ pp.26-28; pp.105–8.

✓ pp. 10–15.

▶ pp. 126–28 is an alternative to pp. 126–128. Most publishers prefer the full number, and in any case for numbers less than 100; pp. 95–98 and not pp. 95–8.

Some publishers prefer the spaced dash: pp. 95 – 98.

J. Periods

It is a matter of choice as to whether one uses *1756–91* or *1756–1791*. The latter is often easier to read and will result in consistency insofar as it is necessary to write *1788–1823*, for example. The dashed date is suitable for dates of birth and death, but in other cases the preposition is correct.

✓ Mozart (1756–1791) wrote 41 symphonies.
✓ The dispute lasted from 1932 until 1939.
✓ Rationing lasted from 1945 to 1952.

A common mistake when referring to a period is treat the dash as meaning 'until':

✗ Rationing lasted from 1945–1952.

K. Digits or text?

▶ Generally, text should be used at the beginning of a sentence.

Precise references to numbers, mass, volume, etc.

▶ Where a precise amount is given or required, numbers should be used. Weights etc. are abbreviated.

✓ The sacks measured 0.9 by 1.6 m and contained 56 lbs of grain.

▶ Technical articles and references to measures use numbers:

✓ In general terms 1 dm^3 is approximately 0.57 pints; 1000 litres is precisely 1 m^3.

This also applies to percentages. Proportions and ratios in technical articles use numbers, otherwise text.

✓ The increase was 26 percent. The ratio was 1:3. One in seven migrated.

Text and numbers may both appear in the same sentence where the context is clear:

✓ The three involved received 2, 6 and 9 months jail respectively.

General references to numbers, mass, volume, etc.

a) Low numbers

Text should be used for numbers in the range 1 to 10 (one to ten). Some publishers use 1 to 99 (one to ninety-nine). Text may also be used according to discretion for higher numbers (discussed below).

✓ He was two years old at the time...

Just fifty votes decided the issue or Just 50 votes decided the issue.

▶ Where text is used for values in the range 21 to 99, these are hyphenated: twenty-one, sixty-three, and also in higher values if the text form is chosen: one hundred and twenty-one....

Abbreviations should not be used for mass in general references etc.

✓ The box was about five cubic feet and contained some ten kilograms.

✓ The consignment was about 150 kilograms short.

b) Reference to numbers greater than 100

▶ Values divisible by one hundred up to and including 1000 may employ text. Some publishers apply this rule for round values up to a million.

✓ The petition contained more than eight hundred names.

✓ About five hundred of the six hundred applicants were under 18.

– although numbers are also acceptable:

✗ About 500 of the 600 applicants were considered qualified.

If the numbers are not round hundreds, figures are preferable.

✓ There were 250 applicants for the post.

The rule about commencing sentences with a number still applies:

✗ 500 of the 600 applicants were considered qualified.

A number may precede 'million'. There is no rule here, but 5 is normally the lower limit.

✓   The city had almost one million inhabitants in 1980; twenty years later it exceeded 5 million.

Numbers larger than a thousand *may* commence a sentence, but *only* if re-writing is difficult. Here, for example, the number at the beginning makes an impact. (Try re-writing the sentence with the figure elsewhere, or even place 'Some' at the beginning of the sentence. It doesn't have quite the same effect.)

   3,655 out-patients had been waiting for more than three months.

Exceptions to the 'text rule' are dates, time, references to pages or chapters, etc., ages (the 8-year old boy, *etc.*), units of measurement (a 6-inch plank), percentages and statistics. Numbers should be used in connection with symbols: 212°, 5%, $10. This will, of course, apply to mathematical symbols such as $+$, $-$, $\pm$, $<$, $>$ or similar: -4, ± 6, <30.

▶   A combination of text and numbers may be employed for the sake of clarity:

✓   The school had two hundred and ten pupils. Thirty-three of these were from overseas: 4 were from four different Asian countries, 14 were from nine African countries, and 15 from eleven different European countries.

But not a few readers are number-blind! Can *you* remember any details from the previous paragraph? There is much to be said for listing the above:

✓   The school had two hundred and ten pupils. Of these, thirty-three were from overseas countries as follows. (Numbers in parentheses show the number of countries.)

Asia	4	(4)
Africa	14	(9)
Europe	15	(11)

c) General comments on large numbers

▶   Commas are used to separate thousands, millions, etc.

✓   The population of the USA is 285,538,566

▶   Some publishers require a comma for all values above 999; others permit 9999 rather than 9,999. However, if the value is a round 100, the comma may be dropped: 2500 instead of 2,500. Numbers 10,000 and higher always use a comma: 10,643; 123,321.

▶   Having said that, it appears to be increasingly the practice to omit commas, replacing these by a space: 3 456; 10 121; 103 666 000. This certainly provides a clearer picture in tables. But, beware that your word-processor may automatically break line at a space thereby splitting the number. Further, spacing may appear excessive where right-margin justification is used. This can be fixed in Microsoft Word (for example), by highlighting the numbers and then using Format – Font – Character spacing – Condensed – By . . . and then set to 0.7 or other appropriate value.

One exception to the above rule for commas or spacing is where a number is assigned to a product or commodity. For example:

✓ It is stated in Act no. 25466 that the fishing rights are protected according to international convention.

✓ The relevant stock part no. 423959 had been replaced by no. 2444324.

L. Ranges

Ranges are often incorrectly defined. > 10 means 'greater than 10', i.e. 10.05, 10.1, 10.5 etc. and above, depending upon the interval used, but *excluding* 10.0. > = 10 (greater or equal to 10) will include 10.0 and above, although more conveniently given as a range such as 10.0 – 19.9. Tables must be precise, each category registering the smallest unit involved, here tenths.

Ideally, 0 should be written as 0.0 indicating that intervals are in tenths. The scale indicates precisely what measurements have been employed.

0.0 – 9.9
10.0 – 19.9
20.0 – 29.9
etc.

The following is ambiguous and therefore wrong (even if decimal .0 is employed):

0 – 10
10 – 20
20 – 30
etc.

Avoid 0 – 10; 11 – 20; 21 –, etc. Keep the tens in the same groups: 0 – 9; 10 – 19; 20 – , etc.

Technical articles however, may employ:

0 – < 10
10 – < 20
etc.

M. Other

The practice of using # for number is common in the US, but is rarely used (at present) in the UK. *He lives in Block 2, Apt. #5.* On the other hand, it is now quite common to see salaries quoted as 12K, seemingly an inheritance of the data era where K = 1000. In connection with the millennium year 2000, it was not uncommon to see this referred to as Y2K.

Ordinal values (first, second, third etc.) are frequently used to list points to be made. The adverbial forms (firstly, secondly, thirdly etc.) are more colloquial and should be used sparingly.

The apostrophe is not normally found in the following:

This year, Miss Jones will teach the under 8s.

'The under eights' is also acceptable. The under 8's may be encountered in the genitive form such as the under 8's books are now available.

In a book from 1921 I found: Edward III.'s reign. The full point is not really necessary today: Edward III's reign. (Note that non-serif fonts do not produce the Roman 'I'.)

PAGES

The standard A4 page is 297 mm x 210 mm. This corresponds to the British A4 measuring 8½" × 11". Standard margins are 1.27 cm or 1". Camera-ready copy may require mirror margins where the inside margins are wider to allow for binding.

Page numbering

See Manuscript: structure and layout.

PARENTHESES [( )]

See also Brackets, Full point, D.

Parentheses is the correct term for curved brackets [( ] and [ )]. These are used in pairs.

Parentheses have several uses:

A. Explanation

✓ Mr Logan told Mr Berrigan that his wife (Mrs Logan) was responsible.

✓ The committee arranged to meet again at the same time next week (Wednesday).

B. Clarification

▶ Parentheses may be useful in clarifying a point. When a hyphened prefix is involved there is no space following the closing parenthesis:

A (semi-)conductor is used on the template.

▶ Placement of punctuation signs may be inside or outside the closing parenthesis depending on the context:

✓ What was the expected increase (in the government bonds)?

✓ The election was declared void (because the president lost?).

In preparing this manuscript I wrote 'Sample statistics are used for estimating the parameters of a population, often of unknown size'. This could be understood that the parameters were of an unknown size. Parentheses proved better: '...parameters of a population (often of unknown size)', more so than '...parameters of a population the size of which might be unknown.'

If an *entire* sentence is within parentheses, the final full point is *within* the closing parenthesis:

✓ (He confirmed this later.)

– otherwise outside:

✓ She said she had (although later denied this).

C. Style

In addition to explanation and clarification, the use of parentheses can add to the style to your writing, reducing the need for commas and semicolons.

✓ The market was described as anticipatory (?) but not optimistic!

✓ The shares did rise (slightly) towards the end of dealing following rumours of a merger (later shown to be groundless).

The amount of text in parentheses should be considered. (Sometimes an entire sentence – or even two – is included within parentheses, but this gives the impression that the author is not certain whether to include it or not. Further, this may displace the closing parenthesis such that the reader loses track of where the opening parenthesis lay. This is, of course, a typical example.)

If a sentence ends with an exclamation or question mark within the closing parenthesis, a final full point is required, e.g. She received his card (he remembered!). But then...

D. Parentheses in lists

Parenthesised numbers in lists can be appropriate if items are listed:

✓ The following three posts were to be appointed: (1) Chairman, (2) Secretary, (3) Accountant.

Numbers are preferable here, rather than (a), (b), etc., as three specific posts are mentioned.

▶ When used at the beginning of a line, it is a matter of taste whether single or paired parentheses are used for letters.

Several points were mentioned in the debate:

PUNCTUATION AND USAGE

   a) the state of the roads
   b) alternative financing of the toll roads
   c) the establishment of a new Inspectorate.

▶ The full point occurs only at the end of the final item on this list.

If items are contained in the text, then the paired parentheses (a) provide more clarity and, (b) are easier for the reader to locate. Lower case letters and Roman numerals are often preferable: (a), (b), (c); (i), (ii), (iii) etc. However, listed items in a text (rather than in rows as above), can be more confusing than revealing:

✗   Twenty-six delegates from four countries attended: 1) The U.K. (12); 2) France (3); 3) Germany (5); and 4) Japan (6).

Why, indeed, bother to number the items at all?

E. Braces

In mathematics parentheses the curly brace may be encountered { }. These form the highest order of parentheses. Square brackets are the secondary level and normal parentheses are the primary form {..[..(...)..]..} and should be used accordingly:

   a. $(2/3)(6-2) = 2.667$
   b. $[2+(6 \times 3)-5] = 15$
   c. $2 + \{\sqrt{[(6 \times 3)-(2 \times 4.5)]+3}\ \}^2 = 38$

PLURALS

   'The council were interested in the mayor's comments. The committee was not interested at all.'

▶ Singular or plural, i.e. *was* or *were*? Not really a problem. Did you regard the council as a group of old so-and-so's who didn't have too much to say for themselves? Then they should be regarded as a unit or entity and be considered as singular! (The council was....) But what if you had regarded them as a bunch of cantankerous individuals, each with a mind of his/her own? Well, o.k., they all reached the same agreement, but now you could well refer to them in the plural: The council were...(they were...).

In a newspaper we might read: Every year 20 million cubic metres of gas is exported through this port. The writer is taking the standpoint that this is an entity and not twenty million separate packages. Strictly speaking we are referring to metres (in the plural) and should be treated as such. Occasionally an apparent plural form may be treated as singular: Russian politics is a subject much discussed today.

▶ Data. 'The data was analysed...' or, 'the data were analysed...'. Data was originally, almost exclusively, a plural term. Thus 'data were...'. Today, this has changed and 'data' is normally regarded as a collective noun, hence 'the data was analysed...'. But either form is correct (as long as you are consistent!).

▶ 'None' may be either singular or plural idiomatically, but 'none' means 'not one'. 'None of them says that it is a satisfactory contract' rather than 'None of them say that...'

This also illustrates the point that an intervening phrase may displace the association between the subject and the verb: The impression was that the contents of the Act, in spite of the vociferous opposition of Labour members as well as that of a number of Liberals, was acceptable. (The *contents*...were acceptable.)

Losing sight of the verb can result in syntactic disasters. The issue of pollution, which included such varied factors as run-off from farmyards, exhaust from diesel-driven vehicles, fumes from cattle pyres, were all secondary features of the foot-and-mouth epidemic. (The *issue*...*was*.)

▶ Plurals of abbreviations *may* employ a full point where the singular form uses a full point: ed., eds., but chs without a full point. However, there is no consistency in this among the standard dictionaries.

PREFIXES AND SUFFIXES

See Affixes; Chapter 12, Prefixes; Chapter 13, Suffixes.

A. Prefixes

A prefix is an affix such as un-, anti, co-, etc. The following is a selection of the most commonly encountered prefixes and suffixes. A number of adjectives and adverbs may also be used as a prefix, under-, over-, etc., to form compound words. The main problem for the writer is to know when prefixed words should be hyphenated. Such hyphenation is referred to as 'hard hyphenation' in contrast to 'soft hyphenation' which occurs when the word-processor divides a word in connection with wrap-around at the end of a line. The problem arises in that the spell-checker does not distinguish between a hard and a soft hyphen.

Prefixes
anti – against
arch – chief (archbishop)
auto – self (autobiography)
bi – two (biennial)
circum – around (circumscribe)
contra – against (contradict)

multi – many (multiply)
over – beyond (overextend)
per – through/by (perennial)
post – after (postpone)
pre – before (precede)
pro – forward/support (protagonist)

PUNCTUATION AND USAGE

de – separate (decompose)
demi – half (demigod)
dis – reversal (disconnect)
for – away/without (forgo)
fore – in advance (forefront)
homo – alike (homogenous)
hyper – excessive (hyperactive)
il – not (illegal)
im – not (impossible)
in – not (incontrovertible)
meta – change (metamorphic)
mis – wrong (misdeed)
mono – one (monoplane)

pseudo – false (pseudonym)
re – back (retreat)
retro – backward (retrograde)
semi – half (semitone)
sub – under (subterranean)
super – above (superintendent)
trans – across (transport)
tri – three (triangle)
ultra – beyond (ultrasonic)
un – reverse (undo)
under – lower (underneath)
uni – one (universal)
vice – in place of (viceroy)

An overview of prefixed words is given in Chapter 12.

Some generalisations can be drawn about the use of a hyphen:

1. Prefix ends with vowel; word commences with vowel. Normally hyphenated:

   anti-imperialist, pre-engage, semi-illiterate, co-ordinate (or coordinate)

   The general exception is the prefix re- which is not normally hyphenated (e.g. redistribution), neither before a vowel (reassign, reinstate, reoccupy, reuse) except before 'e': e.g. re-elect. (US English does not hyphenate reentry.)

2. Prefix ends with vowel; word commences with consonant. Hyphenated.

   anti-fade, anti-racism

3. Prefix ends with consonant; word commences with vowel. No general rule.

   over-abundance, over-emotional, to overachieve, overindulgence

4. Prefix ends with consonant; word commences with consonant. No general rule, but verbs often conjoined, adjectives and nouns hyphenated.

   overhear, underbid, over-sexed, under-jaw

5. 'Double-consonant rule'. If the final consonant of the prefix is the same as the first letter of the following word, a hyphen is *normally* used, but there are many exceptions to this rule.

   under-represented, out-tray; overreact, midday, outthink

7. mis- does not use a hyphen: misuse, misspelled or mispelt (US misspelt).

8. A hyphen is used where a prefix is used before a word with a capital (i.e. a proper noun):

✓ pre-Christian.

9. A hyphen is used to separate a suffix where this would result in a triple character, or where the suffix commences with the same letter as the stem: She was childlike with a doll-like face; his brain was ball-like – round and rubbery! The off-fore leg.

▶ Most texts maintain that when an affix such as anti-, pre-, pro-, etc. are applied, then all three elements should be hyphenated.

   a. The Stone Age sites were designated as ancient monuments.

   The boundaries of the pre-Stone-Age sites had yet to be determined.

   b. The women priests' lobby adopted a new approach.

   The anti-women-priests' lobby was defeated when it came to the vote.

However, when a hyphenated term is affixed with 'non-', for example, the original hyphen *may* be dropped. Wages were originally gender-related. The new regulations stipulated that these were to be non-gender related.

The prefix co- is normally hyphenated in both UK and US English (e.g. co-chairman), but there is no consistency between dictionaries for words such as cooperation (co-operation) or coordinate (co-ordinate). Some recommend the one version; others accept both.

B. Suffixes

The following suffixes are the most commonly encountered.

Suffixes

–able – capable of (predictable)
–age – place/state (marriage)
–ance – state/action (resemblance)
–asm – state/being (enthusiasm)
–dom – state/jurisdiction (martyrdom)
–eer – occupation (auctioneer)
–ence – state/action (independence)
–ency – state/action (ascendancy)
–eous – pertaining to (advantageous)
–escence – act of becoming (convalescence)
–escent – becoming (obsolescent)
–fold – many (threefold)
–genous – yielding/generating (homogenous)
–hood – state/nature (childhood)
–ible – capable of being (possible)
–kind – sort (mankind)
–lence – completeness (excellence)
–lent – state of being (excellent)
–less – without (topless)
–like (resembling) child-like
–logy – study (geology)
–ly – in the manner of (quietly)
–ment – state of (endorsement)
–mony – state of (matrimony)
–most – superlative (uppermost)
–ness – state of (illness)
–ory – pertaining to (obligatory)
–ose – full of/possessing (verbose)
–ous – abounding with (glorious)
–pathy – state of feeling (sympathy)
–scope – aiding sight (telescope)
–ship – state (friendship)

PUNCTUATION AND USAGE

–ile – pertaining to (bibliophile)
–ish – resembling (childish)
–ism – state/doctrine (egoism)
–ite – supporter (Israelite)
–ity – state of (accountability)
–ize – to make/do (idolize)

–some – full of (loathsome)
–tion – state/action (continuation)
–tude – state of being (magnitude)
–ward – direction (eastward)
–wards – direction (homewards)
–wise – manner (clockwise)

The problem of hyphenation – or not – arises with suffixes such as hideout, worn-out, even out, although to a lesser extent than prefixes insofar as there are fewer terms which are hyphenated. The general rule (generalisation) seems to apply here: nouns conjoined, adjectives hyphenated, verbs separate words.

Chapter 13 provides a comprehensive overview of words often encountered as a suffix.

QUESTION MARKS [?]

A. Questions

The question mark is used in direct speech.

✓ How could he have known that he would be nominated?

▶ In a quotation the question mark is retained within the inverted commas.

✓ She asked him directly: 'Are you available for re-election?'

No final full point is required.

✗ She asked him directly: 'Are you available for re-election?'.

In the following, the question mark relates to what is actually being asked. For example:

✓ How do you say in Lithuanian '*I love you*'?

✓ How do you ask in Lithuanian '*What time is the train?*'

Note that only one question mark is necessary, but two different punctuation marks may be used as required:

✓ Did I hear him exclaim 'damn it!'?

▶ In indirect speech the question mark is not used:

✓ She enquired whether he was available for re-election.

✗ He asked her if she could make herself available?

Recently, I read: 'Larry knocked on the door and said who the guests were and when was I coming down?! I replied...'

I leave this punctuation to the reader's own judgement, but might add that the book was a best seller.

▶ A final full point is required in the following:

✓ The publisher said the material was 'not suitable' for the journal (meaning it was nonsense?).

But not if the entire sentence is within parentheses:

✓ (What were the reasons for this?)

▶ Some sentences may permit the use of several question marks. This is really a question of style.

✓ Are you interested in re-election? – in leading the opposition? – or just going into retirement?

▶ If listed or bulleted, only a final question mark is required:

✓ Was he interested in standing for (a) Chairman, (b) Secretary, (c) Registrar?

▶ An apparent question which is essentially a comment or remark still requires a question mark.

'You don't really believe that, do you?', the lawyer muttered, not expecting any response.

But Shakespeare wasn't too fussy:

'To be, or not to be, that is the Question.'(*Ham*. iii. i. 56)

▶ Probably the most common error is to confuse the direct and the indirect question. The latter requires no question mark. I recently read:

✗ In the fourth section, we ask to what extent and how we can define and measure the effectiveness of EU environmental policy?

This would be correct if we place the actual question in apostrophes:..., we ask: 'to what extent...?'

▶ In speech, a question mark may be encountered even though, strictly speaking, a statement rather than a question is presented:

'I must be wrong in thinking that there was a signed contract?'

This draws attention to the fact that there was some doubt behind the statement and is quite permissible.

Can more than one question mark occur in a sentence? I read this in *Famous trial of Marshall Hall* by Edward Marjoribanks: 'Was there any means of avoiding the settlement? or, if not, did that make each will irrevocable?' Unusual, but effective.

B. Editorial questions

Questions concerning dates and names (for example) may be in parentheses.

✓ He was originally elected in March(?) 1933.

✓ The new member was called Dick W(illie?) Hampton.

QUOTATIONS

See also Quotation marks.

Collins English Dictionary defines a quotation as 'a phrase or passage from a book, poem, play, etc., remembered and spoken, esp. to illustrate succinctly or support a point or an argument'.

▶ Short quotations are normally retained within the text. To illustrate the point one might quote Blaise Pascal who stated 'anything that is written to please the author is worthless'. (Some readers may well agree!)

▶ As a general rule, longer quotations of three lines or more (called an 'extract') form their own paragraph and are indented throughout. They may also use a point size smaller than the general text. Extracts are not placed in inverted commas unless these comprise the spoken word.

> In this text we are referring to quotations as a sentence or part thereof, contained within the text. These will employ quotation marks (inverted commas). A longer quotation – extract – will appear as an indented paragraph (as this), concluding with the author reference in parentheses which does not employ a final full point. (Taylor, 2001)

When reverting to the normal text, the first line of the subsequent paragraph following is not indented even though initial lines of subsequent paragraphs are indented.

QUOTATION MARKS [" ", ' ']

See also Quotations.

Quotation marks are also referred to as Inverted commas. In this section we are essentially concerned with the typographical application.

A. General usage, typing

As the name suggests, quotation marks encase the quoted word – that which is spoken. The spoken word may be placed in either single [' '] or double [" "] quotation marks. Strictly speaking these are called the prime and double prime quotation marks. It is important to be consistent in their use. Sometimes double inverted commas are referred to as sixty-six ["] and ninety-nine ["]. These are also referred to as 'smart quotes' as opposed to 'straight quotes' [' and "]. The single and double quotes shown on the keyboard are straight quotes and appear as such in non-serifed typefaces (e.g. Arial). It is with serifed typefaces such as Times Roman that both smart quotes and straight quotes are available. The latter have special uses (see F below).

The primes '6' or '9' [' '] appear automatically, dependent whether the inverted commas are preceded by a space or not. This means that typing the phrase *it was a "hit"/"miss" affair*, has produced a '99' instead of a '66' before "miss". This is clearly not what is required. Type this using a space following the slash: The wedding was a "hit"/ "miss" affair. Now delete the space following the slash giving: The wedding was a "hit"/"miss" affair.

B. Quotes within quotes

Where the main quotation employs double inverted commas, the quote within the quote employs single inverted commas. (see Quotation marks, C)

✓ 'I told you,' Mary repeated, 'that the author's words were "success comes before excess", although "pride comes before a fool" might have been more appropriate'.

The first internal quote ("success...") is the author's words: the second ("pride...") is an unreferenced citation that Mary has used to make her point to the person she is addressing.

The final full point precedes the final quotation marks indicating the close of Mary's statement.

✓ 'I told you,' Mary repeated, 'that the author's words were "success is usually followed by excess".'

Note the comma after 'you' in the above and which is placed *inside the quotation mark*. A comma following the quotation mark ['I told you', Mary repeated...] – would appear to be more logical, but this is one of those inexplicable points of English punctuation.

▶ My impression is that US publishers generally prefer the double quotes as the basis. Conversely, UK publishers appear to prefer the single quotes. Using a basis in double quotes for the spoken word – and single quotation marks for those seldom occasions when quotes within quotes are encountered, enables the single quotation marks also to be used for that "special" word. I have encountered this on a few occasions and where the use of the single quotes, or apostrophes, may be regarded as an alternative to using italics. This practice thus enables a clear distinction to be made between the 'spoken word', and terms which take on a "special" meaning.

C. Nested quotes

(Quotes within quotes within quotes)! Yes, these can be found. Alternate the single and double inverted commas at each level.

> 'Well,' he said, 'I distinctly heard Tom say "The Director's exact words were 'Get out of here'," and I have no reason to doubt his word.'

Better to use italics:

PUNCTUATION AND USAGE

✓ 'Well,' he said, 'I distinctly heard Tom say "The Director's exact words were *Get out of here*," and I have no reason to doubt his word.'

▶ A final full point is not included inside the quotes as well as at the end:

✗ I commented (in French): "The Dijon train is late – again.".

D. The single quotes (apostrophes)

▶ Inverted commas marks are often used to emphasise particular words or unusual use of words, or even 'constructed' words!

✓ Milton Berle once described a Committee as a group of men who keep minutes and waste hours (and 'ours')!

✓ Her parties were large as was her physique. She was indeed the hostess with the 'mostest'.

▶ If an unusual term or word used in a manner contrary to normal understanding is placed within inverted commas, this punctuation is required only for the first time of use:

Blair's speech had an 'attractivity' about it. The essence of this attractivity lay not in the appeal of the presentation, but in the attraction of the content to the voter.

Some authors have a tendency to put many words and phrases in quotes apparently only with the purpose of emphasising them. Here is an example from an article I recently read:

✗ In sum, it appears that a 'model' which stresses the institutions' authority....

The term 'model' is not being used metaphorically or in any unusual sense. Why, then, the inverted commas? The flow of the sentence is interrupted, leaving the reader to wonder exactly what the author really meant if he did not mean a 'model'!

▶ Book and article titles should be in italics. Chapter titles are kept in single inverted commas.

✓ In Child's book, *The Essentials of Factor Analysis*, Thurstone's theory of simple structure is discussed in Chapter 4, 'The rotation of factors'.

E. '. or .' – where to place the full point

The other question is the placement of the final prime – before or after the full point?

✓ He said: 'The shares have recovered.'

✓ 'Yes,' she replied, 'I've had the chairs re-covered.'

A HANDBOOK FOR WRITERS OF ENGLISH

The spoken word, when introduced by a comma or colon, contains the punctuation within the closing quotation marks. Complete sentences concluding with the full point or other punctuation are contained within the quotes. Common sense should normally determine the placement of the punctuation as the following examples illustrate.

✓ She wanted know. 'Isn't that pure nonsense?'

✓ He reflected briefly. Did she really mean that it was 'pure nonsense'?

I recently received instructions from one publisher stating 'Punctuation should follow the British style, e.g. "quotes precede punctuation".' This was aimed at standardisation, but for the majority of publishers the following would be incorrect:

✗ He said: 'The shares have recovered'.

▶ If an exclamation mark is included in a quotation which itself is within quotation marks, punctuate as follows:

✓ He quoted them both: 'Russell stated: "Better Red than dead" but I am not certain who said "Better bed than Red!".'

A final comment. I have one book (by P. G. Wodehouse) where the spoken word is within single quotes, but with a following or leading space:
' I am downstairs, ' he called out. Strange – and not unproblematic on the PC as a space before the closing quote mark will produce an opening quote (try it).

F. Prime and double prime

As stated above, primes (' ... and " ...) as given on the keyboard will appear as smart quotes (' ... and " ...) in serifed typefaces, but straight quotes in non-serifed typefaces. The modern word-processor will also convert straight to smart quotes (or vice versa) if a typeface is changed for a document or passage. However, we may have to control for these as primes are required for in certain cases.

✓ The box was exactly 4' 2" wide. (Four foot, two inches.)

✓ North Cape is located at N 71° 7' 59". (North, seventy-one degrees, seven minutes and fifty-nine seconds.)

✓ The cyclist reached the mile mark in 1' 24.18". (One minute, 24.18 seconds.)

When using serifed typefaces (Times Roman for example), the 'straight quotes' [' "] – here used to denote measurement – will have to be inserted using the 'Insert – Symbols' feature.

REFERENCES

References to authors' works in the text, literary sources, further reading and references are important elements in your book or paper. There are a number of rules and standards for references within the body of the text, and in the literature list. These are dealt with comprehensively in Chapter 4.

ROMAN NUMERALS

Upper case should be used for chapters (e.g. Chapter VIII). Lower case is used for the prelims pages (i, ii, iii, iv, etc.). It is unusual to find values over 100 in lower case (c = 100; CC = 200).

i	I	1
v	V	5
x	X	10
l	L	50
c	C	100
	D	500
	M	1000

In principle, values are accumulated beginning with the highest order. The values for thousands, hundreds, tens and units are treated in sequence.

Up to three similar characters may be adjoined. (III = 3; CCC = 300) although IIII (4) can be observed on church clocks, and even CCCC (400) rather than CD is occasionally encountered.

A symbol with a lower value 1, 10, 100, 1000 etc. may be placed before the next higher value indicating that this lower value is to be subtracted, IV = 4, IX = 9; XC = 90. XCIV = 94. XCIX = 99 (and not IC. IX is an exception to the 'next higher value' rule). There are nevertheless different ways of writing certain numbers, and even the Romans weren't too strict about the method used.

A bar may be found over the character increasing the value by 1000. $\overline{D}$ would be 500,000.

Finally, when listing Roman numbers, they are *right* justified.
Most writers will be concerned with numbering the prelims, so we may summarise:

i	1	vi	6	xi	11	xvi	16
ii	2	vii	7	xii	12	xvii	17
iii	3	viii	8	xiii	13	xviii	18
iv	4	ix	9	xiv	14	xix	19
v	5	x	10	xv	15	xx	20

Non-serifed typefaces may not produce Roman numbers satisfactorily, e.g. III rather than III.

The full point, formerly used, is now rarely encountered in the possessive form: Edward VIII.'s abdication (with or without period).

SEMICOLON [;]

See also Colon.

In many foreign languages, the semicolon[3] is seldom encountered. It has a more specific role in English and is frequently used to combine two sentences which are closely related, or to divide a long sentence where the contents comprise a sequence or list.

A. Dividing sentences

If many commas appear in a long sentence, a semicolon may be introduced at an appropriate place, particularly if this is preferable to rewriting as two or more sentences. Only one semicolon should be used within the sentence for this purpose.

✓ There were two views. The government emphasised the importance of monetary policy as an essential element in reviving the economy which, according to virtually all indicators, was now at the low-point of a depression; but the advisory committee – comprised of government-appointed economists – disagreed, and pointed out the need to introduce measures which, in the short term, would reduce unemployment as a first step on the road to recovery.

The semicolon can be used to clarify the different elements in a sentence:

✓ The distribution of appointments was as follows: Sociology, two new lecturers – one of whom was to be a woman; Philosophy, a research assistant – provided that funds were made available for the new project; and two secretaries to the Faculty of Arts.

B. Lists

The semicolon is used to separate items in a list which contains commas:

✓ The following cities had applied to hold the International Bricklayer's Championship for 2006: London, U.K.; Paris, France; Oslo, Norway; Tirana, Albania.

A semicolon may be used in a sequence.

✓ Two maids a-milking; three French hens; four turtle-doves. Two maids, fine: three chickens?

C. Clauses

The semicolon is used between independent clauses joined by however, indeed or nevertheless, where an association remains. Note that the clause

---

[3] Previously spelled with a hyphen, semi-colon. Modern spelling seems to favour the conjoined word.

PUNCTUATION AND USAGE

also comprises a complete sentence. (This requirement does not apply to the colon.)

✓ The government attached importance to monetary policy; however, this remained secondary to issues of employment.

✓ He was acquitted of the charge; nevertheless, the public still remained sceptical.

Similarly, the semicolon is used in dividing complementary clauses, particularly where these are sequential or explanatory:

✓ The Opposition supported the Government in the debate; the bill was nevertheless defeated by backbenchers of all parties.

✓ Look before you leap; he who hesitates is lost.

✓ 'I will not say that women have no character; rather, they have a new one every day.' (Heine, 1797–1856)

D. Expressions

The semicolon may be used between two independent clauses in a spoken sentence interrupted by an expression:

✓ 'What we need is a monetary policy,' the Minister emphasised; 'there is no alternative.'

It may be considered that a full point should follow 'emphasised'. Nevertheless, the words spoken suggest that the basis is a divided sentence: 'What we need is a monetary policy; there is no alternative.' The semicolon contributes to the flow of the text.

SENTENCE CONNECTORS

Style (or lack of it) is often manifest by repeated phrases, particularly sentence connectors. It is surprising how many times some authors use 'however' when other connectors or adverbs will add a little variety. Consider using some of the following alternatives. Sentence connectors, where indicated, are defined as such in Collins Dictionary, but many adverbs (among others) and phrases may also serve as connectors. Avoid colloquialisms such as 'anyhow', 'anyway'.

but	Verb transitive when used to present an objection (But for that . . .)
consequently	Adverb
consequentially	Adverb
even so	(= nevertheless. Adverb)
for example	
further	Adverb
furthermore	Adverb

hence	Adverb. Sentence connector
however	Adverb. Sentence connector
meanwhile	Adverb.
more so	[Note: two words]
moreover	Adverb. Sentence connector
nevertheless	Adverb. Sentence connector
on the contrary	
on the other hand	
otherwise	Adverb. Sentence connector
still	Adverb. Sentence connector
therefore	Adverb. Sentence connector
thus	Adverb. Sentence connector
yet	Adverb. Sentence connector

SLASH/BACKSLASH [/,\]

A. Forward slash

The forward (or oblique) slash [/] is used to separate alternatives.

✗ The Chairman and/or The Secretary will be present during the counting of votes.

The forward slash can also mean 'and/or' (both):

✓ New factory opening. Skilled/unskilled workers needed.

But this could be ambiguous, meaning 'either'.

The tenure may be freehold/leasehold by agreement.

Consideration should be given to rewriting the text when such ambiguities may arise. The forward slash may also mean just 'or':

✓ The name of the winner be announced at 12.30 p.m. He/she will be formally installed on Monday.

Avoid using s/he for she/he.

It may also indicate 'and – also':

✓ The London/Birmingham/Liverpool train is diverted to Coventry/Stafford/Liverpool.

▶ The oblique slash also means 'per' as in 'per hour'. It should only be used in advertisements and lists in this form. Room to let: £50/week. Fresh cod $10/lb. In scientific articles we may encounter: Fat content 5.6g/100g.

It is also referred to as the solidus in dates: 10/12/58. The solidus is also encountered in mathematics: 10/2 = 5.

B. Backslash

▶ The backslash [\] is not frequently encountered but has become familiar to Internet surfers:

PUNCTUATION AND USAGE

✓ Our Home Page: http://www.microflop.com\progs\help

SORTING
Sorting records, not only bibliographic material, can present some difficulties and may be an important part of the preparation of your manuscript. A description of a routine for sorting diverse records is given in Chapter 4, Q.

SPELLING

Spelling is no longer a major problem for many writers in that all major word-processors include a spell-checker. We no longer have to struggle with *–able* or *–ible* and *-ability* or *-ibility*![4] Naturally, the fewer mistakes in your manuscript, the less time taken to correct. Further, certain errors will not be discovered such as typing *further* for *farther,* or *farther* for *father,* and indeed, dropping the 'h' in *farther* may not be amusing reading in the Company's Annual Report! (This will not be detected by the spell-checker.) Unfortunate typing errors can occur with a number of words, either when a letter is dropped, changed or added. A common problem with the PC keyboard is that keys can 'stick', as I found out when checking an article I had translated about middle class women. Unfortunately, they came out as 'idle class women' (but were re-instated during proofreading!). I do not have to point out the necessity of checking the spelling of *public places*.

The first draft of this book contained a comprehensive guide to spelling where I tried to accumulate all the 'rules'. It did not take long to discover that exceptions to the rule outnumbered the norm in many instances. I was recently asked about the use of double 'll' in English. A colleague supplied the following guide:

> The 'l' is doubled in British English after a single unstressed vowel, e.g. travel, traveller, travelled, travelling (compare US English traveler, traveled, traveling). In both UK and US English, if the final syllable is stressed 'll' is mandatory, e.g. compel, compelled, compelling. In both variants of English a single 'l' is used after a double vowel, e.g. fail, failed, failing.

I am sure that this is correct – but don't ask me to remember the rule for this. I'll continue to rely on my spell-checker!

Of course, the spell-checker cannot be relied upon for distinguishing between 'maybe' and 'may be'. Consider for example: 'Maybe he will arrive later. It may be that he took the bus instead.' Neither is the grammar checker much help here! Incidentally, the first is an adverb, the second 'may' an auxiliary verb.

---

[4] See Burt, Angela (2000) for some excellent tips on spelling and usage.

For those intent on learning the rules, there are a great number of textbooks where several sections, if not an entire chapter, will enlighten the curious reader. See, for example, Swan (1991, §§568–579), and Phythian (1998, Ch. 9). Marion Field's book in the *How To* series, *Improving Your Spelling*, is a very readable text covering many aspects.

One source of confusion and inconsistency is UK English and US English spellings. Certain words, particularly those ending in *–ise* or *–ize* may be spelt using either form in both languages, although even here there are exceptions. The fact that both *advertise* and *advertize* are acceptable in UK English underscores the need for consistency. There are also some grammatical differences. Chapter 15 discusses a number of these.

A. Unrecognised words

Your spell-checker will probably react to a number of words that you consider to be o.k. There may be several reasons for this. Apart from the fact that you had actually misspelt the word, you may have invented a new word! Now this is not such an infringement of the rules as might be thought. Elsewhere in this text I have pointed out that new words may be encountered the whole time, and indeed, it is to be expected of a living language. Proofreaders frequently encounter new 'inventions'. As a proofreader I have learnt that it is unwise to pounce on every word which the spell-checker reacts to and to inform the author that 'this word does not exist'. The mere fact that you have just read it suggests that it *could* exist. Some words encountered in a recent article were 'bilateralist'. The full expression was 'the bilateralist Barents Sea regime' and which referred to the agreement by which Norway and Russia regulated fish stocks in this ocean. This is interesting as it is the suffix which appears unusual. But when we consider the use of the suffix, then it may be acceptable.

> -ist *suff.* 1.a. One that performs a specified action: lobbyist. ... 4. One that is characterized by a specified trait or quality: romanticist
> *American Heritage Dictionary*

But what about *fishable*! This arose in the same article. Now, something capable of being fished, using rod, line, net or trawl, is precisely that, i.e. 'fishable' – capable of being fished. But in the context of this article, which was concerned with fish stocks and fishing agreements, the term was used to mean fish stocks that were economically exploitable. Almost any sea creature is capable of being fished, but whether they are 'fishable' in an economic sense depends upon the market conditions. (I have since heard this word on the BBC.) The suffix 'able' is defined in one dictionary:

> -able or -ible *suff.* 1. Susceptible, capable, or worthy of a specified action: debatable. 2. Inclined or given to a specified state or action: changeable.
> *American Heritage Dictionary*

PUNCTUATION AND USAGE

In other words, do not discount the unusual word. As a writer, you may feel that there is something appealing about the unusual. If you are in doubt, place it in inverted commas the first time you use it.

✓ To what extent capelin was 'fishable' was dependent upon market prices. It was certainly as fishable as herring at that time.

If you are convening a new expression, check that the prefix or suffix is appropriate. See Prefixes and suffixes. Finally, consult *The Oxford Dictionary of New Words* or *The New Oxford Dictionary of English*. These are rich sources of new material, the latter also being available on CD-ROM. See also Chapter 19, C for useful Internet sites.

B. Foreign letters and symbols

Foreign words, where less familiar, use italics. Absorption into the English language may have resulted in the italics (and accents) disappearing, but the correct spelling should be retained: *café* rather than *cafe*. Retaining the original French can reflect your personal style. It is still possible to encounter an *hôtel* rather than a hotel. Other original spellings are also endearing: *Aesop's Fables* should preferably be written as *Æsop's fables*. We also find fetus or foetus rather than fœtus. Its is a matter of choice as to whether one puts these words in italics, but phrases such as *œufs en cocotte* (boiled eggs) should be italicised. Occasionally the diesis ["] should be used in such words as *naïve*. While given in most dictionaries (including US dictionaries), many writers overlook this. A dieresis is defined as a mark placed over a vowel indicating a change in the quality of the vowel. We find this in the name of *Emily Brontë*, author of *Wuthering Heights*. Foreign characters and symbols are obligatory in proper names. A number of words employing foreign symbols have become archaic such as *cañon* (*canyon*).

Foreign letters and symbols are often a headache for the writer. A summary of the keystrokes in WordPerfect and Microsoft Word is given in Chapter 5.

C. Misspelt words

Spell-checkers do not recognise errors when the misspelt word comprises another word. For example, when proofreading one of the most common examples encountered are *fir – for*, *my – may*, and *form – from*. But also many three-letter words may be erroneously typed as a two-letter word and accepted by the spell-checker such as *to* for *two*.

Inversion of vowels is another source of such errors, for example, *lion* and *loin*. It could be noted that there are a number of words where adjacent letters on the keyboard can result in misspelt words. For example, the vowels *u, i, o* are consecutively located and may result in mistyping *fun* for *fin*, *firm* for *form*, etc. It is also possible to hit two keys virtually simultaneously

A HANDBOOK FOR WRITERS OF ENGLISH

giving *suit* for *sit*, *moist* for *most*, etc. Another error is to misplace the consonant in certain words, e.g. *bread* for *beard*.

I keep a note of those words which I have a habit of typing erroneously and take a final check of my manuscript. The following list covers those which I have discovered to be among the most common.

The following two letter words are accepted by the spell-checker, but the intention may well have been a three letter word. For example, *bi* might have been a mistype for *bib, bid, big, bim, bin, bio, bis, bit* or *biz* – all accepted by my spell-checker!

au	de	hi	lo	pa	vi
bi	do	ho	me	pi	vu
ca	ea	ka	mi	se	we
co	fu	la	mo	so	zo
cu	ha	le	no	to	ye

All of these are the stem of at least one – and often several three- (and four-) letter words. There is no quick remedy for checking these, but if you are writing an article on the great auk, then it may prove fruitful at the end to check for any typing errors *au*< space > or even < space >uk.

The following words are easily mistyped and, clearly, not detected by the spell-checker.

Intended	Mistyped	Intended	Mistyped	Intended	Mistyped
but	buy	he	the	sail	sial
buy	but	heal	hale	sale	seal
cerate	create	lair	liar	seal	sale
corp	crop	liar	lair	sial	sail
dairy	diary	loin	lion	sit	suit
dale	deal	mist	must	sit	site
deal	dale	mist	most	site	sire
diary	dairy	mist	moist	tale	teal
eat	east	most	mist	tan	than
fair	fiar	most	moist	tat	that
fiar	fair	must	mist	teal	tale
field	filed	my	may	tem	them
fin	fun	none	neon	ten	then
form	from	pale	peal	the	then/m
from	form	peal	pale	vale	veal
fun	fin	relies	replies	veal	vale
gaol	goal	replies	relies	wit	with
goal	gaol			with	wit
hale	heal				

SYMBOLS

There are a wide number of symbols available in the modern word-processor. These may be used for many purposes such as:

a) currencies £ $ € ¥ ¢
b) foreign letters å ø æ ç
c) bullets ● ○ *
d) typographical symbols: § ¶
e) mathematical signs etc.: ∑ √ ≈ ¹/₃ ⁷/₈
f) business symbols: © ® ™
g) Dingbats, a printer's symbol. Microsoft Word has several defined as:
   i) Webdings, e.g.: 🄸 ♪
   ii) Wingdings, e.g.: ✦ ☋ ☞

– and others. None of my dictionaries explain the difference between Webdings and Wingdings, but the term 'Dingbats' seems to cover all of these.

Formerly, footnotes and other references used a variety of typographic symbols. Conventionally, they appeared in the following order: * † ‡ § ¶. The advent of the word-processor seems to have made this historical, particularly as the ASCII values of these symbols produces another order when sorting.

The word-processor contains a set of standard bullets, but it is possible to select any chosen symbol such as ❑ ➪

TENSES

▶ A common error is to mix tenses *in the same sentence*.

✗ Even though the resolution is now approved, it had been subject to long debate.

This should read: 'Even though the issue has now been approved....'

Care should also be given to changing tenses in the same paragraph, although rules concerning mixed tenses are not so strict as previously. Of course, there may be good reason to change tense in mid-paragraph.

TIME

The 24-hour clock is now common practice in those countries which previously used a.m. and p.m.

▶ a.m. and p.m. may also be encountered as 'am' and 'pm'. This should be avoided although may be accepted in brochures and timetables:

Brochure: The coach departs Victoria at 9 am. Arrival in Paris 2 pm.

Article etc.: The meeting commenced at 11 a.m. and was concluded at 1.20 p.m.

Previously, capitals were encountered: A.M. and P.M. These always used full points. This format is seldom today. (Note that AM = *anno mundi*, in the year of the world; PM = Prime Minister.)

The dash means 'to' and should not be used following 'between' or 'from':

✗ The museum is open between 14.00–17.30.

✓ The museum is open between 14.00 and 17.30.

The 24-hour clock should preferably use the full point:

✓ The museum is open 14.00–17.30.

✗ The museum is open 1400–1730.

The latter form is common, however, in timetables!

A space around the dash is occasionally encountered, but is not to be preferred. The 'from' is not only superfluous but erroneous, unless the dash is replaced by 'to':

✗ The museum is open from 14.00–17.30.

The term 'o'clock' is colloquial and should be reserved for informal literature.

▶ The 24-hour clock may also employ a colon: 12:45, 16:30, particularly where attached to dates.

▶ Per year or per annum? The former normally applies to a calendar year, from January 1 to December 31. 'Per annum' is mainly used in connection with finance and relates to any twelve-month period. For example, the tax year in the UK is the year commencing April 5th.

TYPEFACES AND FONTS

A **typeface** is a specific type design such as TIMES ROMAN, ARIAL, COURIER NEW, *Palace Script*, etc. Modern word-processors contain 150–200 different typefaces, but many of these, such as the script typeface shown above, are only suitable for particular purposes such as brochures, guides, handbooks and similar. Some pleasing typefaces may be downloaded over the Internet. Note that some may be a proprietary name and you may have to apply for the rights to use these.

Typeface style may be normal, **bold**, *italic*, or ***bold italic***; and underlined normal, **bold**, *italic*, or ***bold italic***. Typestyle may be small or large, indicated by the point size.[5] This is 10-point; this is 14 point; this is 18 point.

A **font** is a specific typeface, style and size; 'a complete assortment of types of one sort, with all that is necessary for printing in that kind of letter, (Chambers). ***This font is Times Roman 14 pt bold italic.*** This is Century Gothic 12 pt font.

Frequently, the publishing house will require a serif typeface for the text such as Times Roman 12 pt. It has to be stated, however, that certain non-

---

5 Point size is technically defined as a multiple of a twelfth of a pica, theoretically one twelfth of an inch (72 points = 1 inch). The higher the point value, the larger the typeface.

serif (proportional) fonts such as Arial or Gothic are attractive and easy to read, particularly in smaller point size. The latter are especially useful in figures and diagrams.

I find it irritating that Microsoft Word provides autoselection for point sizes 12 pt, 14 pt, 16 pt etc., but not 13 or 15 pt. However, these may be selected by typing in the value in the Font Size box. It is also possible to select 12.5 pt. This, or 13 pt is an ideal default font size.

A. Typefaces and PCs

PCs have annoying habits: for the man they have the temperament of the girl-friend – unpredictable! For the woman, they are like the man who forgets the anniversary – irritating! Transferring a file from one PC to another is something like sending a woman into a hat shop. By the time she has pulled off the trimmings and added some others, it isn't quite the same hat! And neither might your file be. Certain typefaces have a frustrating habit of not being accepted or converted easily with the result that Greek symbols may appear instead of italic apostrophes, for example. You may find that you have to change the typeface, but try transferring as a bitmap as a last resort. This can result in the file size increasing threefold in this event.

If you decide to change the basic typeface of a manuscript, or even a part of it, or to transfer it to another PC or word-processor, then it is advisable to make an experimental file, especially where you are using a font not commonly encountered. Include in it a number of normal symbols. I use the following test file, initially written in Times Roman:

Here is a test text (..); [..]; {..}. Here are the symbols which have been used:
– (end-dash),
$ (dollar);
@ (alpha);
© copyright;
£ (GBP).
check ".." and '..' (inverted commas).

Of course, insert any other symbols that you may have used. *Now mark and copy this text, inserting it at the end of the file above. Mark this new section and convert to italics.* Next, mark and copy the entire file and change to the proposed typeface. This file should now be 28 lines long. Save the file under any name. Close it, and then open it again and check the fonts. Of course, emailing it to yourself may reveal some problems, but it is the recipient's PC which is the key factor.

UNDERLINING (UNDERSCORING)

Generally, underlining should be avoided. It is an indication to the typesetter that the underlined text is to be printed in italics. This dates back to the days of the typewriter although the more 'modern' of these latter-day machines had interchangeable wheels and spherical attachments such as the IBM 'golf-ball' enabling italics to be typed. Some publishers still require text to be italicised in the printed document to be underlined in the manuscript.

▶ Underlining might be used where a phrase is already in italics in order to emphasise a particular word:

Caution: *It is essential* to renumber the pages after editing.

▶ There are a few limited uses for the underscored text, particularly in emphasising the initial letters of an acronym for example, UNESCO (United Nations Educational, Scientific, and Cultural Organization).[6]

▶ A line can be drawn across the page to 'underline' a section by entering three minus signs: - - - and then < Enter > :

Similarly, typing three asterisks and < Enter > produces the following:

■ ■

---

6 Acronym: a pronounceable name made up of a series of initial letters or parts of words.

4
References and Bibliographies

A. Reference lists

As well as a bibliography, references to sources may also appear in the main body of the text. Occasionally a list of references is given following each chapter, or these may be given in a single list under chapter headings at the end. However, it is more usual to contain all references within a single list. This list may be headed 'References' or 'Bibliography', occasionally 'Literature List'. In texts especially designed for students, material specifically recommended as 'Further reading' may form a separate section in the bibliography.

There is, perhaps, a subtle difference between *References* (i.e. a reference list) and *Bibliography* (i.e. a literature list). The former essentially contains specific material references by the author in his research for the publication. A *bibliography* is usually more comprehensive in that it will also contain references to other associated material which may be of general interest to the reader. The material referenced in the bibliography may refer to a variety of different types of material, published and unpublished, including books, articles, parliamentary acts (laws), etc. The following covers the main types of material encountered. As a general rule material that is normally available through libraries contains an entry in italics (either book title, journal name). Other material such as congress papers, circulars, and unpublished material do not normally employ italics.

The reader will have noticed the terms 'normally' and 'may'. This leaves the choice open, and it is therefore essential to check the style of reference to be used with the publisher. There are two main styles: 1. The Vancouver style, largely used by biomedical journals and where references follow a numbering sequence; 2. The Harvard system – following author, date.

The Harvard system is probably that with which most readers will be familiar. However, there are many variations to be found. A glance at the reference list in half-a-dozen books will almost certainly reveal four or five variants. (Should eds employ a full point eds. for example? Does a comma follow the date?) Many papers written as internal documents, theses and seminar papers will probably not be subjected to the scrutiny of a proof-editor. This really emphasises the need for consistency. But if you are aiming at publication, then check the house style first. Checking reference lists is a number of books by the same publisher may well reveal the fact that the publisher accepts a number of variations but he won't accept inconsistency!

The following example includes all types of literary references commonly encountered, here from a book published by Hutchinson. Many publishers employ virtually the same formats. Variations are discussed below.

Alternatives to Domestic Rates, (1981). Cmnd 8449, HMSO.

Clegg, H. A. (1976a), *Trade Unions under Collective Bargaining*. Oxford: Blackwell.

Cousins, P. (1977), 'Theories of democracy and local government'. *Public Administration Bulletin*, vol. 23, pp. 40–53.

Friedman, M. (1970), *The Counter-Revolution in Monetary Theory*. Institute of Economic Affairs, Occasional Paper 33, London: IEA.

Glasgow District Council (1985), 'Housing Policy and the Private Sector'. Glasgow: GDC.

Leach, S. (1989), 'Strengthening local democracy? The government's response to Widdicombe'. In J. Stewart, and G. Stoker (eds.), *The Future of Local Government*. London: Macmillan.

Lloyds Bank. Annual accounts

Local Government (Scotland) Act 1973.

Madgwick, P. and Rose R. (eds.) (1982), *The Territorial Dimension in United Kingdom Politics*. London: Macmillan.

Parry, R. (1982), 'Who runs Scottish social policy?'. Paper presented to Political Studies Association Work Group on United Kingdom Politics.

Regina v. *Hindley*. Court of Appeal: Criminal Division, 17 October 1966.

Walker M. (1990). *The Guardian,* 7 February, p. 3.

Young, T. (1984), 'The politics of public participation in planning', University of Sussex, M.Phil. thesis (unpubl.)

http://www.yourdictionary.com/cgi-bin/mw.cgi

B. Books

1   2 3 4   5   6

Clegg, H. A. (1976a), *Trade Unions under Collective Bargaining*. Oxford: Blackwell.

1. **Author's name** employs initials.

Where possible confusion may arise the first name(s) may be given in full: Jones, John; Jones, Jane, alternatively Jones, J(ohn), etc. Space after full point for initials: Clegg, H. A. (1976) and not Clegg H.A. (1976).
 A few publishers prefer the full first name irrespectively:

Smith, David M. (1975), *Patterns in Human Geography*. Harmandsworth: Penguin.

Some publishers previously used upper case for author's names and this may occasionally be encountered today.

REFERENCES AND BIBLIOGRAPHIES

Editor is abbreviated ed. The plural form is often given as eds. (with a full point), but may be encountered without.

Joint authors
   Madgwick, P. and Rose R. (eds.) (1982), *The Territorial Dimension in United Kingdom Politics*. London: Macmillan.

Some publishers do not use the conjunction 'and'. A more recent trend is to use the ampersand: Madgwick, P. & Rose, R. This is also found in references contained in the main body of the text: (Madgwick & Rose, 1982:16). The ampersand is best reserved for publishers' names.

A former practice, still found occasionally, is to reverse the order of the *initials* of the second and subsequent authors. This also applies where the full first name is employed.

   Madgwick, P. and R. Rose (eds.) (1982), *The Territorial*....

Where there is more than one author, all authors' names should be given in the bibliography. In the main text, however, a normal method of referencing is that only the first author is used followed by et al. (*et alli*). It is not normal to italicise 'et al.' as this is now a familiar term.

The placement of 'ed.' may vary. In one book I encountered this following the date:

   Harloe, M. (1970) (ed.), *Captive Cities*...

2. **Date** in parentheses followed by a comma.

A comma is normal following the date, but a colon or a full point may be found. Some publishers use none of these, just a space.

   Smith, David M. 1975: *Patterns in Human Geography*. Harmandsworth: Penguin.

In older publications the date is found at the end (following the publisher), and not placed within parentheses. This practice seems to have been changed when electronic sorting became commonplace.

3. Several publications by **same author** numbered (1976a), (1976b), etc.

Some older publications used an em dash [—] (should be a double em) for successive publications by the same author. This is not often practised today (see Em Dash).

If the date is not given, then (n.d.) is used (no date), alternatively (undated).

4. **Title** in italics. Initial letters capitalised (except conjunctions, prepositions etc.)

Note that this does not apply to articles in journals. Very few publishers employ upper case for the title of an article. Most publishers place a full point at the end of the title; some use a comma prior to the publisher place and name.

5. **Publisher** shown by Place: Publisher. (Colon or comma separator.)

Nearly all publishers use an ampersand in their trade name: A & C Black; Allen & Unwin. Exceptions are found: Secker and Warburg; ...and Company, but ...& Co. (not and Co.).

Another version I recently encountered placed all the publishers details in parentheses at the end: (John Murray, London, 1971) No final full point, and place following the publisher's name. Not really to be recommended!

I have also encountered just the publisher's name without the place. The place name is particularly useful where a book is published in both London and New York, for example.

6. **Pages**. A very few publishers previously stated the number of pages in the book. e.g. 230 pp.). This does not seem to be practiced today. Page numbers of an article in a journal should be given.

Edition may be entered at the end of the reference:

> Hays, W. L. (1998), *Statistics*. Chicago: Holt, Rinehart & Winston. 4th edn.

Another method is to state the dates of the current and original editions:

> Hays, W. L. (1998) [1926], *Statistics*. Chicago: Holt, Rinehart & Winston.

Some publishers use:

> Hays, W. L. (1998), *Statistics*. Chicago: Holt, Rinehart & Winston. (First published in 1926).

C. Articles in periodicals

A periodical is a numbered journal appearing at regular intervals and *dated*. For *undated* series, see F. Papers.

> Cousins, P. (1977), 'Theories of democracy and local government', *Public Administration Bulletin*, vol. 23, pp. 40–53.

Title of article not italicised, employs lower case initial letters, placed within single inverted commas, concluding with a comma. Journal name italicised.

A few publishers use capital initial letters for the title. Double inverted commas around the title are found in older publications. Continental publications may use « » in place of inverted commas.

Alternatives to **volume** number, pages etc. (Check publisher's guidelines.)

> Vol. 23, pp. 40–53.
> (23) 40–53.
> 23: 40–53.
> XXIII: 40–53.

REFERENCES AND BIBLIOGRAPHIES

Note the dash (not a minus sign); space after the colon. Some publishers use the spaced dash: pp. 40 – 53.

Lower case may also be encountered: vol. 23, no. 1.

Where a periodical is published several times a year, reference may be made to the part, normally in parentheses:

> Rugg, D. (1941), 'Experiments in wording questions: II'. *Public Opinion Quarterly,* Vol. 5 (1), pp. 8–22.

Some publishers prefer a more specific date:

> Rugg, D. 'Experiments in wording questions: II'. *Public Opinion Quarterly,* Vol. 5, No. 1, March 1941.

D. Papers etc. in anthologies

> Leach, S. (1989), 'Strengthening local democracy? The government's response to Widdicombe'. In J. Stewart, and G. Stoker (eds.), *The Future of Local Government.* London: Macmillan.

Date refers to date of publication of main entry (the anthology may have been compiled in a later year). Title of paper (or chapter) *not italicised,* but within single quotes, lower case initial letters. Main entry: author(s) initials before surname as above, but some publishers prefer the reversed entry: In Stewart, J. and Stoker. G. (eds.)

Note ed. (editor, with full point); eds. (editors, normally also full point).

No date. Some publishers use a comma before 'in'...Widdicome', in J. Stewart...

Title of anthology in italics, upper case initial letters. However, the page numbers are normally omitted although the chapter number can be given. The precise page(s) referred to will, of course, appear in the main text as, for example, (Leach 1989: 101 ff.)

Where a bibliography refers to many articles from the same anthology, it may be practised that only the editor(s) is given:

> Leach, S. (1989), 'Strengthening local democracy? The government's response to Widdicombe'. In J. Stewart, and G. Stoker (eds.) (1993), pp. 101–22.

The full work will then be given under Stewart J., and Stoker G. (eds.). Some publishers prefer this form to be used, with the main work as a separate entry, even where only one chapter is cited.

E. Chapters in books

These are similar to the above, except that the chapter will be included. The page numbers are frequently added, although there are exceptions:

> Fielding, N. G., and Lee, Raymond M. (1998), *Computer Analysis and Qualitative Research.* Ch. 5, 'Analytic Pathologies', London: Sage, pp. 119–128.

The chapter title may be omitted.

F. Papers: numbered series

This includes working papers, circulars, etc. which are numbered but appear at *irregular* intervals.

> Friedman, M. (1970), *The Counter-Revolution in Monetary Theory*. Institute of Economic Affairs, Occasional Paper 33, London: IEA.

Title italicised. Upper case for titles. Name of series *not* italicised. However, note that in the same reference list I did encounter:

> Maybey, C. (1973), 'Social and ethnic mix in schools and the relationship with attainment of children aged 8 and 11', *CES Research Paper 9*, London: Centre for Environmental Studies.

The latter reference is treated as a journal and emphasises the point that a distinction between occasional and regular publications is not always clear.

G. Papers (unnumbered)

> Parry, R. (1982), 'Who runs Scottish social policy?' Paper presented to Political Studies Association Work Group on United Kingdom Politics.

Title not normally italicised but contained within single quotes. Where known, a place should be given for the publisher, or at least where a copy may be obtained.

H. Institution or organisation etc. as author

> Glasgow District Council (1985). *Housing Policy and the Private Sector*. Glasgow: GDC.

If the institution is given as the publisher, the title is italicised with upper case. If this is not stated, then the title is not italicised, placed in inverted commas and with lower case.

> Save the Whale Action Group (n.d.). 'The statistical evidence'. [Pamphlet.]

I. Acts of parliament

> Local Government (Scotland) Act 1973.

The title of the Parliamentary Act is not italicised (even though the publication may be available in libraries). The date is not contained in parentheses as this is part of the title. By implication it is also the date of publication. Other official publications where the publisher is stated are italicised.

Alternatives to Domestic Rates, (1981). Cmnd 8449, HMSO.

J. Legal cases

The names of plaintiffs and defendants should be italicised. Details may follow.

Regina v. *Hindley*. Court of Appeal: Criminal Division, 17 October 1966.

K. Other printed material

Newspapers. Where possible, state the page and column of an article referred to, although the following examples (drawn from the same publication as many of the above) show one publisher's accepted styles:

Walker M. (1990). *The Guardian,* 7 February, p. 3.

The Economist, 9 July 1994.

Other publications. General titles not italicised.

Lloyds Bank. Annual accounts

L. Unpublished material

Young, T. (1984), 'The politics of public participation in planning', University of Sussex, M.Phil. thesis (unpubl.)

Johnson M., Cross, M., and Parker, R. (1981), 'Ethnic minorities and the inner city'. Unpublished paper presented to the Institute of British Geographers Conference.

Title not italicised but placed within single quotes. Initial letters not capitalised. The place of the conference may be given, but is really of little assistance in locating a copy of the paper.

Some publishers might require more detail on the thesis, e.g. Ph.D. Thesis in Sociology. But you may also be advised by the publisher not to included unpublished material in the references! However, for the researcher this may provide a clue to other works by the same author published at a later date.

M. The Internet

Internet addresses are now frequently included in reference lists and footnotes, preferably at the end. If your paper is distributed as a file or is available electronically, you may establish hyperlinks such that the reader may click on the address and go straight to a site. Otherwise remove the hyperlink. Give the whole location in full:

http://www.yourdictionary.com/cgi-bin/mw.cgi

N. References in the text

A reference in the main body of the text is an indicator to the full bibliographic information given in the bibliography. References in the text will be concise, for example (Clegg, 1976: 16). Space usually follows the colon. This form seems to be more common than (Clegg 1976, p. 16). (Note space after p.).

It should be mentioned here that many references are frequently superfluous. For example, in a recent text I read 'Oil prices fell again towards the end of the year (Withers, 2000).' Now, my immediate reaction is to enquire as to why this reference should be so very important. There is nothing to indicate this. If the sentence had been '...end of the year due to conflicts between the OPEC members (Smithers 1999: 44)', then I would immediately have understood that this was something of interest had I been a student of oil politics.

The golden rule is to use references in the text with discretion. Here is a gem from a manuscript I received quite recently:

> Historical studies of certain phases in history, focused on a specific time and place, typically generate singularising questions and answers. Marx's answer to the question of how money can beget money (1867: chs 4, 5, 6) and Weber's (1956: chs 3, 10, 11) and Dahl's (1970) answers as to what constitutes legitimate power are examples of answers which have a high degree of generality. According to Aubert, sociology as a science must work to achieve a coherent view of all social behaviour and the entire structure of society (1979: 14). ...He is reducing 'experience' to 'immediate impressions of the senses' (1943: 178, 180–181, 190, 193, 195–196).

The above illustrates how the visual appearance of the text is broken up by continual reference to other works. It will also break up your reader's concentration. Sometimes the impression is given that the author is saying to the reader: 'just see how well read I am – how much I know about my subject.' What he should be asking is whether the reference really is necessary. I also recently read a paper where many statistics concerning the Norwegian metallurgical industry were presented. These had been obtained from another book and where the original author had manifestly obtained these from an official source. It was clearly not necessary to quote the source and the page number for this information at the end of every sentence containing a statistic (which this article did). As a general rule, use only references which are specific and necessary, preferably with the relevant page numbers.

References in the text normally use only the author's surname. Page numbers or chapters should be given where reference is being made to a specific statement etc. Otherwise we may question the validity of the reference. The following formats, and probably some others, are to be found.

(Smith, J., 1997: 22)   Initial letter only if several authors with same name.

REFERENCES AND BIBLIOGRAPHIES

(Jackson 1976: 76)	Option: no comma between name and date.
(Doulgie, 1982a: 55)	Option: comma between name and date.
(Pearson et al., 1987: 22)	'et al.' (not italicised). Applies where three authors or more. [No full point after et!] Cite all authors in the reference list.
(Homer 1982: 102, Leach 1989: 77)	Different works separated with comma.
(Jackson, 1976: 34; Black, 1992a: 9)	Semicolon between works if comma after author.
(Bone & Head 1977)	Ampersand is not recommended for author references, whether in the text or the bibliography.

Where information is gathered from a wide range of sources and are commented upon, then it may be felt desirable to quote all relevant references. To avoid cluttering up the text with references to different pages in the same work and detailed sources in technical documents, the use of footnotes rather than author references in the text is to be preferred. This does not prevent the use of author references elsewhere, but the footnotes should be annotated otherwise we will have a hybrid system of references where authors are referred to in the footnotes *and* in the text.

> Smith (1994) reached his initial conclusions after studying the parliamentary debate (Hansard, April 7, 1989: 1116 – 1228). His findings were particularly criticised in a number of subsequent articles (Bradshaw 1995a: 18; 1996: 212 – 217).This criticism was found to be justified when the Minister at the time published his memoirs (Smythe-Aitchison 1997), and which subsequently led to a re-evaluation by Smith (Smith 1997a, 1997b).

– as opposed to:

> Smith (1994) reached his initial conclusions after studying the parliamentary debate.[1] His findings were particularly criticised in a number of subsequent articles.[2] This criticism was found to be justified when the Minister at the time published his memoirs,[3] and which subsequently led to a re-evaluation by Smith.[4]

Note that the footnote reference numbers come after the comma and the full point.

Occasionally, a source is not known. In this case it is sufficient to include the author's dates of birth and death where known. As the sources to these quotations are unknown, no reference will appear in the bibliography.

Someone once said: 'When in Rome, do as the Romans do.' Possibly Balzac (1799–1850) had it right when he said: 'When in Turkey, do as the turkeys do.' However, when in Scotland, do *nothing* that the Scottish do! (Taylor 1937–)

References in the text should refer directly to the author and the year of publication. Avoid superfluous instructions and excessive parentheses.

✗ This model is widely used (e.g. Jones (1978), Black & Green (1979)).

✓ This model is widely used (Jones, 1978; Black and Green, 1979).

Where the genitive case is used, place the reference date at the most convenient point after the object:

✗ Smith's (1996: 22) point was that it had not been proved.

✓ Smith's point (1996: 22) was that it had not been proved.

or even:

✓ Smith's point was that it had not been proved (1996: 22).

▶ Avoid familiarity: the surname is sufficient. However, the initials may be useful for clarity. But the following is a bit condescending:

✗ The historian, Jacqueline Bywaters (1972), disputes this finding.

✓ This finding is disputed by Bywaters (1972).

Nevertheless, where an author is widely known by his full name, the familiar approach is occasionally better.

✓ It was disputed by James Joyce, but not by Shakespeare!

▶ Several authors are referred to as Smith et al.(1970). Avoid, however, the genitive 's: Smith et al.'s theory was... Rewrite as The theory advanced by Smith et al. was that....

▶ References in footnotes occasionally include the term 'passim', e.g. Smith, Ch. 11, *passim*. This term means 'throughout'.

O. Dates

The following forms may be used:

Taylor (1937–)	Author still living
Purcell (1623– ?)	Date of death unknown
Tacitus (55?–130?)	Date of birth and date of death uncertain
Aristotle (384?–322 BC)	Date of birth uncertain
Oscar Wilde(?)	Indicates uncertain source.

The spaced dash may be considered more appropriate for some of these.

REFERENCES AND BIBLIOGRAPHIES

P. References in footnotes and endnotes

Where references are included in footnotes and endnotes the following are used:

ibidem (ibid.)
In footnotes ibid. (not normally italicised) is used meaning 'in the same book'. This refers to the book cited in the immediately preceding footnote or reference. In this case the author's name is not restated. Some publishers do not approve of using 'ibid.', preferring the whole reference to be repeated.

opere citato (op. cit.)
Op. cit. as in Waldorf (op. cit.) refers to the last reference made to the work by Waldorf. This may be even be in a footnote on a previous page.
Originally, being Latin terms, they were italicised. Not so today. Convention is that foreign terms in everyday use are no longer italicised. Here is a sample set of footnotes to illustrate the principle:

1. Waldorf (1997: 12). The internal split ultimately led to a cabinet reshuffle.
2. The Upper House was unanimous on the issue, but only 67 members were in attendance.
3. Jones (1996) considers that trade union membership declined as a result of the vote.
4. (ibid.). A similar workers' reaction to the EU regulation occurred in Denmark.
5. Waldorf (op. cit.: 55) bases his statement on conversations with the Minister (now retired).

Here, ibid. (4) refers to Jones (3) and op. cit. (5) refers to Waldorf (1). Where possible, these should give precise references to page(s).

▶ The terms 'ibid.' and 'op. cit.' are not used within the main body of the text and where the full reference must be repeated.

Some research papers refer to personal notes or correspondence with other researchers. Publishers do not like entries such as 'Jones R., Personal communication.' Nevertheless, a footnote such as 'Prof. R. Jones, Brunel University, Department of Engineering. Personal communication.' can certainly have a place in a research document.

Finally, this chapter has discussed various alternatives for bibliographic information, and you should have no difficulty in finding almost all of these. The list at the beginning of the chapter summarises the most frequently encountered formats. A lot of work will be involved if you have to change the style on account of the publisher's preferences. These must be checked first. Otherwise select your own choices and stick to them.

Q. Sorting your own records

Frequently, bibliographic information (and other types of record such as addresses) is entered into a file and sorted later. Sorting lines or paragraphs is not difficult on the modern word-processor. However, a line break at the end of the line has the same effect as marking the end of a paragraph and may present difficulty in sorting some types of records.

Bibliographic references are usually easy to sort as these are written as a single string, the wrap-around at the end of the line being taken care of by the word-processor. This means that a (concealed) paragraph mark is placed only at the end of each reference, and in all probability a second one to provide a blank line before the next reference. Line breaks and thus the end of the paragraph may be revealed by clicking the ¶ symbol on the 'Standard' tools bar.

The paragraph marks can be referred to as 'hard returns', as opposed to 'soft returns' introduced casually by the word-processor to wrap a line. This means that there is a problem in sorting addresses and similar lists where information for each record may occur on several lines. You may deliberately have chosen to register bibliographic records on several lines. The problem arises from the fact that there is a paragraph mark at the end of *each* line prohibiting effective sorting of a *group* of lines. Here are three records which will illustrate the procedure.

The problem with which one is faced is to sort records containing a hard return so as not to regard each line as a paragraph. In this event the lines would be sorted independently.

The original records
Norway
Oslo

Lithuania
Vilnius

Estonia
Tallinn

Sorting these by lines would produce the following:

Estonia
Lithuania
Norway
Oslo
Tallinn
Vilnius

Clearly we wish to retain the record lines together. This may be done using the following steps in the Search&Replace procedure. Each line concludes with a Paragraph Mark (revealed by clicking the ¶ symbol). It is not necessary

REFERENCES AND BIBLIOGRAPHIES

to reveal these in order to sort, but they form part of the procedure. Note that a record is separated from the next by two Paragraph Marks, one at the end of the record followed by just a Paragraph Mark on the next line (this being a blank line, of course, separating the records).

When replacing the paragraph marks, we use 'Special' and then 'Paragraph Mark' on the Search&Replace screen. These appear as ^p on the search and replace panels.

Stages 1 to 3 reconstruct the records as lines. Check that there is no blank line at the end of the file following the last record. Use ¶ to check this.

Stage	Replace	With
1	^p^p	*
2	^p	+
3	*	*^p

The file now appears as follows:

Norway+Oslo*
Lithuania+Vilnius*
Estonia+Tallinn*

If the records comprise long lines, these will wrap onto the next line and are essentially single line paragraphs, the + signs representing the former hard line breaks.

Stage 4
Using the Sort procedure under tables, sort the lines (i.e. paragraphs).

The final stages reconstruct the records after the lines have been sorted.

Stage	Replace	With
5	*	^p
6	+	^p

Remove any blank lines from the end of the file. The end result is:

Estonia
Tallinn

Lithuania
Vilnius

Norway
Oslo

This method works even if records have different numbers of lines. You may find a way to refine this procedure or, ideally, record the steps as a macro.

5
Characters and Symbols

A. Typographic symbols

There are a number of general typographic symbols where it is convenient to know the name. These are frequently associated with foreign words but also encountered in general usage. These include:

á, é	acute accent
&	ampersand
'	apostrophe
*	asterisk
{ }	braces
[ ]	brackets
ˆ	caret
ç	cedilla
ˆ	circumflex
:	colon
,	comma
†	dagger
°	degree
ä, ï, ö	diæresis (dieresis)
‡	double dagger
—	em dash
–	en dash
&c.	et cetera (obsolete)
!	exclamation
à, è	grave accent
¶	line return (paragraph)
.	full point (period)
?	question mark
§	section/legal paragraph
;	semicolon
~	tilde

WordPerfect 5.1 – the classic word-processor – had a remarkable range of characters. These may be viewed in either the CHARMAP.TST file or the CHARACTER.DOC file. The range is similar in Corel WP 9 and later, and appear on the CHARMAP.WPD file. It could be added here that the spell-checker was very flexible in WP5x allowing searches to be made for AD???TLY or REIN*. The first would find ADEPTLY, the second would find all words commencing with REIN such as REINCARNATION, REINDEER. Ideal for crossword enthusiasts. (Chambers Electronic dictionary allows use of the asterisk; Cassells

CHARACTERS AND SYMBOLS

Electronic Dictionary is also excellent for 'wild-card' searches.)
    Corel WordPerfect and **Microsoft Word** contain similar character sets. The following are to be found in the latter:

- Latin
- Greek
- Cyrillic
- Hebrew
- Arabic
- General Punctuation symbols
- Currency symbols
- Number forms (including fractions)
- Mathematical operators
- Miscellaneous Dingbats,
- Specials
- Area for inserting own symbols.

Each typeface has its own set of symbols, but these are often limited. There is no difficulty in applying the 'normal text' symbols to any font although some are not particularly suited.
    Generally speaking, the characters available on the monitor are printable. However, certain characters may appear on the screen as □. These will also be printed correspondingly.
    Modern word-processors have the possibility of programming key-strokes for selected symbols. This might be useful for the mathematician who is constantly using $\sum \sqrt{} \Phi$ and so forth.
    There are two sets of symbols which one should be aware of: Webdings and Wingdings. Otherwise known as Dingbats, these are printer's symbols where those such as telephone symbol may be useful [☏] or the confirm box ☑. There is a considerable variety here. Many may be downloaded from the web.
    If you wish to see all of the available symbols in Microsoft Word, go to the toolbar at the top of the screen which shows the typeface currently in use. Click on the down arrow to the right to view all the available typefaces. Now select those which show symbols in the typeface field. According to your version of Microsoft Word these may include:

- Common bullets
- Holidays MT
- Monosorts
- Monosorts 2
- MS Outlook
- Vacation MT
- Webdings
- Wingdings
- Wingdings2
- Wingdings3

Now type all the keys on the keyboard! Next, repeat these holding down the shift key!! For example, hitting the (capital) letter 'R' (with the shift key) on Wingdings2 will produce ☑. You might require to use a larger font size for a better effect. However, it is worth noting those symbols for which you have regular use. Further simplification of achieving these is to designate a short cut key. This will eliminate the necessity of using the 'Insert (symbol)' procedure.

B. Pre-programmed symbols

The previous section outlined symbols that could be inserted. This demands quite a bit of activity with the mouse. It is possible to programme keystrokes for those symbols used regularly. However, many foreign letters and punctuation signs are already pre-programmed

The following table shows the keys to be entered to print the character shown. The table shows those symbols for which there are pre-programmed short cut keys for WP5.1, Corel WordPerfect 8 +, and Microsoft Word 98/ Office 2000.

WordPerfect

Complete tables (the CHARMAP files mentioned above) are shown in the WP handbooks for several hundred symbols. For the following 'Ctrl' and 'V' keys are held and released simultaneously, and the Key strokes must then be entered (including the comma).

Keys given in parentheses for WP 5.1/Corel WP (early versions) provide similar although not identical symbols to those shown in the table. The latest versions of Corel WP simplify insertion of symbols with the use of Ctrl + W.

Microsoft Word

In Microsoft Word the keys in the first column in the table below are held and released, and the keys in the second column are then entered where required. Where Ctrl + : is required (for example), this will also necessitate the Shift key to obtain the colon. (The ' + ' sign is *not* entered.) This may be confusing to the beginner, but a couple of experiments will reveal all. Numbers following Alt + must be entered on the number pad (press Num Lock first). The AltGr key is the same as Alt + Ctrl except where stated. Num− means the minus sign on the number keys.

The keystrokes for any symbol may be changed. This may be particularly useful where a given symbol is used regularly but the default keystrokes are a bit demanding! You can enter your own selection in the column to the right.

It could be added that the table has been sorted on Column 1 using the Sort feature in Microsoft Word.

CHARACTERS AND SYMBOLS

Symbol	WP 5.1 Ctrl + V, then number pad Corel WP (Win) Ctrl + W, then number pad	Microsoft Word (Win) Hold these, release, then press		MS Word (alternative strokes) Hold Alt + number pad	My keys
–	4,33	Ctrl + Num-			
—	4,34	AltGr + Num-			
^	1,3	Ctrl + ^	< space >		
~	0,126	Alt + ~		127	
¡	4,7	AltGr + !		173	
|		Alt + 166			
¨	1,7	Ctrl + :	< space >	249	
―	6,38	Alt + 0175			
´	1,6	Ctrl + '	< space >		
'	(1,10)(1,13)	Ctrl + '	< space >		
¸	1,12; 1,27	Ctrl + ,	< space >		
¿	4,8	AltGr + ?		168	
˜	1,7	Alt + 0152			
`	4,27	Ctrl + `			
'	4,29				
"	4,32	Ctr +	"		
"	4,31	Ctrl +	"		
±	6,42	Alt + 0177		241	
«	4,9	Ctrl + `	<	174	
»	4,10	Ctrl + `	>	175	
¢	4,19	Ctrl + /	c		
¤	4,24	Shift + 4		207	
¥	4,12	Alt + 165		190	
§	4,6	Shift + |		245	
©	4,23	AltGr + c		184	
¬	6,20	Alt + 0178		170	
®	4,22	AltGr + r		169	
°	6,36	Alt + Ctrl + 2	< space >	248	
µ	8,25	AltGr + m			
¶	4,5	Alt + 0182		204	
·	4,3	Alt + 0183			
…	4,56	AltGr + .			
¼	4,18	Alt + 0188		172	
½	4,17	Alt + 0189		171	
¾	4,25	Alt + 0190		243	
¹	4,78	Alt + 0185		251	

Symbol	WP 5.1 Ctrl + V, then number pad Corel WP (Win) Ctrl + W, then number pad	Microsoft Word (Win) Hold these, release, then press		MS Word (alternative strokes) Hold Alt + number pad	My keys
²	4,20	Alt + 0178		253	
³	4,26	Alt + 0179		252	
ª	(4,15)	Alt + 0170		167	
Á	1,26	Ctrl + '	Shift + a	181	
á	1,27	Ctrl + '	a	160	
À	1,32	Ctrl + `	Shift + a	183	
à	1,33	Ctrl + `	a	133	
Â	1,28	Ctrl + ^	Shift + a	182	
â	1,29	Ctrl + ^	a	131	
Ã	1,76	Alt + Ctrl + ~	Shift + a	199	
ã	1,77	Alt + Ctrl + ~	a	198	
Ç	1,38	Ctrl + ,	Shift + c	128	
ç	1,39	Ctrl + ,	c	135	
Ð	1,78	Ctrl + '	Shift + d	209	
ð	1,87	Ctrl + '	d		
É	1,40	Ctrl + '	Shift + e	144	
é	1,41	Ctrl + '	e	130	
È	1,46	Ctrl + `	Shift + e	212	
è	1,47	Ctrl + `	e	138	
Ê	1,42	Ctrl + ^	Shift + e	210	
ê	1,43	Ctrl + ^	e	136	
Ë	1,44	Ctrl + :	Shift + e	211	
ë	1,45	Ctrl + :	e	137	
ƒ	(4,14)	Alt + 0131		159	
Í	1,48	Ctrl + '	Shift + i	214	
í	1,49	Ctrl + '	u	161	
Ì	1,54	Ctrl + `	Shift + i	222	
ì	1,55	Ctrl + `	u	141	
Î	1,50	Ctrl + ^	Shift + i	215	
î	1,51	Ctrl + ^	u	140	
Ï	1,52	Ctrl + :	Shift + i	216	
ï	1,53	Ctrl + :	u	139	
Ñ	1,56	Alt + Ctrl + ~	Shift + n	165	
ñ	1,57	Alt + Ctrl + n	n	164	
º	(6,36)(1,14)	Alt + 0186		248	
Ó	1,58	Ctrl + '	Shift + o	224	
ó	1,59	Ctrl + '	o	162	

CHARACTERS AND SYMBOLS

Symbol	WP 5.1 Ctrl + V, then number pad Corel WP (Win) Ctrl + W, then number pad	Microsoft Word (Win) Hold these, release, then press		MS Word (alternative strokes) Hold Alt + number pad	My keys
Ó	1,64	Ctrl + '	Shift + o	227	
ó	1,65	Ctrl + '	o	149	
Ô	1,60	Ctrl + ^	Shift + o	226	
ô	1,61	Ctrl + ^	o	147	
Õ	1,82	AltGr + ~	Shift + o	229	
õ	1,83	AltGr + ~	o	228	
Œ	(1,166)	Ctrl + &	Shift + o		
œ	(1,167)	Ctrl + &	o		
Š		Alt + Ctrl + ^	Shift + s		
š		Alt + Ctrol + ^	s		
ß	8,3	Ctrl + &	s	225	
þ	(1,88)	Alt + 0254		232	
™	4,41	AltGr + t			
Ú	1,66	Ctrl + '	Shift + u	233	
ú	1,67	Ctrl + '	u	163	
Ù	1,72	Ctrl + `	Shift + u	235	
ù	1,73	Ctrl + `	u	151	
Û	1,68	Ctrl + ^	Shift + u	234	
û	1,69	Ctrl + ^	u	150	
Ý	1,84	Ctrl + '	Shift + y	237	
ý	1,85	Ctrl + '	y	236	
Ÿ	1,74	Ctrl + :	Shift + y	153	
ÿ	1,75	Ctrl + :		152	
Ü	1,70	Ctrl + :	Shift + u	154	
ü	1,71	Ctrl + :	u	129	
Ž	1,206	Alt + 0142			
ž	1,207	Alt + 0158			
Æ	1,36	Ctrl + &	Shift + a	146	
æ	1,37	Ctrl + &	a	145	
Ä	1,30	Ctrl + :	Shift + a	142	
ä	1,31	Ctrl + :	a	132	
Ø	1,80	Ctrl + /	Shift + o	157	
ø	1,81	Ctrl + /	o	155	
Ö	1,62	Ctrl + :	Shift + o	153	
ö	1,63	Ctrl + :	o	148	
Å	1,34	Alt + Ctrl + 2	Shift + a	143	
å	1,35	Alt + Ctrl + 2	a	134	

In addition to the above, many editing functions are pre-programmed. This particularly applies to alphabetic and F-keys in connection with the Ctrl key (or CTRL + ALT/SHIFT). However, the ALT-keys are relatively free, only ALT-E, F, V and W, and just ALT + SHIFT + I being pre-programmed. As the four former ALT key functions are also available via the menu bar these are not really needed. This virtually enables one to programme a complete alphabet in upper and lower case using the ALT key.

The following are some of the 'normal text' symbols which are not pre-programmed in Microsoft Word but for which you may have frequent use in some texts. You may assign your own short cut keys. The above table will show which short cut keys are already programmed, but you will be warned if you try to assign short cut keys already assigned.

^{n} $^c/_o$ $^1/_3$ $^2/_3$ $^1/_8$ $^5/_8$ $^7/_8$ ϑ Δ Π Σ $\sqrt{}$ ∞ $\cap$ $\int$ $\approx$ $\neq$ $\leq$ $\geq$ ♀ ♂ ♠ ♣ ♥ ♦ ■ □

In addition there are a number of statistical signs which may be programmed (see below).

C. Paragraph symbols

The paragraph mark for typographic purposes is ¶. In legal and other documents the section mark § is often referred to as the paragraph symbol. This may be used where paragraphs are numbered: See §6. This is also referred to in §§2, 9, 12–13. In some countries a space follows the § sign [see § 6]. This practice is occasionally encountered in the UK and USA. Note that §§ means 'paragraphs'.

The paragraph icon is also used by Microsoft Word to indicate a 'hard return'.

D. The Greek alphabet

The statistician will have considerable use of Greek characters. A number of other symbols will also be of interest to the mathematician. Many articles use only symbols for the mean (μ), and standard deviation (σ). These are not pre-programmed in Microsoft Word and must provisionally be inserted from the symbols function. However, they are easily programmed, and some authors may require to apply their own key strokes for rapid insertion of these characters.

A word of caution here. Make sure that the keys you choose are not already programmed such as Ctrl + A (blocks all the text in Microsoft Word). Indeed, many of the Ctrl + and Alt + combinations are already pre-programmed. Many 'AltGr' keys (= Alt + Ctrl), and several combinations of these (Alt + Ctrl + ...) are pre-programmed, but not all. You will be cautioned if you try to programme the keys and a particular combination is already in use.

Certain fonts, particularly non-serif fonts, are not always suitable for Greek characters, for example:

CHARACTERS AND SYMBOLS

Times Roman: Γ Λ Ξ Ψ γ π ψ
Arial: Γ Λ Ξ Ψ γ π ψ

In the following table you may note the key combinations you may prefer for selected Greek characters. Consult the previous table for a summary of pre-programmed keys.

Character	Upper case	My keys:	Lower case	My keys:
alpha	A		α	
beta	B		β	
gamma	Γ		γ	
delta	Δ		δ	
epsilon	E		ε	
zeta	Z		ζ	
eta	H		η	
theta	Θ		θ	
iota	I		ι	
kappa	K		κ	
lambda	Λ		λ	
mu	M		μ	
nu	N		ν	
chi	Ξ		ξ	
omicron	O		o	
pi	Π		π	
rho	P		ρ	
sigma	Σ		σ	
tau	T		τ	
ypsilon	Y		υ	
phi	Φ		φ	
chi	X		χ	
psi	Ψ		ψ	
omega	Ω		ω	

E. Mathematical symbols and notation

Mathematical analysis

$|a|$	absolute value of a
∠	acute angle
∡	angle
≈	approximately equals
⌒	arc

$\because$	because
$\bigcirc$	circle
$/$	divide
$\div$	divide
$\Leftrightarrow$ or $\leftrightarrow$	double implication
$\cong$	equal or nearly equal to
$=$	equals
$\equiv$	exactly equals
Δ	finite difference
f	function
$\geq$	greater or equal to
$>$	greater than
$\Leftarrow$ or $\leftarrow$	implied by
∞	infinity
$\int$	integral
$\in$	is an element in
$:$	is to
$\leq$	less or equal to
$<$	less than
Π	mathematical consonant, pi = 3.14159265
$\log e$	mathematical constant, base of natural logarithms = 2.71828
$\mp$	minus or plus
$N!$	N factorial
$\neg a$	not a
$\neq$	not equal to
$\|\|$	parallel
$\perp$	perpendicular
$\pm$	plus or minus
Π	product
$::$	proportion, so is
$,$	quadrant
$\Rightarrow$ or $\rightarrow$	results in, implies
$\llcorner$	right angle (90°)
$\sqrt{}$	root
$\square$	square
$-$	subtraction (minus)
Σ	sum
$\therefore$	therefore
$\neq$	unequal to/different to
δ	variation
$\propto$	varies as, proportional to
$\top$	vertical

CHARACTERS AND SYMBOLS

F. Statistical symbols and notation

A surprisingly large number of articles which I am required to look at contain statistical symbols which are not used according to custom. By definition a *statistic* is a measure calculated on the basis of a sample. *Statistics* is the analysis of data by which estimates are made about the *parameters* of a *population* (often of unknown size), the basis of the estimate frequently being a *normally distributed representative sample*.

There are a number of statistics which may be used to describe a sample, for example, the sum, mean, standard deviation and so forth. *Latin alphabetic characters* are used to denote the *sample statistics*. *Greek symbols* are used to denote the *population parameters*, i.e. the sum, mean, etc., of the population. Statistical formulae are given in *Dictionary/Outline of Statistics* by J. E. Freund and F. J. Williams, Dover Publications 1966. Definitions and examples are given in *Dictionary of Statistics* by Roger Porkess, Collins Reference 1988.

The following statistical symbols are normally encountered:

Symbol[1]	statistic
χ^2	chi square statistic
(x,y)	a joint event where x is paired with y
$|AD|$	MAD = mean absolute deviation
μ	estimated population mean
ANCOVA	Analysis of covariance
ANOVA	Analysis of variance
cf	cumulative frequency (= running total)
cov(X,Y)	covariance of two random variables X and Y.
e	error or a measurement
$E(X)$	expectation of a random variable
F	F-ration computed from a sample
f	frequency (of a variable or class)
G^2	likelihood ratio test statistic
i	used as a subscript for the i_{th} variable
K or κ	kappa statistic
MANOVA	Multiple analysis of variance
MS	Mean Square in ANOVA
n	size of a sample
N	size of population (occasionally used for sample size!)
p	probability of a given event
Q	proportion of classes in the upper tail of a sampling distribution
Q, Y	Yules' index
r_s	Spearman's rank-correlation coefficient

---

[1] This list has been sorted using Microsoft Word sort routine. The order may differ using other sort procedures.

s	standard correlation coefficient (corrected) for a sample
S	standard correlation coefficient for a sample
S	standard deviation of a sample
S^2	sample variance
SS	Sum of Squares in ANOVA
t	Student's t-statistic
T	Total number of potential observations in a finite population
var(X)	variance of the random variable X.
w	a weighting factor
X	a random variable; independent variable
x	a value which a random variable X may assume
Y	a random variable; the dependent variable
z	standardised score
Z	value of Fisher's r- to Z transformation
α	Type I error (Probability of rejection of H_0 when it is true)
β	Type II error (Probability of failure to reject H_0 when it is true)
θ	theta. General symbol for a population parameter
θ_2	Value of θ specified by the null hypothesis
λ	lambda – measure of asymmetric association
ρ	intraclass correlation coefficient for a population
σ	standard deviation of a random variable
σ^2	variance of a random variable
$\sigma_{\text{diff.}}$	standard error of the difference between two means
τ	tau. Kendall's coefficient of rank-order agreement
ϕ^2	index of mean square contingency for a sample contingency table
Φ^2	index of mean square contingency for a population contingency table

G. Other symbols

Auto correct

It is possible to use the auto-correct feature to make symbols. Word includes several examples. For example, a colon will nearly always be followed by a space and we are unlikely to meet an opening parenthesis immediately following a colon, such as :(. The auto correct feature automatically changes :(to ☹ while :) is automatically changed to ☺. So how did I manage to print :(and :) ? Just use the delete back key (top right of the alphabetic keyboard) and the characters reappear. You may also switch off the auto-correct feature to do this. Using the auto-correct feature you can program any sequence of letters to produce any symbol that you may be using regularly. As described earlier, another method is to programme the ALT keys (see Chapter 5, B).

Overstrike

In WordPerfect for DOS it is possible to superimpose (overstrike) two characters such as O and / to make Ø. Use Shift F8, 4, 5, 1 to create a symbol and follow the instructions on the screen. Windows word-processors contain so many characters and symbols that I have never had use for these features although I suspect they do exist there as well.

Euro symbol

The Euro currency symbol [€] is included in Windows 98 and shown on modern keyboards where one may use the AltGr + e, or AltGr + 5 keys. This feature is not available in earlier Windows versions of WordPerfect or Microsoft Word nor with Windows 95. Use the overstrike feature in WordPerfect for DOS (see preceding paragraph) to create a character C and =. This will produce the Euro symbol. However, this will appear on the screen as C = (i.e. not as an overstrike symbol).

Warning!

When exporting files to another user, by email or on diskette, you should ensure that he/she has the same, similar or convertible fonts. *This is 'Linoscript' and may appear attractive on a brochure for the church bazaar,* but it may appear as gobbledegook on another PC, even though this too has Microsoft Word, or whatever. Different versions of Microsoft Word or WordPerfect may not necessarily contain the same set of fonts as your PC. If you are planning to use a special font and/or symbols, send an email trial to the recipient first, as an attachment.

6
Tables

It is surprising how many manuscripts omit the use of tables, as well as figures and diagrams, where these could be usefully employed. This is very largely the result of ignorance as to how to produce these on the word-processor. A half-hour using the 'help' menu will cure this ailment and will add 'life' to your manuscript. The intention behind four or five lines of confusing text is readily assimilated when presented graphically or in a table. A frequent mistake on the part of many academic authors is to insert too much statistical data in the text. The inclusion of too many statistics confuses many readers and the points to be emphasised may be lost. Even where only a few statistics are to be described, they may be usefully summarised in a table. Take the following, for example:

> In 1931, Norwegian landings of salmon amounted to 879 tons. Landings of plaice were four times greater, totalling 3484 tons, while halibut exceeded 5200 tons. In 1941 salmon landings of 823 tons while both halibut and plaice landings were only about a quarter of the level of a decade earlier at 1352 tons and 880 tons respectively.

We had lost the trend at the end of the second line, I suspect. Now glance at the first two columns in Table 1 below. The point is readily understood.

The layout of the table will make the task easier for the reader to grasp the essential points. Modern word-processors provide a number of alternative layouts whereby your table will be formatted automatically. These may include colour and fancy fonts, but keep in mind your readership. If you are designing a brochure, a 'modern' design might be appropriate, but a table in a Ph.D. thesis will probably require a more conservative approach.

Headings for tables and figures

Normally, *table headings* will be *above* the table; *figure headings*, *below*. Curiously, a number of publishers place the title of the figure in italics whereas the title of the table is not. Further, the font size for either or both may be one point smaller.

Numbering tables etc.

Tables and diagrams may be numbered consecutively throughout the book, or by chapter: *Table 1-1, 1-2; 2-1, 2-2*, etc. The same applies to diagrams (figures). If the publisher is converting your text from a standard word-processor file, then tables and diagrams are usually required to be delivered as a separate file. The text should then include a note: [*Table 1-5 about here*]. This will enable the typesetter to insert the table at the most appropriate place to avoid an unnecessary page-break or white space.

TABLE DESIGN

Very frequently we get carried away both with the detail to be included in tables and the layout. The result is that we may have to use a smaller font which, when reduced to the book page-size, is scarcely readable. Further, excessive vertical lines in a table do not contribute to the appearance; horizontal lines should also be kept to a minimum. It is important to keep in mind the scale of reduction required, and where necessary, divide a table into two.

Broad tables may be printed 'landscape', that is, turned anti-clockwise 90° such that the top of the table is on the left-hand margin of the page. But this is not an ideal solution. It may be better to redesign and split the table and then to present it on facing pages in normal ('portrait') layout.

It should not be forgotten that the table is frequently a summary of what may or could have been written as text as well as supplying supplementary information. A detailed table is useful in this respect but should be designed such that the essential statistics and trends are easily observed.

Commence by constructing a framework selecting the 'Tables' function and defining the number of rows of columns. You can easily add or delete columns and rows as required. The table framework is automatically adjusted to the width of the margins. At this stage we are concerned only with entering data; formatting comes later. Here only four rows are shown; the complete table is given later. Time series should be on the horizontal scale (row). Data may be sorted by row or column. Care should also be given to the title. Short statements make for clarity. These should summarise the column (here, species) and row (time series) information and the measurement used (unless the table contains diverse information and units).

Table 1: Norway. Fish landings by species 1931–1971. Tons.

	1931	1941	1951	1961	1971
Salmon	879	823	896	1335	1704
Halibut	5293	1352	5273	4292	1981
Plaice	3484	880	1414	1424	520

You do not need to boldface the row and column titles at this stage, but should mark the *data* and give this a *right margin alignment*. Headings may be centred. You may want to change the font for the table. Use the sort feature to sort the rows or columns, or both. Preferably, set equal column widths and centre the table. Here is the result for the full table:

Table 2: Norway. Fish landings by species 1931–1971. Tons.

	1931	1941	1951	1961	1971
Cod	106834	129686	149070	77580	169457
Haddock	22435	12768	18260	46677	35595
Halibut	5293	1352	5273	4292	1981
Herring	305446	214475	888006	69042	6894
Mackerel	8388	4760	18490	14973	229825
Plaice	3484	880	1414	1424	520
Salmon	879	823	896	1335	1704

Now highlight the table and select one of the autoformats. The first is the simplest choice. Note that the table width is automatically reduced to a convenient size.

Table 3: Norway. Fish landings by species 1931–1971. Tons.

	1931	1941	1951	1961	1971
Cod	106834	129686	149070	77580	169457
Haddock	22435	12768	18260	46677	35595
Halibut	5293	1352	5273	4292	1981
Herring	305446	214475	888006	69042	6894
Mackerel	8388	4760	18490	14973	229825
Plaice	3484	880	1414	1424	520
Salmon	879	823	896	1335	1704

Modern processors provide a variety of autoformatted tables, but you may frequently find that it is worth spending some time on applying your own shading to selected columns in order to distinguish between the variables. A 15% density shading is used in Table 4.

Table 4: Norway. Fish landings 1931–1971. Tons and Per cent of total, by species.

Species	1931	%	1941	%	1951	%	1961	%	1971	%
Cod	106834	23.6	129686	35.6	149070	13.8	77580	36.0	169457	38.0
Haddock	22435	5.0	12768	3.5	18260	1.7	46677	21.7	35595	8.0
Halibut	5293	1.2	1352	0.4	5273	0.5	4292	2.0	1981	0.4
Herring	305446	67.5	214475	58.8	888006	82.1	69042	32.1	6894	1.5
Mackerel	8388	1.9	4760	1.3	18490	1.7	14973	7.0	229825	51.5
Plaice	3484	0.8	880	0.2	1414	0.1	1424	0.7	520	0.1
Salmon	879	0.2	823	0.2	896	0.1	1335	0.6	1704	0.4
TOTAL	452759	100.0	364744	100.0	1081409	100.0	215323	100.0	445976	100.0

The following shows the various shades of grey and white on black. These subtleties may not, however, appear on all laser printers (better on an inkjet printer). These effects are easily achieved by marking the column and selecting the background colour. Then choose the font colour (black or white).

Table 5: Shading: Percentage grey shading.

0%	5%	10%	15%	20%	25%	30%	35%	W/Gr	W/B
106834	23.6	129686	35.6	149070	13.8	77580	36.0	169457	38.0
22435	5.0	12768	3.5	18260	1.7	46677	21.7	35595	8.0
5293	1.2	1352	0.4	5273	0.5	4292	2.0	19.81	0.4
305446	67.5	214475	58.8	888006	82.1	69042	32.1	6894	1.5
8388	1.9	4760	1.3	18490	1.7	14973	7.0	229825	51.5
3484	0.8	880	0.2	1414	0.1	1424	0.7	520	0.1
879	0.2	823	0.2	896	0.1	1335	0.6	1704	0.4
452759	100.0	364744	100.0	1081409	100.0	215323	100.0	445976	100.0

The white on grey (W/Gr) is quite effective, here on 60% shading. This seems to be more effective than the black background (W/B).

A final comment is that by this time it should be clear that Excel is not a suitable substitute for the Tables feature in Microsoft Word. The same applies to other word-processors and associated spreadsheets. One important reason is that the text in column headings does not wrap around to fit the column width. Further, the spreadsheet lacks the flexibility for design such as lines between columns, for example. It is frequently a question of revealing or hiding the grid entirely. Further, import of spreadsheets into a word-processor table is not unproblematic.

7
Statistics

Survey data plays an important part in many research papers and articles. The data may cover an entire *population*, or may comprise a *sample* upon which the *parameters* of a population (of known or unknown size) are to be predicted. Nevertheless, the descriptive statistics of our survey data can be very illuminating. Unfortunately, familiarity with descriptive statistics seems to be quite restricted. The essential descriptive statistics are obtainable in worksheets such as Excel or Quattro Pro.

When describing a data set we are often interested in a) the degree to which values of individual cases are concentrated around the mean value, conversely the *spread* of the data, and b) the *skew* of the distribution, i.e. the degree to which data is symmetrically located around the mean.

Let us consider the following cases, assuming these to be the ages of children born to a sample of four families, each who have been married 12 years. (I am aware that some families will have several children within the first few years of marriage, but the following will serve to illustrate descriptive statistics.)

These can be presented diagrammatically:

Age of child

Data set	1	2	3	4	5	6	7	8	9	10	11
1		+	+				+	+		+	
2	+			+		+		+	+		
3		+	++		+	+					+
4		+			++		+				+

The mean values for each data set are shaded.

Statistical summary:

Data values, sets 1 to 4	Note	2 3 7 8 10	1 4 6 9 10	2 3 3 5 6 11	2 5 5 7 11
Number of cases (N =)		5	5	6	5
Sum		30	30	30	30
Mean (Sum/N)		6	6	5	6
Minimum value		2	1	2	2
Maximum value		10	10	11	11
Range (Max. Min.)		8	9	9	9
Mid-range (Max. + Min.)/2	1	6	5.5	6.5	6.5
Median		7	6	4	5
Mode		-	-	3	5

STATISTICS

1. quartile (Q1)	2	3	4	3	5
2. quartile((Q2)	3	7	6	4	5
3. quartile(Q3)	4	8	9	5.5	7
Interquartile range (Q3-Q1)		5	5	2.5	2
Low spread (Q2-Q1)		4	2	1	0
High spread (Q3-Q2)		1	3	1.5	2
Quartile devn (Q3-Q1)/2		2.5	2.5	1.25	1
Mean absolute deviation	5	2.8	2.8	2.3	2.0
Coeff. of mean deviation	6	0.47	0.47	0.46	0.33
Quartile coeff. of dispersion	7	0.45	0.38	0.29	0.17
Standard Deviation (SD)	8	3.39	3.67	3.29	3.32
St. Error of the mean	9	1.52	1.64	1.34	1.48
Coefficient of variation	10	0.565	0.612	0.658	0.553
Coefficient of skewness	11	-0.19	-0.35	1.47	0.69
Coefficient of kurtosis	12	-2.23	-1.29	2.21	1.13

Notes:
1. The mid-range is that value located at the mid-point between the lowest and highest values.
2. The 1. quartile indicates that value for which one fourth *or less* of cases are below. Where N is divisible by 4, this is easily calculated. For other values of N, Q1 = 1(N+1)/4. For data set 1 this is (6/4) = 1.5. We round this *up* to 2. Q1 is thus the value of the 2nd case (=3). Q3 = 3(N+1)/4 = 4.5. This is rounded *down* to 4. Q4 is thus the value of the 4th case (=8).
3. The 2nd quartile, Q2, is the median, that value where 50% of cases lie above, and 50% below.
4. Similar to Q1, 75% of cases are *below* this value, 25% above.
5. The Mean Absolute Deviation (MAD) is the mean of the absolute values of the each case value minus the mean. For Data set 1 this would be the mean of |2-6|, |3-6|... giving (4+3+1+2+4)/5 = 2.8. A useful statistic for this type of data.
6. The Coefficient of mean deviation is given by MAD/mean. This is a measure of dispersion (spread) about the mean.
7. Quartile coefficient of dispersion. This is given by (Q3-Q1)/(Q3+Q1).
8. The Standard Deviation is a measure of spread around the mean. Approximately 68% of all cases will lie within the mean ± 1 SD in a normal distribution.
9. The Standard Deviation of the mean (confusingly also called the Standard Error) is used to estimate the true error of the population in predictive statistics. It provides an estimate of the range within which the true (but unknown) mean of the population will lie.

10. The Coefficient of variation is the SD/mean, usually given as a percentage (* 100).

11. The coefficient of skewness indicates the number of cases to the left (positive skew) or right (negative skew) of the mean. That is the extent to which the distribution is skewed in comparison to a normal bell-shaped symmetrical distribution. A symmetrical (bell-shaped) distribution will have a coefficient of 0. Date set 3 shows is the most skewed. The youngest child is just three years under the mean age; the oldest is six years over.

12. Kurtosis is also a similar measurement to indicate the 'peakedness' of a distribution. Another way of expressing this is the degree to which the tail values are spread with respect to the mean. Data set 3 has the highest coefficient suggesting that it has the most 'peaked' distribution. In fact, three of the six children are aged 2 or 3. Data set 1 has the 'flattest' distribution.

The fact that the quartiles are easily calculated enables the quartile deviation to be given. Also known as the semi-interquartile range, this is a measure of dispersion of data around the mean.

Clearly, there is a considerable amount of quite basic information which can be presented using descriptive statistics. Statistics in **boldface** are obtainable in Excel using Tools – Data Analysis – Descriptive statistics (OK) – Summary statistics. Other statistics may be calculated using a formula in the spreadsheet. Virtually all the above statistics (and some others) are available in programs such as SPSS, SAS, SYSTAT, MINITAB, etc.

Descriptive statistics are only concerned with a specific data set. Which statistics are selected to describe the data may depend on the objective as well as the type of data. The above data was 'quantitative'. Other data may be 'qualitative' and are subjective (or based on personal evaluation). For example, persons interviewed might be asked to rank answers 1 to 5 to the question: 'Should foreign aid be increased/reduced?' 'Much Increased', 'Partly increased', 'Kept the same', 'Partly decreased', 'Much decreased'. If half the respondents say 'Much increased' and the other half state 'Much decreased', it is clearly misleading to suggest as the mean value was 3, people meant 'on average' that foreign aid should 'remain unchanged'.

Predictive statistics are used to estimate parameters of the whole population. The standard error of the mean, for example, is used to estimate the mean of the population within given limits. As we are not measuring the entire population, we can only predict such values as the population mean.

I have included a number of very readable texts in the reference lists which provide introductions to statistics for the non-statistician. (See Chapter 20 D)

8
Metric Conversion

There always seems to be one problem when converting data – one can never find the conversion factor required. The British steadfastly retain their pint, and indeed the pound weight as well as their pound in the pocket! Conversions involving population density, miles per gallon, hectares, etc., always seem problematic. This is reflected in the fact that many authors do not even add a footnote explaining the continental or US equivalent. I have found the following to be a convenient aid to conversions – it is alphabetical. One unit of the first column represents so many units of the third, the middle column being the conversion factor. A number of non-metric units are also included.

unit	equiv. to	unit
acre	0.404856	hectares
are (100 sq. m)	119.6	sq. yards
centigrade	x(9/5) + 32	Fahrenheit
centimetre	0.3937	inches
cubic centimetre	0.6102	cubic inches
cubic foot	0.0280	cubic metres
cubic inch	1.6380	cubic centimetres
cubic metre	35.3147	cubic feet
cubic metre	1.3080	cubic yards
cubic yard	0.7650	cubic metres
Fahrenheit	-32 x (5/9)	centigrade
foot	0.3048	metres
gallon (UK)	1.2010	gallons (US)
gallon (UK)	4.5461	litres
gallon (US)	0.8327	gallons (UK)
gallon (US)	3.7854	litres
gram	0.0353	ounces
hectare	2.4711	acres
hundredweight (cwt.)	50.8020	kilograms
inch	2.5400	centimetres
kilogram	0.0197	hundredweight (cwt.)
kilogram	2.2046	pounds
kilogram	0.1575	stones
kilometre	0.6214	miles
kilometre	0.5400	nautical miles
kp per sq. cm	14.2233	psi (lbs per sq. in.)
lbs per sq. inch	.07031	kp per sq. cm
litre	0.2200	gallons (UK)
litre	0.2642	gallons (US)
litre	1.7596	pints (UK)
litre	2.1133	pints (US)
litre per mil (10 km)	28.244	miles per gallon

A HANDBOOK FOR WRITERS OF ENGLISH

metre	3.2808	feet
metre	1.0936	yards
metric tonne	0.9843	tons
mile	1.6093	kilometres
nautical mile	1.8520	kilometres
ounce	28.3400	grams
pint (UK)	0.5883	litres
pint (US)	0.4732	litres
pound	0.4536	kilograms
square centimetre	1.5500	square inches
square foot	0.0929	square metres
square inch	0.6452	square centimetres
square kilometre	0.3861	square miles
square metre	10.7639	square feet
square metre	2.2960	square yards
square mile	2.5900	square kilometre
square yard	0.8361	square metres
stone	6.3500	kilograms
ton	1.0160	metric tonnes
yard	0.9144	metres

A note on tons, tonnes and tonnage

Collins English Dictionary provides useful definitions:

ton
1. **long ton.** *Brit.* a unit of weight equal to 2240 pounds or 1016.046 kilograms.
2. **short ton, net ton.** *U.S.* a unit of weight equal to 2000 pounds or 907.184 kilograms.
3. **metric ton, tonne.** a unit of weight equal to 1000 kilograms (2204.6 pounds).

tonnage or tunnage
The capacity of a merchant ship expressed in tons, for which purpose a ton is considered as 40 cubic feet of freight or 100 cubic feet of bulk cargo, unless such an amount would weigh more than 2000 pounds in which case the actual weight is used.

So now we know!

A note on miles

British and U.S. mile = 1760 yards or 5280 feet
Nautical mile: UK = 6080 feet (1.8532 km); US = 6076.1 feet (1.852 km).

METRIC CONVERSION

A note on gallons

1 gallon (imperial) UK = 4.546 litres (277.4 cubic inches); U.S. = 3.785 litres (231 cubic inches).

A useful guide to conversions and scientific data in general is: Tennent, R. M., *Scientific Data Book*. Open University Press: Edinburgh 1971.

9
Compound Growth Rates

Rates of growth are an element in many studies, not only finance. The following table shows the factor growth yielded on a principle amount at various rates of interest compounded over a given number of periods. For example, at 10% growth rate (or interest), capital will have virtually doubled after just over 7 years. The formula is given by $F = K*(1+i/100)^P$ where F = factor growth, K = capital (or principle), i = interest, and P the number of periods. If the world's population is increasing at 5% p.a., it will almost double every 14 years.

Periods	Annual Rate of Growth (percent)									
	1.00	1.50	2.00	2.50	3.00	4.00	5.00	6.00	8.00	10.00
1	1.01	1.02	1.02	1.03	1.03	1.04	1.05	1.06	1.08	1.10
2	1.02	1.03	1.04	1.05	1.06	1.08	1.10	1.12	1.17	1.21
3	1.03	1.05	1.06	1.08	1.09	1.12	1.16	1.19	1.26	1.33
4	1.04	1.06	1.08	1.10	1.13	1.17	1.22	1.26	1.36	1.46
5	1.05	1.08	1.10	1.13	1.16	1.22	1.28	1.34	1.47	1.61
6	1.06	1.09	1.13	1.16	1.19	1.27	1.34	1.42	1.59	1.77
7	1.07	1.11	1.15	1.19	1.23	1.32	1.41	1.50	1.71	1.95
8	1.08	1.13	1.17	1.22	1.27	1.37	1.48	1.59	1.85	2.14
9	1.09	1.14	1.20	1.25	1.30	1.42	1.55	1.69	2.00	2.36
10	1.10	1.16	1.22	1.28	1.34	1.48	1.63	1.79	2.16	2.59
11	1.12	1.18	1.24	1.31	1.38	1.54	1.71	1.90	2.33	2.85
12	1.13	1.20	1.27	1.34	1.43	1.60	1.80	2.01	2.52	3.14
13	1.14	1.21	1.29	1.38	1.47	1.67	1.89	2.13	2.72	3.45
14	1.15	1.23	1.32	1.41	1.51	1.73	1.98	2.26	2.94	3.80
15	1.16	1.25	1.35	1.45	1.56	1.80	2.08	2.40	3.17	4.18
16	1.17	1.27	1.37	1.48	1.60	1.87	2.18	2.54	3.43	4.59
17	1.18	1.29	1.40	1.52	1.65	1.95	2.29	2.69	3.70	5.05
18	1.20	1.31	1.43	1.56	1.70	2.03	2.41	2.85	4.00	5.56
19	1.21	1.33	1.46	1.60	1.75	2.11	2.53	3.03	4.32	6.12
20	1.22	1.35	1.49	1.64	1.81	2.19	2.65	3.21	4.66	6.73
50	1.64	2.11	2.69	3.44	4.38	7.11	11.47	18.42	46.90	117.39
100	2.70	4.43	7.24	11.81	19.22	50.50	131.50	339.30	2199.76	13780.61

It is also possible to read the table in another manner. If the population of a country has increased by 50 percent in ten years, what is the mean annual growth rate? The factor growth will be given as 1.5 (150% of the base level). Look along the horizontal row for the 10-year period until we come to 1.5. The nearest value is 1.48 indicating an annual growth rate of about 4 per cent (the value at the top of the column). For the curious, the formula is:

$$i = [(T/P)^{(1/Y)} - 1] * 100$$

COMPOUND GROWTH RATES

where: i = nominal interest rate
P = amount at beginning of period
T = amount at end of period
Y = number of years

10
Currencies and Prices

Prices are normally given using the symbol or abbreviation for the currency: Gold is now $290 per ounce; silver is around £3 per ounce.

The normal form for US dollars used to be $US. This appears to be changing and US$ is now used, corresponding to Can$, HK$, NZ$ and S$ (Canada, Hong Kong, New Zealand and Singapore, respectively). Only the Australian dollar remains as $A with the symbol placed first.

Currencies are often required to be referred to in financial and economic articles, company reports, and so forth. Some years ago international three-letter currency codes (ICC) were introduced. It has become popular to use these in financial documents, currency conversions, world market prices. etc. The norm appears to be that these are placed after the amount.

> The value of French exports of nitrates to Spain was 2 million FRF.

There is also a tendency in financial documents to place M in front for millions:

> Norwegian exports rose to 250 MNOK (21.5 MUSD) in January.

In some countries the new international currency code appears on price labels in tourist shops, menus in restaurants and brochures rather than the currency symbol, and normally before the amount: NOK 250.

Country	Currency	ICC	Symbol
Algeria	Dinar	DZD	DA
Australia	Australian dollar	AUD	$A
Austria*	Schilling	ATS	AS
Belgium*	Franc	BEF	BF
Bulgaria	Lev	BGL	Lv
Canada	Dollar	CAD	Can$
China	Yuan	CNY	yen
Cyprus	Cypriot pound	CYP	C£
Czechia	koruna	CZK	Kc
Denmark	Krone	DKK	DKr
EMU	Euro (ECU)	EUR	€
Estonia	Estonian kroon	EEK	EEK
Finland*	Marka	FIM	M
France*	French franc	FRF	F
Germany*	Deutsche mark	DEM	DM
Greece*	Drachma	GRD	Dr
Hong Kong	Hong Kong dollar	HKD	HK$
Hungary	Forint	HUF	Ft
Iceland	Krona	ISK	IKr

CURRENCIES AND PRICES

Country	Currency	Code	Symbol
India	Indian rupee	INR	Re
Ireland*	Irish pound	IEP	Ir
Israel	New Israeli shekel	ILS	NIS
Italy*	Lire	ITL	L
Japan	Yen	JPY	yen, ¥
Korea, South	Won	KRW	W
Kuwait	Kuwaiti dinar	KWD	KD
Latvia	Lat	LVL	LVL
Lithuania	Litas	LTL	Lt
Luxembourg*	Lux. Franc	LUF	Luxf
Malaysia	ringgit	MYR	M$
Malta	Maltese lira	MTL	LM
Morocco	Moroccan dirham	MAD	DH
Netherlands*	Gilder/florin	NLG	f.
New Zealand	NZ dollar	NZD	NZ$
Norway	krone	NOK	NKr
Poland	zloty	PLN	Zl
Portugal*	Escudo	PTE	Esc
Russia	ruble	RUR	R
Saudi Arabia	Saudi riyal	SAR	SR
Singapore	Singapore dollar	SGD	S$
Slovenia	tolar	SLT	SLT
South Africa	rand	ZAR	R
Spain*	Peseta	ESP	Pta
Sweden	Krona	SEK	SKr
Switzerland	Swiss franc	CHF	SFR
Tunisia	Tunisian dina	TND	TD
Turkey	Turkish lira	TRL	TL
U.K.	Pound	GBP	£
USA	Dollar, cent	USD	US$

A comprehensive list is found in *The Economist Style Guide,* Profile Books, London.

Currency rates may be found on www.bloomberg.com/markets/currency/currcalc.html.

*Countries indicated with an asterisk adopted the Euro on 1 January 2002.

11
Abbreviations

Earlier editions of *The Concise Oxford English Dictionary* contained a list of several hundred abbreviations covering everything from military medals (H.L.I.: The Highland Light Infantry), organisations (L.G.U.: Ladies' Golf Union), membership (FSA: Fellow of the Society of Antiquaries), medical terms (A.I.D.: artificial insemination by donor) and miscellaneous (w.a.f. – with all faults!). These are now published separately in *The Oxford Dictionary of Abbreviations*.

It should not be assumed that standard abbreviations in a particular area are familiar to all readers, such as NPM (New Public Management), MBO (Management by Objectives). These should be stated in the text or a footnote at the first occurrence.

It is often convenient to use one's own abbreviations where a term is used constantly throughout an article. The popular mode is to use an acronym for certain types of abbreviations: BAMMO – The Battered and Maltreated Mistresses Organisation! It is essential that these are defined at the first time of use.

A. Upper and lower case

Some abbreviations require capital letters whereas others do not. For example, plc (public limited company) [lower case], Inc. (Incorporated) [upper case], Ltd or ltd (Limited) is optional. No fast rules here!

A number of energy units are named after their discoverer/inventor: W (Watt), J (Joule). The abbreviations retain the capital (15 kW, 10J), but the terms watts and joules do not. The symbol for megahertz (no capitals) is MHz.

B. The full point

Not all abbreviations use a full point. For example, Ltd (Limited) does not require a full point (although is often given one); Co. and Inc. do. A general rule is that if the abbreviation concludes with the final letter of the word, then a full point is not normally required. But there are exceptions here as in Coy. (military company). If the abbreviation comprises the initial letters of two or more words, then a full point is not required, e.g. MP (Member of Parliament). The exception here is where this might cause confusion. Thus, M.P. means Military Police. Previously IBM (International Business Machines Corporation) could have been confused with I.B.M. (Intercontinental Ballistic Missile). The latter is now formally abbreviated ICBM.

Metric measurements do not use a full point: m is used for meters, while m. indicates million. The former abbreviation for 'miles per gallon' was m.p.g. It is normally encountered today as 'mpg', and similarly mph for

ABBREVIATIONS

'miles per hour', although some dictionaries still retain the full point (m.p.h.).

Naturally, the full point is required at the end of the sentence. Should an abbreviated term not requiring a full point occur at the end, and where confusion might arise, then rewriting the sentence might be advisable. E.g. 'The distance was only 6 m.' (miles or metres?). A double full point is never used. Use the full term (miles *or* metres).

Mr and Mrs do not now use a full point although this was previously the practice. The same also applies to other titles today: OBE, DSO, etc. It has been suggested that the full point here was originally dropped as a war-time measure for saving ink! Indeed, there is a general tendency towards dropping full points for abbreviations in general, such as USSR rather than U.S.S.R. Dr. and Rev. may be encountered with and without a full point.

Where the singular form employs a full point (ed., ch.), some publishing houses employ a full point for the plural, others do not: eds. (eds), but chs (no full point) is normal.

Recently, I was glancing at a publication by Collins covering abbreviations. It was interesting to observe that not a single full point was used at all.

C. Single letter abbreviations

Most single letter abbreviations are either upper or lower case (a very few may employ either upper or lower case); some end with a full point, others do not.

> Coastal site in Brittany for sale, 23 a, FF 200,000.

Sounds like a bargain, all those acres at that price! But 23 a for a Frenchman means 23 *ares*. An *are* is 100 sq. m and is signified without the full point. The abbreviation for *acre* is a. (with a full point), although it might be preferable to use the alternative ac. or A. (upper case with full point). This is one of the few single letter abbreviations employing either upper or lower case.

The following is a summary of the most common abbreviations encountered. Commonly used Latin abbreviations do not employ italics; other less frequently encountered Latin abbreviations and terms employ italics. However, some dictionaries may not indicate italics at all.

MEASURES (ABBREVIATIONS)

There used to be a general rule that metric measurements did not use the full point in abbreviations whereas imperial and UK measurements did. However, there is a tendency to drop these in the UK, although the US still retains the full point in some measurements (e.g. feet; UK = ft, US = ft.). Some scientific journals tend not to use the full point for measurements where these may be given in the following.

A HANDBOOK FOR WRITERS OF ENGLISH

A. Imperial and other UK measurements

area
acre	a., ac. or A.	4840 square yards

capacity
gallon	gall. or gal. (occ. g)	8 pints
gill	gl.	¼ pint
pint	p. or pt or pt.	
quart	q. or qt or qt.	2 pints

length
chain	ch.	Gunter's ch. = 66 ft.; engineer's ch. = 100 ft.
foot	ft or ft.(US)	12 inches
furlong	f. or fur.	1/8 mile; 220 yards
inch	in. (not i.)	
mile	m. or mi.	1760 yards; 5280 feet
nautical mile	naut. m. (or mi.)	(UK) 6080 feet, ca. 1.15 miles
yard (s)	yd or yd. (yds)	3 feet; 36 inches

It is important to use the correct sign (straight quotes) for feet and inches: 2' 6" and not the single and double quotation marks (smart quotes): 2' 6'.

mass
grain	gr.	1 oz = 437.5 grains
hundredweight	cwt or cwt.	112 lbs
ounce	oz or oz.	
pound	lb or lb.	16 oz.
quarter	qr.	28 lbs
stone	st.	14 lb.
ton	t or t.	20 cwt; 2240 lbs

temperature
Fahrenheit	F	

volume
bushel	bsh.	8 imperial gallons (but mainly used for grain, ca. 15.5 cu. ft)

B. Metric measurements

area
are	a	100 sq. m.
decare	da	1000 sq. m; 10 ares
hectare	ha	10 000 sq. m; 100 ares

capacity
centilitre	cl	
decilitre	dl	
litre	l or lit.	

ABBREVIATIONS

length
centimetre	cm
kilometre	km
metre	m
millimetre	mm

mass
gram	g
hectogram	hg
kilogram	kg
tonne	tonne

temperature
Celsius; centigrade   C

ORGANISATIONS

The following is a list of major international and selected national and commercial organisations where the abbreviated form is often encountered. It should not be assumed that all readers of your manuscript are familiar with these and a footnote is recommended the first time the abbreviation is used. Many thousand acronyms are to be found on www.acronymfinder.com.

AEA	Atomic Energy Authority (UK)
AEC	Atomic Energy Commission (USA)
AFL	American Federation of Labor
ANC	African National Congress
ANSI	American National Standards Institute
AONB	Area of Outstanding Natural Beauty
AP	Associated Press
APEX	Association of Professional, Executive, Clerical and Computer Staff
ASE	American Stock Exchange
ASA	American Standards Association
ASCII	American Standard Code for Information Interchange
ASEAN	Association of South-East Asian Nations
AU	The African Union
BIS	Bank for International Settlement
BSI	British Standards Institution
CAP	Common Agricultural Policy
CARICOM	Caribbean Community
CARIFTA	Caribbean Free Trade Area
CBI	Confederation of British Industry
CCJ	Council of Christians and Jews
CCTA	Central Computer and Telecommunications Agency
CDC	Commonwealth Development Corporation
CENTO	Central Treaty Organization
CERN	Organisation Européene pour la recherche nucléaire (formerly, Conseil Européen pour la recherche nucléaire)
CHAPS	Clearing House Automated Payments System

CHIPS	Clearing House Interbank Payments System
CIA	Central Intelligence Agency
CIO	Congress of Industrial Organizations
COBOL	Common Business Oriented Language
COMECON	Council for Mutual Economic Assistance
EBU	European Broadcasting Union
EC	European Community
ECA	European Commission on Agriculture
ECM	European Common Market
ECO	European Coal Organization
ECOSOC	Economic and Social Council (of the United Nations)
ECGD	Export Credits Guarantee Department
ECSC	European Coal and Steel Community
ECTG	European Channel Tunnel Group
ECU	European currency unit
EDC	European Defence Community
EDF	European Development Fund
EEOC	Equal Employment Opportunity Commission
EFC	European Forestry Commission
EFTA	European Free Trade Association
EMS	European Monetary System
EP	European Parliament
EPA	Environmental Protection Agency
ESA	Environmentally Sensitive Area
ESA	European Space Agency
ESOC	European Space Operations Centre
ESRO	European Space Research Organization
EURATOM	European Atomic Energy Community
FAO	Food and Agriculture Organization
FTC	Federal Trade Commission
GATT	General Agreement on Tariffs and Trade
GMC	General Medical Council
GMT	Greenwich Mean Time
IBRD	International Bank for Reconstruction and Development
ICC	International Chamber of Commerce
ICFTU	International Confederation of Free Trade Unions
ICJ	International Court of Justice
IEA	International Environmental Agreement
IEA	International Energy Agency
IFC	International Finance Corporation
ILO	International Labour Organization
IMF	International Monetary Fund
IMO	International Migration Office
ISO	International Organization for Standardization
IUCN	International Union for the Conservation of Nature and Natural Resources
IWC	International Whaling Commission
LAFTA	Latin American Free Trade Association
LCE	London Commodity Exchange

ABBREVIATIONS

LDC	Less developed country
LSE	London Stock Exchange (also London School of Economics)
LEA	Local Education Authority
LIFFE	London International Financial Futures Exchange
LME	London Metals Exchange
NAFTA	North American Free Trade Association
NASA	National Aeronautics and Space Administration
NASDA	National Space Development Agency
NASDAQ	National Association of Securities Dealers Automated Quotation
NATO	North Atlantic Treaty Organisation
NHS	National Health Service
NYFE	New York Futures Exchange
NYSE	New York Stock Exchange
OAU	Organization of African Unity
OECD	Organization for Economic Co-operation and Development
OEEC	Organization for European Economic Co-operation
PAC	Pan-African Congress
SHAEF	Supreme Headquarters Allied Expeditionary Force
SHAPE	Supreme Headquarters Allied Powers, Europe
SONAR	sound navigation and ranging
TUC	Trades Union Council
UAE	United Arab Emirates
UNCED	United Nations Conference on Environment and Development
UNCTAD	United Nations Conference on Trade and Development
UNDC	United Nations Disarmament Commission
UNDP	United Nations Development Programme
UNEP	United Nations Environment Programme
UNESCO	United Nations Educational, Scientific and Cultural Organization
UNFAO	United Nations Food and Agriculture Organization
UNGA	United Nations General Assembly
UNHCR	United Nations High Commissioner for Refugees
UNHRC	United Nations Human Rights Commissioner
UNICEF	United Nations Children's Fund (formerly UN International Children's Emergency Fund)
UNIDO	United Nations Industrial Development Organization
UNO	United Nations Organization
UNRWA	United Nations Relief and Works Agency for Palestine Refugees in the Near East
UNSC	United Nations Security Council
UNSG	United Nations Secretary General
UNTT	United Nations Trust Territory
UPU	Universal Postal Union
WFTU	World Federation of Trade Unions
WHO	World Health Organization
WMO	World Meteorological Organization

A HANDBOOK FOR WRITERS OF ENGLISH

BRITISH ACADEMIC TITLES

A number of the following are historic but may be found in the literature.

The modern tendency is to use BSc rather than B.Sc. (for example). No space after full point (B. etc.). Associates and Fellows are very numerous. See *Letter Writing* by Louise Lang.

B.A.	Bachelor of Arts
B.Agr.	Bachelor of Agriculture
B.Ch.	Bachelor of Surgery (Chirurgy)
BChD	Bachelor of Dental Surgery
B.C.L.	Bachelor of Civil Law
B.D.	Bachelor of Divinity
B.D.S.	Bachelor of Dental Surgery
B.Ed.	Bachelor of Education
B.Eng. or BEng	Bachelor of Engineering
B. ès LL.	Bachelor of Literature (Bachelier ès Lettres)
B.L.	Bachelor of Law
B.LL	Bachelor of Laws
B.Litt. or BLitt	Bachelor of Letters
B.Med or B.M.	Bachelor of Medicine
B.Mus. or BMus	Bachelor of Music
B.Phil.	Bachelor of Philosophy
B.S.	Bachelor of Surgery
B.Sc or BSc	Bachelor of Science
ChB	Bachelor of Surgery
Ch.M. or ChM or CM	Master of Surgery
D.C.L. or DCL	Doctor of Civil Law
D.D. or DD	Doctor of Divinity
D.D.S. or DDS	Doctor of Dental Surgery
D.Litt. or DLitt	Doctor of Literature, Doctor of letters [L *Doctor Litterarum*]
D.Mus.	Doctor of Music
D.Phil. or DPhil	Doctor of Philosophy
D.Sc. or DSc	Doctor of Science
D.T.	Doctor of Divinity
DTh	Doctor of Theology
JCD	Doctor of Civil Law, Doctor of Canon Law
JD	Doctor of Laws
JUD	Doctor of Canon and Civil Law
Litt.B.	Bachelor of Literature
Litt.D.	Doctor of Literature
LittD	Doctor of Letters (as above)
LL.B.	Bachelor of Laws
LL.M.	Master of Laws
M.A. or MA	Master of Arts
M.B. or MB	Bachelor of Medicine
M.Ch., M.Chir. or MCh	Master of Surgery [*Magister Chirurgiae*]
M.Comm. or MComm	Master of Commerce
M.D.	Doctor of Medicine

ABBREVIATIONS

M.Econ.	Master of Economics
M.Ed. or MEd	Master of Education
M.Litt.	Master of Letters [L *Magister Litterarum*]
M.Mus.	Master of Music
M.Phil.	Master of Philosophy
Mus.B	Bachelor of Music
Mus. D.	Doctor of Music
M.S. or MS	Master of Surgery
M.Sc. (Econ.)	Master of Science (Economics)
M.Sc. or MSc	Master of Science
M.Tech.	Master of Technology
MA. or M.Arts	Master of Arts
MB	Bachelor of Medicine [L *Medicinae Baccalaureus*]
MBA	Master of Business Administration
MusB	Bachelor of Music
MusD	Doctor of Music
Ph.D. or PhD	Doctor of Philosophy
ScB	Bachelor of Science
ScD	Doctor of Science

Many first degrees previously suffixed Hons., indicating 'With honours' – a first or second class degree. Regarded as 'snobbishness' by many, it is less frequently encountered today.

COMMERCIAL ABBREVIATIONS

A/C	Account
A/c	account of
APR	annual percentage rate
A/S	account sales
a/d	after date
B/E	Bill of Exchange
B/L	Bill of Lading
B/S	Bill of Sale
CCJ	County Court Judgement
CD	Certificate of Deposit
CEO	Chief Executive Officer
C.O.D.	Cash on delivery
CPI	Consumer Price index
d/a	days after acceptance
d/d	day's date
d/s	day's sight
f.o.b. or fob	free on board
GDI	gross domestic income
GDP	gross domestic product
GNP	gross national product
ICC	Internat. Currency Code
IEA	International Environmental Agreement
IOU	letter of debt

IRR	internal rate of return
J/A	Joint account
L/c	Letter of Credit
LIBOR	London Inter-Bank Offered Rate
MBO	Management by objectives
Mc	Metallic currency
m/d	month's date
MLM	Multi-level Marketing
m/s	month's sight
NFP	not-for-profit (org.)
NPM	New Public Management
NPV	net present value
o/a	on account
OTC	over the counter (price, market etc.)
PAYE	Pay-as-you-earn (tax)
P/E	Price-Earnings ratio
PERT	Program Evaluation and Review Technique
plc or PLC	public limited company
P/N	Promissory Note
PPBS	Planning, Programming, Budgeting System
PPI	Producer Price Index
PPP	purchasing power parity
pv	present value
R&D	Research and development
RPM	resale price maintenance
VAT	Value-added tax
WPI	Wholesale price index

OTHER ABBREVIATIONS

(*sic*)	So or thus. Before text to show that it is correctly quoted although appears doubtful.
A	absolute; ampere; area
A.D.	(previously used for AD) Note 1999 AD *or* AD 1999 *but* 1999 BC
a.m.	*ante meridian*: before noon
abbrev. or abbr.	abbreviation/abbreviated
ABM	antiballistic missile
AD	*anno Domini (In the Year of Our Lord)*.
AGM	annual general meeting
amp	ampere
amu	atomic mass unit
AOB	any other business
APL	A Programming Language
APR	annual percentage rate
ASCII	American standard code for information interchange
ASM	air-to-surface missile
AU	astronomical unit

ABBREVIATIONS

AV	audio-visual
b.	born [John Smith b.1927]
B.C.	(previously used for BC)
BASIC	Beginners All-purpose Symbolic Instruction Code
BC	Before Christ. See AD
c	cent-; cubic (also cu.)
c.	century; cent(s); circa (also ca.); copyright (also ©)
C.	Conservative (party)
c.i.f.	cost, insurance, freight
C.O.D.	cash on delivery
c/o	care of
ca.	*circa* (or circa): about
CAD	computer-aided design
CAI	computer-aided instruction
CAL	computer-aided learning
CAM	computer-aided manufacture
CASE	computer-aided software engineering
CATV	cable television
CBL	computer-based learning
CCD	charge-coupled device
CCR	camera cassette recorder
CCTV	closed circuit television
CD	compact disc
CD-ROM	compact disc read-only memory
cent.	century
cf.	*confer*: compare
cg.	centigram
cgs	centimetre-gram-second
CGT	capital gains tax
ch.	church; chain (unit of measure)
circ.	*circa*: about
Co.	Company (e.g. Co. Ltd, limited company)
col.	column
Coll.	College
Coy.	Company (military)
CPU	central processing unit
CRT	cathode-ray tube
CTT	capital transfer tax
D	The first derivative of a mathematical function
d.	died [John Smith d.1992]
DBMS	database management system
DBS	direct broadcasting from satellite
dc	direct current
DCF	discounted cash flow
DDP	Director of Public Prosecutions
dept	department
Dr	Doctor
dr.	drachma
DST	daylight saving time

DTP	desk-top publishing
d.w.t	dead weight tonnage
E	East; English
e.g.[1]	*exempli gratia*: for example (avoid eg)
ed.	editor; edited.
edn	edition
eds	editors
ENG	Electronic News Gathering
et al.	*et alli*; and others (frequently used where several authors).
et seq.	*et sequentia*: and the following
etc.	*et cetera*; and so on
F	franc(s)
f	function (math.) If possible, use symbol f
f.	fathom(s); female; following page (see ff.)
f.o.b.	free on board
FAQ	Frequently asked questions (frequently encountered on the Internet).
ff.	following pages (or FF.); folio
fig.	figure
fr.	francs
Fr.	French
ft.	foot; feet
fur.	furlong
G	giga; gigabytes; gravity (e.g. 3G)
GDI	gross domestic income
GDP	gross domestic product
GMT	Greenwich Mean Time
GNP	gross national product
h.	hour(s); height; hundred; husband [Anne h. John]
h.& c.	hot and cold
ho.	house
hp	horsepower
hr	hour
hrs	hours
I.	Institute; International; Island
i.	interest (finance)
i.a.	*in absentia*. (NOT inter alia = among other things)
i.e.	*id est:* that is (avoid ie, although this is increasingly encountered)
i/c	in charge
ibid.	ibidem: in the quoted reference. Does not use italics.
id.	*idem*: the same
Inc.	Incorporated
J	joule(s)
j	unit vector along the y-axis
J.	Judge (plur. JJ.)
jr	junior
K	kilobytes; Köchel (or K.) [Mozart; K454]
k.	karat(s)
kp	kiloparsec
kv	kilovolt

ABBREVIATIONS

kw	kilowatt
L	lire
l.	length (or L.)
L.	Liberal (party); Licentiate
l.c.	lower case
LAN	local area network
LED	light-emitting diode
ll.	lines
loc.cit.	*loco citato*: at the place cited
log	logarithm
long.	longitude
LPG	liquefied petroleum gas
lpt	line printer
Ltd, ltd	Limited
m	meter(s); mile(s); million(s); minute(s)
M	Million, marks
m.	male; married; meridian; month
M.	Monsieur; million
M.P.	Military Police
math.	mathemat/, -ical. (Not maths.)
memo.	memorandum
Messrs	Messieurs
mg	milligrams
MHz	megahertz
misc.	miscellaneous
MM or MM.	Messieurs
MP	Member of Parliament
mpg	miles per gallon (formerly m.p.g.)
mph	miles per hour (formerly m.p.h.)
Mr	Mister (Not Mr.)
Mrs	Refers to married woman (originally abbrev. of Mistress)
Ms	abbreviation for Miss/Mrs (Not Ms.)
ms. or MS.	manuscript
mss. or MSS.	manuscripts
MW, MWh	megawatt(s), -hours
mW	milliwatt(s)
n	nano-
N	North
n.	noon; note; number
N.B.	Please note
n.d. or nd	not dated
NAFTA	North American Free Trade Association
N°	No.; number
o	used in logic for a negative category
o.	only
O.K. or OK	'all correct'. 'o.k.' may be used, but not 'ok'
o/s	out of stock
ob.	obit: died (on tombstones)
op. cit.	*opere citato*. Does not use italics.

151

p	pence
p.c.	per cent
p.m.	*post meridian*: after noon
pc	parsec
PC	personal computer
per pro	by proxy
PIN	personal identification number
plc	public limited company
pop.	population, occasionally popn
POS	point of sale
POW	prisoner of war
pp	*post procurationem*; for and on behalf of [usually written *per pro*]
pr	used for *per*; pair (plural prs)
pr.	price
PROM	programmable read-only memory
QC	Queen's Counsel
R	(currency) rand; rupee
R&D	research and development
RAM	random access memory
recd	received
repr.	reprinted
Rev or Rev.	Reverend
Revd.	Reverend
rms	root-mean-square
ROM	read-only memory
RPI	retail price index
RPM	resale price maintenance
rpm	revolutions per minute
RSVP	Please reply (*Répondez s'il vous plait*) (prev. R.S.V.P.)
Rt Hon	Right Honourable (Prev. Rt. Hon.)
s	second (time)
S	Society; South; (currency) schilling
s.	semi-; signed; singular
S.	Socialist; Society; Saint (plur. Sts)
s.d.	several dates
sae	stamped addressed envelope
SAS	Statistical Analysis System (data program)
SD	Standard Deviation of a Population (math.)
sd	Standard Deviation of a Sample (math.)
sec.	second (time)
Sec.	Secretary
sect.	section
Soc.	Socialist; Society
SONAR	sound navigation and ranging
sov.	sovereign (coin)
SPSS	Statistical Package for the Social Sciences
sq.	square
SQL	structured query language
st (or s.t)	short ton (2000 lbs)

ABBREVIATIONS

St.	Saint, Statute
suppl.	supplement
t	tonne(s)
t.	tare (commerce)
trs.	transpose
U	Unionist; University (or U.)
U.	union (maths.); unit
u.c.	upper case
u.d.	undated
u.p.	under proof
v	velocity; volume (specific v of a gas)
v	*versus*
V	volume (capacity)
v.	very; version; volume (series)
VAN	value-added network
VAT	value-added tax
vv.	verses
W	watt; West
w.	with; week; weight; width; wife [John w. Anne]
w.f.	wrong font
W/L	wave length
X	denoting an unknown variable etc.
x	ex. (commerce); algebraic variable
x-i.	ex interest
x-n.	ex new shares
Y	denoting an unknown variable etc.
y.	year(s)
yf	Yours faithfully
yr.	younger
yrs	yours
ys	yours sincerely
Z	zone; denoting an unknown variable etc.
z.	zero; zone

Notes to the above:

[1] e.g.

This should be understood as meaning 'examples include'.

▶ + A common error is to use this abbreviation in a phrase such as:

✗ He thought, for e.g. that the font size should be increased.

✗ See e.g. Jones (1953).

instead of:

✓ He thought, for example, that the font size should be increased.

✓ See, for example, Jones (1953).

This abbreviation may be used before lists implying 'including the following examples'.

✓ He proposed a number of changes, e.g. larger typeface, wider line spacing, broader margins.

▶ 'e.g.' is not followed by a colon. It is not necessary to use the conjunction *and* before the final item in this list.

It may be of interest to know that I originally used the Microsoft 'Sort' function for the above list of abbreviations, but even though it was set to *case sensitive,* there were still a number of problems. These arose due to the fact that the full point is treated as a symbol. I would have preferred MP to be followed by M.P. However, the full point has a lower ASCII value than the letter 'a' resulting in the above order, and not least placing '(*sic*)' at the head of the list!

Abbreviations in titles and text

Avoid abbreviations or acronyms in titles of books and chapters unless they are very familiar:

✓ THE ROLE OF IBM IN INTERNATIONAL TRADE

but not:

✗ Chapter IV: THE CDM: CHALLENGES AND OPPORTUNITIES

– unless CDM has been previously defined in the book.

Note the following:

> The Clean Development Mechanism (CDM) established in the 1997 Kyoto protocol is designed to...... However, it is unclear whether soil carbon sequestration projects will be possible under the CDM.

In the second sentence, CDM stands for The Clean Development Mechanism (i.e. including the definite article). As a general rule the article should be given even if it is already implied in the abbreviation or acronym.

12
Prefixes

Prefix: an element placed at the beginning of a word to adjust or qualify its meaning (e.g. *ex-*, *non-*, *re-*) or (in some languages) as an inflection (*New Oxford English Dictionary*). There are about 200 prefixes such as un- (unhappy), dis- (disenfranchise), etc. In the following we concerned with prefixed words and other prefixes which may employ a hyphen.

Where the prefix is a word in its own right, such as 'back', 'cross', 'over', etc., these may form (a) a hyphenated word (*back-door, over-optimistic, under-fed*); or (b) a conjoined word (*backbone, overhasty, underpass*). Further, certain terms are neither hyphenated nor conjoined (*[to] back down, [a] cross compiler, under age*). I prefer to use the expression 'compound term' for these. Are there any 'rules' concerning separate, hyphenated or conjoined terms? A colleague ventured to suggest that terms in occasional use are separate words; those in common use tend to be conjoined. This would also apply where the conjoined term forms a distinct unit, e.g. *semicircle*. A useful guideline perhaps. But beware! The norm may be the exception! For example we have *over-represented* but *underrepresented*. Why? The only reason I can find is that these are the norms! But no-one would deny that *under-represented* is also legitimate.

The following lists have been compiled from several dictionaries and where the most commonly encountered form has been selected. It may be noted that Oxford and Collins tend favour conjoint terms more so than Chambers which still tends to retain hyphenated versions.

Note: In the following summaries the columns are in alphabetical order vertically.

a, a-
A few words retaining the Old English prepositional form: afire, a-hunting, alike, akin

above
The following terms are hyphenated:

above-board	above-mentioned	above-the-line
above-ground	above-named	

all, all-
Frequently found in compound words and expressions. Adjectival forms are generally hyphenated. Whilst commonly encountered, *alright*, is colloquial and less preferable than *all right* or *all-right*. The most frequently encountered terms using 'all' are shown.

all-American	All-hallowtide	all-round
All Blacks	all-important	all-rounder
all-clear	all-in	all-seater (stadium)
all comers *or*	all in all	all square
all-comers	all-inclusive	all standing
all-day	all-or-nothing	all-star
all done	all-out	all-telling
all-electric	all-over	all-terrain bike
All Fools' Day	all-powerful	all-time (high, low, record)
all found	all-purpose	all-to
All-Hallows	all right *or* all-right	all-up service
All Hallows' Day	(alright = coll.)	all-weather

ante, ante-, *ante* (Latin: before, prior to). Do not confuse with *anti-*.

Latin origin. Latin terms in everyday use are not italicised.

ante lucem	antechoir	ante-Nicene
ante meridiem	antedate	anteorbital
ante mortem	antediluvial	antepast
ante-bellum	antefix	antependium
antecede	antelucan	antepenultimate
antecessor	antemeridian	ante-post
antechamber	ante-mortem	anteroom
antechapel	antenatal	anteversion

anti, anti- (Greek: against, opposing, counteracting). Do not confuse with *ante-*.

Hyphenate before a capital: *anti-American, anti-Establishment, anti-Communist, anti-Zionist*.
Hyphenate before a vowel: *anti-imperialism*
   Note: *antichrist, anticapitalist, antifascist* but *anti-roman*.

anti-abortion	anti-evolution	antipacifist
anti-abrasion	antifaction	antipathogen
anti-ageing	anti-fade	anti-personnel
anti-aircraft	antifascist	antipolitical
anti-alien	anti-federal	antipollution
anti-American	anti-federalism	anti-predator
anti-apartheid	anti-federalist	antiprohibition
anti-aristocratic	anti-feminist *or*	anti-Protestant
antibacterial	antifeminist	antipuritan
antiballistic	anti-flash	antiracism
antibiblical	anti-Freudian	anti-racist
anti-Bolshevik	antifundamentalist	antirational

PREFIXES

anti-British	anti-Gallican	antireligious
anticapitalist	anti-hero	antirepublican
anti-Catholic	antihumanist	antirevolutionary
anti-chip	anti-imperialist	antiriot
antichrist	anti-inflammatory	anti-roll
antichristian	anti-inflationary	antirust
antichurch	anti-Jacobin	antiscientific
anticlassical	antilabour	anti-Semite
anticoagulating	anti-lock	antishock
anti-Communist	anti-marketeer	anti-social *or* antisocial
anti-competitiveness	antimaterialistic	anti-Soviet
anticonscription	antimatter	antispiritual
anticonstitutional	antimicrobial	antisubmarine
anticorrosive	antimilitarist	anti-tank *or*
anti-Darwinian	antimodernist *or*	antitank
antidemocratic	anti-modernist	antiterrorist
anti-devolutionist	antimonarchist	antitheft
anti-ecclesiastical	antinarcotic	antitheist
anti-episcopal	anti-national	antivirus
anti-erosion	antinationalist	antivivisection
anti-establishment	anti-Nazi	antiwar
anti-Establishment	antinoise	anti-Zionist

auto-
(Greek: self, same. e.g. autobiography). All conjoined except auto-suggestion.

back, back-
Adjective (e.g. *back* door) and verb (e.g. *back* down). When hyphenated, may form a noun (e.g. *back-cloth*) *or* an adjective (*back-door* deal).

backache	backhand	backside
back-bench	back-handed	back-slang
backbencher	back-hander	back-slapping
backbite	back-heel	backslide
back-block	backing-down	backspace
back-board	backlash	backspin
backbone	backlift	backstage
backbreaker	back-light	backstairs
back burner	back-load	backstays
back-calculate	backlog	backstitch
back-chain	backlot	backstop
backchat	backmarker	back street
back-cloth	backmost	back-stroke
back-comb	back-number	backswing
back-country	back-office	back-to-back

backcourt	backpack	back to earth
back-crawl	back passage	back to front
back-cross	backpay	back to nature
back-date	back-pedal	back-to-nature
back-door	backpiece	back to square one
backdown	back-plate	backtrack
back-draught	back pressure	back-up
backdrop	back-projection	backwash
back-end	backroom·	backwater
backfire	back-rope	back water
back-foot	back-row	backwoods
back-formation	backsaw	backwoodsman
back-friend	backscatter	backword
backgammon	backscratch	backwork
background	back-seat driver	backyard
back-hair	back-shift	

bi, bi- (Latin: two, twice). Do not confuse with *by-*.

Virtually all words commencing with the affix *bi* do not employ a hyphen (e.g. *bidirectional, bifocal, bilateral, biplane*). Exceptions: whereas *biannual, bicentenary* and *biennial* do not use a hyphen, the following do:

bi-monthly	bi-weekly	bi-yearly

by, by- (near, aside, subsidiary, incidental). Do not confuse with *bi-*.

Nouns are hyphenated (*by-lane, by-election, by-product* etc.). Nearly all terms and expressions are not hyphenated (e.g. *by all means*).

Note compass directions *north by east, north by west* – (also *south by east/west*, BUT *east-by-north (-south)* and *west-by-north (-south)*.

'by' is found in many expressions: *by the way, by leaps and bounds*. The following are hyphenated:

by-and-by	by-motive	by-product
by-blow	by-passage	by-street
by-election	by-past	by-thing
by-form	by-play	by-time
by-lane	by-plot	by-work
by-line		

co, co- (jointly, mutual)

No fixed rules. Most words beginning with co-or may also use coor (e.g. *co-ordinate; coordinate*). The following exceptions use a hyphen:

co-agent	co-operative	co-portion
co-author	co-operator	co-presence

PREFIXES

co-ax (but coaxial)
co-chair
co-dependant
co-dependent
co-driver
co-host
co-op
co-operate *or* cooperate

co-opt *or* coopt
co-option
co-optive
co-ordinal *or* coordinal
co-ordinate *or* coordinate
co-pilot *or* copilot

co-respondent
(but correspondent)
co-routine
co-star
co-starring
co-tenancy
co-worker
co-write

counter, counter- (against, counteracting)

Used in many compound words, but no hard-and-fast rules for hyphenation.

counteract
counter-agent
counter-attack
counter-attraction
counterbalance
counterbase
counter-battery
counterbid
counterblast
counterblow
counterbluff
counterbond
countercheck
counter-claim
counter-clockwise
countercondition
counter-culture
counter-current
counterdraw
counter-espionage
counter-evidence
counterfect
counterfeit
counterfoil
counter-force
counter-gauge
counter-guard

counter-influence
counter-insurgency
counter-intelligence
counter-jumper
countermand
countermarch
countermark
countermeasure
countermine
countermotion
countermove
countermovement
counteroffensive
counteroffer
counter-opening
counterpane
counterpart
counter-passant
counterplea
counter-plot
counterpoint
counterpoise
counter-poison
counter-pressure
counterproductive
counterproof
counter-proposal

counter-punch
Counter-Reformation
counter-revolution
counterseal
counter-security
countershaft
countersign
counter-signal
counter-signature
countersink
counterspy
counter-statement
counterstroke
countersubject
countersunk
counter-tenor
counter-terrorist
counter-trading
counter-turn
countervail
counter-view
counter-vote
counter-weigh
counter-weight
counter-wheel
co-worker
co-write

cross, cross- (against, contrary)
Many are conjoined (e.g. *crossbencher, crossroads*). The following are hyphenated. A few exceptions are neither conjoined or hyphenated (e.g. *cross compiler*).

cross-armed	cross-grained	cross-quarters
cross-buttock	cross guard	cross-question
cross-border	cross hairs	cross-reference
cross-country	cross-hatching	cross-ruff
cross cousin	cross-lateral	cross-section
cross-cultural	cross-leaved	cross-selling
cross-current	cross-legged	cross-springer
cross-division	cross-linking	cross-staff
cross-examination	cross-match	cross-stitch
cross-eye	cross-ply tyre	cross-stone
cross-fade	cross-pollination	cross-talk
cross-fertilization	cross-purpose	cross-vaulting

de, de- *de* (Latin: down from, away, reversal)

de facto	*de novo*	de-Americanize
de fide	*de profundis*	de-emphasise
de haut en bas	*de règle*	de-energise
de integro	*de rigueur*	de-escalate
de jure	deactivate	de-ice
de luxe	de-alcoholize	de-Stalinize

demi, demi- (French: denoting a half)

Almost exclusively hyphenated. Exception *demigod*.

demigod	demi-monde	demi-semiquaver
demi-jour	demi-pension	demi-volt

dis (a reversal, negation) (e.g. *disavow*)

No hyphenated words.

down, down-

'down' is used as an adverb, adjective, preposition, verb and noun. As such it may be found in many compound words and expressions.

down-and-out	down-line	down the drain/hatch
down-at-heel	download	down-throw *or*
down-at-the-heel	downmarket *or*	downthrow
downbeat	down-market	downtime
downbow *or* down-bow	down payment	down to earth *or*
downburst	downplay	down-to-earth
downcast	downpour	down tools
down-come *or*	down-quilt	down-town *or*
downcome	downrange	downtown
downdraft	downright	down-train

down-draught *or*
downdraught
downfall
down-going
downgrade
down-haul *or* downhaul
down-hearted *or*
downhearted
down in the dumps
down in the mouth

downriver
downscale
downside
downsize
downslide
downstage
downstairs
downstate
downstream

downswing
downtrend
down-trod
down-trodden *or*
downtrodden
downturn
down under
downward
downwind

eco- (relating to the environment)

Conjoined (e.g. *ecotoxicology*) except the following:

eco-label eco-management eco-tourism

ex, ex-, *ex* (Latin: out, from)

A hyphen is used *when this is a prefix* (e.g. *ex*-wife) as opposed to exhume etc. Many Latin terms commence with *ex*. These are not hyphenated. However, both *ex libris* and *ex-libris* are permissible.

ex also implies 'direct from' as in ex works, ex stores (not italicised).

ex-directory
ex-dividend *or*
ex dividend
ex dono
ex gratia
ex hypothesi

ex improviso
ex int
ex lib
ex libris or ex-libris
ex-librist

ex officio
ex-serviceman
ex stores
ex works

extra, extra-, *extra* (adjective: extraordinary, additional; adverb: unusual, exceptional)

All conjoined (e.g. *extrajudicial, extramarital*) except the following:

extra-axillary
extra-condensed
extra-curricular
extra-illustrate
extra modum

extra muros
extra-parochial
extra-physical
extra-solar

extra-special
extra-uterine
extra-virgin (US)
extra virgin (UK)

far (remote, most distant)
Adjective, adverb and verb transitive. Hyphenated except in expressions such as '*far and wide*'.

far and away
far and near

far-flung
far-forth

far-seeing
far-sighted

far and wide	Far North	far-sought
far be it	far-off	Far South
far cry	far-out	far-spent
Far East	far-reaching	Far West
far-fetched		

fore- (Old English: previously, former, in front)

Most terms are conjoined: *forehead, foreground*, etc. Exceptions:

fore-advise	fore-brace	fore-end
fore-and-aft	fore-cited	fore-notice
fore-and-after	fore-edge	fore-quoted

geo (relating to, or denoting the earth)

all terms conjoined: e.g. *geophysical*

hemi (Greek: half) Not hyphenated.

hemidemisemiquaver   hemisphere

hyper (excessive). Not hyphenated. e.g. *hypersensitive*.

il (the negative form) (e.g. *illegal*)

Not hyphenated

ill (misfortune, evil)

'Ill' is an adjective and not hyphenated when associated with a noun (e.g. ill nature). All non-hyphenated versions are shown. The hyphenated terms are adjectival (e.g. ill-defined, ill-disposed, ill-natured). These are not shown except for the few cases where an adverbial form may be constructed. The one exception occurs when 'ness' is suffixed to the adjective to form a noun (ill-naturedness).

ill blood	ill-natured	ill success
ill luck	ill part	ill temper
ill nature	ill seen	ill-tempered

in, in-, *in* (relating to)
Preposition and adverb. The Latin *in-* form is almost exclusively used to form adjectives.

in-between	in-depth	in-line
in-bond	in-flight	in-service
in-bounds	in-foal	*in situ*
in-built	in-group	in-store *or* in store

in-calf	in-house	in style
in camera	in-joke	in-toed
in capite	-in-law	in-tray
-in-chief	in-laws	in-word

infra (Latin: below, within)

All terms are conjoined, e.g. *infrastructure, infrared.*

inter, inter- (Latin: between, among). Conjoined (e.g. *interactive*) except the following. Latin terms separate words. These are shown.

inter-arts	inter-collegiate (but	*inter partes*
Inter-Bank (transaction)	interdepartmental)	inter-science
inter alia	*inter nos*	*inter se*
inter alios	*inter pares*	*inter vivos*

intra, intra- (Latin: from the inside.) Conjoined (e.g. *intramolecular*) except the following. Latin terms separate words.

intra-abdominal	intra-departmental	*intra vires*
intra-arterial	intra-Fallopian	*intra vitam*
intra-articular	*intra muros*	

macro- (Greek: long, great)

The list shows the most commonly encountered terms. With the exception of those below, all others are conjoined (e.g. *macroeconomics, macroinstruction*).

macro-axis	macro lens	macro-marketing

mega (Greek: large, large scale)

All words conjoined (e.g. *megastore*)

meta- (among, change). All conjoined (e.g. *metamorphosis*).

micro, micro- (Greek: small, minute). No fixed rules. The most common terms include:

microampere	microeconomics	micro-meteorite
microbar	microgram	micro-meteorology
micro-brew	micro-manipulation	micro-organism (UK)
micro drive (PC)	micro-marketing	microorganism (US)

mid, mid-, midi (middle). No fixed rules. The most common terms include:

mid-Atlantic	midmost	midsummer
midday	midnoon	midterm

midfield	mid-ocean	mid-Victorian
midiron	mid-off	midway
midi-skirt	mid-on	mid-week
midi-system	mid-point	Midwest
midland	midrib	mid-wicket
Midlands (The)	mid-season	midwife
mid-Lent	midshipmate	mid-winter
mid-life crisis	midships	mid-year
mid-morning	midstream	

mini, mini- (small, minature). No fixed rules. The most common terms include:

mini-budget	minicomputer	mini-roundabout
mini-buffet	mini-dress *or* minidress	mini-skirt *or* miniskirt
minibus	mini-floppy	mini-skis
minicab	mini-flyweight	mini-sub
mini-car	mini-rocket	mini-submarine

mis (wrong, mistake). All words conjoined (e.g. *mismanage*).

mono, mono- (single)

All words conjoined (e.g. *monorail*) except:

mono-compound	mono-ski

multi, multi- (many, much)

All words conjoined (e.g. *multiracial*) except the following:

multi-access	multi-layered	multi-storey
multi-author	multi-ownership	multi-track
multi-faceted	multi-stage *or*	multi-wall
multi-function	multistage	

neo- (Greek: new)

Hyphenated before a proper noun (e.g. *Neo-Darwin*), but some terms conjoined (e.g. *Neopythagoran*):

Neo-Catholic	neologism	neoplastic
Neo-Christian	neologistic	neoplasticism
neoclassic	Neo-Malthusianism	Neo-Plasticism
neocolonialism	Neo-Melanesian	Neoplatonic
Neo-Darwin	neomycin	Neoplatonism
neodymium	neonatal	Neoplatonist
Neofascism	neo-Nazi	Neopythagorean

PREFIXES

Neo-Gothic	neo-Nazism	neorealism
Neohellenism	neopagan	neorealist
Neo-Impressionist	neophile	Neo-Scholasticism
Neo-Kantian	neophilia	neotoxin
Neo-Latin	neophobe	Neotropical
neologian	neophyte	neovitalism

no (negative)

The following terms are hyphenated:

no-ball	no-man's land	no-win situation
no-go area	no-score draw	
no-good	no-trumps	

non, non-, *non* (Latin: not)

There are well over a thousand words to which the prefix *non* may be attached. There are no hard and fast rules as to whether these should be hyphenated or not. Some dictionaries may give the hyphenated version, others dictionaries suggest the conjoined form. A colleague has suggested that if the term is a commonly accepted word, e.g. *nonhuman*, then it is more likely to be conjoined. Less familiar terms e.g. *non-contentious*, are usually hyphenated. But we do find *non-conclusive* (a familiar term) and *noncontemporary* (hardly a familiar term).

Again, I am not able to find any specific rules or guidelines. In addition to selected Latin terms, the following shows where the conjoined form is the norm or where the hyphenated version is also acceptable. Note hyphenated form before a proper noun (e.g. *non-Catholic*).

Latin terms

non compos mentis	*non multa, sed*	*non placet*
(persona) non grata	*multum*	*non seq*
non licet	*non obstante*	*non sequitur*
non liquet		

nonacademic	nonauthoritative	non-breakable
nonacceptance	nonautomated	noncarbonated
nonaddictive *or*	nonautomatic *or*	noncarnivorous
non-addictive	non-automatic	noncausal
nonagricultural	nonbasic	noncelestial
non-aligned	nonbelligerent *or*	noncellular
nonattendance *or*	non-belligerent	noncentral
non-attendance	nonbiological *or*	noncerebral
non-attributable	non-biological	nonchargeable
nonattributive	nonbreakable *or*	nonclassic

165

nonclassified *or*
non-classified
nonclerical
nonclinical *or*
non-clinical
noncoagulating
noncollegiate *or*
non-collegiate
noncombining
noncommercial *or*
non-commercial
noncommissioned *or*
non-commissioned
noncommunicant *or*
non-communicant
noncommunicative
noncommunist
noncompetitive
noncompliance
nonconciliatory
nonconclusive *or*
non-conclusive
nonconcurrent *or*
non-concurrent
nonconductive
nonconfidential
nonconflicting
nonconformist
noncongenital
nonconnective
nonconsecutive
nonconsenting
nonconstitutional
nonconstraining
nonconstructive
noncontagious *or*
non-contagious
noncontemporary
noncontributing
non-contributory
noncontrollable
noncontroversial *or*
non-controversial
nonconventional
nonconvergent

nonconversant
nonconvertible
non-co-operation
noncorroborative
noncorroding
noncreative
noncriminal
noncritical
noncultivated
noncurrent *or*
non-current
nondeciduous
nondeductible
nondelivery *or*
non-delivery
nondemocratic
nondemonstrable
nondenominational *or*
non-denominational
nondepartmental
nondependence
non-destructive
nondetachable
nondetonating
nondictatorial
nondiffusing
nondiplomatic
nondirectional
nondisciplinary
nondiscriminating
nondistinctive
nondivisible
nondoctrinal
nondogmatic
nondomesticated
nondramatic
nondrinker *or*
non-drinker
nondriver *or* non-driver
nondurable
nonearning
noneconomic
nonedible
nonelastic
nonelection *or*

non-election
nonelective *or*
non-elective
noneligible
nonemotional
nonequal
nonequivalent
nonestablishment
nonethical
nonexchangeable
nonexclusive
nonexecutive *or*
non-executive
non-existence *or*
nonexistence
nonexistent *or*
non-existent
nonexplosive
nonfactual
nonfatal
nonfattening
nonfatty
nonfederal
non-ferrous
non-fiction
nonfictitious
nonfinite
non-flam film
non-flammable
nonflexible
non-flowering
nonfluid
nonformation
nonfreezing
nonfulfilment *or*
non-fulfilment
nonfunctional *or*
non-functional
nonfusible
nongaseous
nongovernmental
nongreasy
nonhabitable
nonhazardous
nonheritable

PREFIXES

nonhistorical
nonhuman
nonidentical
nonidiomatic
noninclusion
nonindependent
nonindictable
nonindustrial
noninfectious
noninflammable
noninflected
noninformative
noninherent
noninheritable
noninjurious
noninstinctive
noninstitutional
nonintellectual
noninterchangeable
nonintersecting
nonintoxicating
nonintuitive
noninvasive *or*
non-invasive
noninvolvement *or*
non-involvement
nonirritant
non-issuable
nonjury
nonkosher
nonlaminated
nonlethal *or* non-lethal
nonlinear *or* non-linear
nonliterary
nonliturgical
nonlocal
nonlogical
nonluminous
nonmagnetic
nonmalignant
nonmaritime
nonmarried
nonmaterialistic
nonmaternal
nonmathematical

nonmeasurable
nonmechanical
nonmedical
nonmedicinal
nonmelodic
nonmember *or*
non-member
nonmembership
nonmetric
nonmigratory
nonmilitant
nonministerial
nonmountainous
nonmystical
nonmythical
nonobligatory
nonobservance *or*
non-observance
nonoccurrence
nonofficial
nonoperable
nonoperational *or*
non-operational
nonoperative
nonorganic
nonorthodox
nonostensive
nonparallel
nonparasitic
nonparental
nonparliamentary
nonparochial
nonpaternal
nonpaying
nonpayment *or*
non-payment
nonpermanent
nonpermeable
nonphilosophical
nonphonemic
nonphysical
nonphysiological
nonplaying *or*
non-playing
nonpoisonous *or*

non-poisonous
nonpolitical
nonpolluting
nonporous
nonpossession
nonpractical
nonpractising
nonprecious
nonpredatory
nonpredictable
nonprejudicial
nonprescriptive
nonpreservable
nonpreservation
nonprofessional *or*
non-professional
nonprogressive
nonproportional
nonprotective
nonpunishable
nonracial *or* non-racial
nonradical
nonradioactive
nonrational
nonreader *or*
non-reader
nonrealistic
nonrecognition
nonrecoverable
nonreflective
nonrefundable
non-regardance
nonregimented
nonregistered
nonreligious
nonrenewable
non-representational
nonrepresentative
non-residence
non-resident
nonresidential
nonrestricted *but*
non-restrictive
nonroutine
nonrural

A HANDBOOK FOR WRITERS OF ENGLISH

non-scheduled
non-scientific *or*
nonscientific
nonseasonal
nonsectarian
nonsecular
nonsegregated
nonselective
nonsensitive
non-sequence
nonsexist *or* non-sexist
nonsexual
nonshrinkable
nonsignificant
nonsinkable
nonskilled
nonsocial
nonsoluble *or*
non-soluble
nonspeaking
nonspecialist *or*
non-specialist
non-specific *or*

nonspecific
nonspeculative
nonspiritual
nonsporting
nonstainable
nonstaining
nonstatistical
nonstrategic
nonstructural
nonsubscriber
nonsuggestive
nonsulphurous
nonsuppression
nonsurgical
nonsustaining
nonswimmer *or*
non-swimmer
nonsymbolic
nonsystematic
nontaxable
nonteaching
nontechnical
non-technical

nontemporal
nonterritorial
nontheatrical
nontoxic *or* non-toxic
nontraditional
nontransferable
nontropical
nontypical
non-U
nonuniform
non-union
non-unionist
nonusage *or* non-usage
nonuse
nonuser *or* non-user
nonvenomous
nonverbal *or* non-verbal
nonverifiable
nonvintage
nonvocal
nonvolatile *or*
non-volatile
nonworking

off, off- (away, not in position)

Adjectival forms usually hyphenated (e.g. *the off-and-on relay switch*). Some common phrases are shown which should not be hyphenated (e.g. *His mood was off and on all day*); others conjoined (e.g. *offset, offshoot, offshore*).

off-air
off-and-on switch
off and on
off balance *or* off-balance
off base
off-beam *or* off beam
off-board
off-break
off-Broadway
off-centre
off-chance
off chance
off colour *or* off-colour
off-come
off-comer
off-cut

off-licence
off-limits *or* off limits
off-line
off-load
off pat
off-peak
off-piste
off-plan
off-putter
off-putting
off-ramp
off-reckoning
off-road
off-sales
off-season
off-shake

off-stage
off-stream
off-street
off the air
off-the-job training
off the map
off the mark
off-the-peg *or*
off the peg
off the rails
off the record *or*
off-the-record
off the reel
off-the-shelf *or*
off the shelf
off the wall

PREFIXES

off-day	off-shakt	off-ward
off duty *or* off-duty	off-site	off-wards
off-fore	off-sorts	off-white
off-job	off-spin	off-year
off-key	off-spinner	

on, on-

Used in several expressions. The hyphenated expressions are adjectival *or* adverbial. Others not listed are conjoined (e.g. *ongoing*).

on-and-off	on-shore *or* on shore	on the offchance *or*
on and off	on sight	on the off-chance
on board *or* on-board	on-stage	on the slate
on-going	on-stream *or* on stream	on the sly
on-job training	on terms	on the spot *or*
on-licence	on-the-job training	on-the-spot
on-line		

out, out-

Generally conjoined (e.g. *outweighed, outplayed*). These are not shown. Used in several expressions without a hyphen. The hyphenated terms may be adjectival, adverbial or nouns. The most common are given here.

out and about	out of pocket	out-pension
out and away	out of the blue	out-pensioner
out-and-out	out of work	out-porter
out-half	out-of-work	out-sentry
out-Herod	out-paramour	out-take
out-of-date	out-parish	out-tray
out of date	out-patient	out-wall
out-of-pocket *or*		

over, over-

Words commencing with 'over' are normally not hyphenated. This applies to verbs (e.g. *overstate, overturn*), adjectives (e.g. *overdone*), and nouns (e.g. *overlay*). The exceptions are shown together with certain phrases which are occasionally and mistakenly hyphenated – or vice versa!

over-absorption	overdiligent	over seas *or*
over-abundance *or*	over-drowsed	overseas
overabundance	over-emotional *or*	over-sexed
over-abundant	overemotional	over-shoe
over-achiever	over-exact	overspread
overactive	overexacting	over-the-counter *or*
over-activity	overexcitable	over the counter

over-age	over-excite *or*	over the hill
overaggressive	overexcite	over the hump
overall (n)	over-exert *or* overexert	over the moon
over-all	over-exposure *or*	over the odds
over-and-under	overexposure	over-the-top
over-anxiety	over-exquisite	over the top
over-anxious *or*	overextend	over the way
overanxious	overhasty	over the wicket
over-anxiously	over-optimistic *or*	over-trade
over-beat	overoptimistic	over-trading
over-breathe	overoptimism	over-weighted
over-breathing	over-precise *or*	over-zealous *or*
overbulky	overprecise	overzealous
overcommon	over-refine	over-60s
over-determined	over-represented	

para- (Greek: beside)

Not hyphenated (e.g. *paraglider*). Exceptions *para-amino acid, para-compound*.

post, post- (Latin: to place, also used to signify 'after'). Conjoined (e.g. *postcode, postgraduate*) except following:

post-bellum	Post-Impressionist	post-partum
post boy	Post-it (label)	post-positionally
post-chaise *or* post chaise	post-lingual	post-primary
post-communion	postmaster	post-production
post-diluvial	post meridian	post-Reformation
post-doc	post-millenarian	post-structuralism
post-doctoral	post-millennial	post-synch
post-echo	post-modern	post-synchronisation
post-entry	post-mortem *or*	post-tension
post-exilian	post mortem	Post-Tertiary
post-existence	post-Nicene	post-traumatic
post-free	post-nuptial	post-vintage
post-glacial	post-orbit	post-viral illness
post-grad *but*	post-office box	post-vocalic
postgraduate	post-office *or* post office	post-war credit
poste-haste	post-operative	post war *or* post-war
post-impressionism	post-paid	

pre, pre-, Pre- (Latin: in front of, before)

Not hyphenated (e.g. *prearrange, preconstruction)*. Only the hyphenated terms are shown. Hyphenate before proper names (e.g. *pre-Christian, pre-Gothic*).

PREFIXES

pre-buy	pre-establish	pre-position
pre-Byzantine	pre-estimate	pre-qualify
pre-Carboniferous	pre-examination	pre-school
pre-conquest	pre-examine	pre-sell
pre-elect	pre-exist	pre-set
pre-election	pre-expose	pre-senile
pre-eminent	pre-glacial	pre-shrink/shrunk
pre-empt	pre-ignition	pre-tax
pre-engage	pre-industrial	pre-tension
pre-engagement	pre-judicial	pre-war *or* prewar
pre-enlistment		

pro, pro- (Latin: before, supporting). Hyphenate before a proper noun (e.g. *pro-Catholic*). All other words are not hyphenated (e.g. *proactive, procapitalist*, exception *pro-life*).

Latin terms are separate words.

pro hac vice	*pro patria*	*pro tanto*
pro indiviso	*pro rata*	*pro tempore*
pro memoria	*pro re nata*	

Note *pro forma* (a matter of form), and *pro-forma invoice*. The latter (adjectival form) is also found unhyphenated.

pseudo (spurious, deceptive). All conjoined also before a vowel, except pseudo-archaic. Hyphenated before a proper noun, e.g. pseudo-Gothic.

quasi (Latin: as it were). Hyphenated.

quasi-contract	quasi-historical	quasi-stellar

re, re- (Latin: repeat, do again)
Not hyphenated, even before a vowel (e.g. *reabsorb, reinstate, reopen, reuse*, etc., except before e: *re-elect* etc.). The exceptions are shown below. Latin terms are separate words, e.g. *re infecta*.

re-ally	re-ignite	re-route *or* reroute
re-alter	re-invent	re-site
re-alteration	re-open *or* reopen	re-train *or* retrain
re-assemble *or* reassemble	re-position	re-type
re-bar	re-release	re-unite *or* reunite
re-e... (all words)	re-roof	re-use

When the hyphen is omitted the following terms take on a different meaning as a noun or as a verb.

re-act	re-formed	re-print
re-cede	re-fund	re-sign

re-collect	re-lay	re-solve
re-count	re-make	re-sort
re-cover	re-mark	re-tread
re-dress	re-order	re-treat
re-form	re-present	re-turn
re-formation	re-press	re-view

retro- (backwards, towards the past) e.g. *retrograde, retrospective*. Not hyphenated except:

retro-operative   retro-rocket

self (personally, oneself)

All words hyphenated (e.g. *self-indulgence*) except:

selfheal   selfhood   selfsame

semi, semi- (Latin: half). Normally hyphenated before a vowel. There are a few exceptions with 'a'. Thus, *semiarid*. All others conjoined (e.g. *semicircle, semifinal*), except the following:

semi-annual	semi-double	semi-officially
semi-annually	semi-drying	semi-opal
semi-annular	semi-ellipse	semi-opaque
semi-aquatic	semi-elliptical	Semi-Pelagian
semi-Arian	semi-evergreen	semi-permeable
semi-Arianism	semi-finished	semi-precious
semi-arid *or* semiarid	semi-grand	semi-rigid
semi-attached	semi-illiterate	semi-ring
semi-automatic *or* semiautomatic	semi-imbecile	semi-sagittate
	semi-independent	Semi-Saxon
semi-axis	semi-jubilee	semi-skilled
semi-bajan	semi-liquid	semi-soft
semi-barbarian	semi-log	semi-trailer
semi-barbarism	semi-logarithmic	semi-tropical
semi-centennial	semi-metal	semi-truck
semi-detached	semi-monthly	semi-tubular
semi-diameter	semi-mute	semi-uncial
semi-diurnal	semi-nude	semi-weekly
semi-divine	semi-occasional	semi-yearly
semi-dome	semi-official	

socio (relating to society)

Not hyphenated. However, both socioeconomics and socio-economics are found.

PREFIXES

sub (Latin: under, near)

All words conjoined (e.g. *suboffice, subprovince*) except:

sub judice	sub-postmistress	sub-species
sub-editor	sub-post-office *or*	sub-standard
sub-machine gun	sub-post office	sub-tropical
sub-postmaster		sub-zero

A few terms may not necessarily be conjoined nor hyphenated, e.g. sub goal. 'Sub' is also an abbreviation for substitute, submarine.

super, super- (Latin: above, superior)

All words conjoined (e.g. *supercharge, supermarket*) except:

Super G	super-flyweight	super-middleweight
super-bantamweight	super-highway	super-rich
super-featherweight	super-intelligent	super-royal

supra (Latin: above)

All words conjoined (e.g. *supralunar, supramolecule*) except:

supra-axillary

tele- (Greek: far)

All words conjoined (e.g. *teleconferencing, telejournalism*) except:

tele-ad(vertisement)

to, to- (preposition)

All words conjoined. Phrases not hyphenated (e.g. *to a fault*).

trans- (Latin: across, beyond)

All words conjoined except the following which are optionally hyphenated.

trans-racial	trans-shape	Trans-Siberian
trans-sexual	trans-ship	trans-sonic

tri, tri- (Latin: threefold)

All words conjoined (e.g. *triaxial, tricolour*) except the following:

tri-jet	Tri-State area	tri-weekly

ultra, ultra- (Latin: beyond)

Hyphenated before a proper noun (e.g. *ultra-Conservative*). All other words conjoined (e.g. *ultrafilter, ultrasonic*) except the following:

ultra-distance	ultra-high	ultra-tropical
ultra-fashionable	ultra-modern	*ultra vires*
ultrafiche	ultra-rapid	ultra-virtuous
ultra-heat-treated	ultrasensual	

un, un- (Latin, Greek: against)

All words conjoined (e.g. *unmusical, unnerved*) except:

un-American	un-English

note: unchristian (no hyphen *or* capital).

under, under- (Old English: below)

All terms conjoined (e.g. *underpass, understeer*), with the exception of the following. Note that some occupations are hyphenated (e.g. *under-secretary*), others are not (*underservant*). These are shown.

under-age *or* under age	underpowered	under-secretary
under-and-over	under-privileged	under-serve *but*
under-board	under-produce *or*	underservant
under-bonnet	underproduce	under-sexed
under-boy	under-production	under-shepherd
under-clerk *or* underclerk	under-representation	under-sheriff
under-constable	under-represented	under-the-counter *or*
under-countenance	*or* underrepresented	under the counter
under-craft	under-ring	under the weather
under-declared	under-ripe	under-trick
under-driven	underripened	under-tunic
under-fed	under-roof	under-turnkey
under-hangman	under-sawyer	under-workman
under-jaw	under-school	under-16s
under-power		

up, up- (a higher level or state)

This prefix is found in many expressions and phrases. Generally, adjectives and adjectival nouns are hyphenated. Other terms not shown are conjoined (e.g. *update, upgrade, uptake*).

up-and-coming	up hill and down dale	up to a point
up and down *or*	up in arms	up-to-date
up-and-down	up in the air	up to the eyes
up-and-over	up-line	up to the hilt
up and running	(one) upmanship	up to the knocker
up-and-under	up-market	up to the mark

PREFIXES

up-beat	up-tempo	up to the minute *or*
up-country	up the creek	up-to-the-minute
up-current	up the pole	up-town
up-draught	up the wall	up-train
up for grabs	up-time (computer)	up-wind
up front *or* up-front	up to (*not upto*)	

vice-, *vice* (Latin: in the place of). All terms hyphenated except the following:

vice anglais　　　　　　viceregent　　　　　　viceroy

It is normal to capitalise when referring to a specific person. The vice-chancellor was present as was Vice-President Johnson.

13
Suffixes

There are about two hundred suffixes. Many are used to form adverbs or adjectives. These include –*ish*, –*ly*, –*ess*, etc., and are exclusively conjoined. In this chapter we are concerned with suffixed words which may be conjoined or hyphenated (there are no rules!). Separate words frequently form a verbal phrase and are not generally included.

Example:

a) *He went **over all** the books once more, but failed to find the mistake.*

b) *This paint will give an **over-all** covering with just one coat.*

c) *He put on his **overall** before starting to paint the room.*

Likewise, we have *pull over, pull-over, pullover*.

In general,

1. Separate words often comprise a phrasal verb: to *break away, give away, knock down, take away*. These are not included in the following.

2. Hyphenated words are normally:
   – compound nouns: *a hold-all is a large bag; the concert was a sell-out;*
   – adjectives: *stand-up comic; knock-down prices.*

3. Conjoined words usually form:
   – a noun: *he had a breakdown, let's get a takeaway, the disguise was a giveaway; he bought a new pullover.*
   – an adjective: *we bought a foldaway table.*

However, to draw hard-and-fast rules would be to deny the flexibility of English. Rather, we should look at customary usage. In fact, one standard text dismisses the problem by stating 'use your own judgement'! Indeed, in one dictionary I found *a foldaway table* and in another *a fold-up bed*.

The following summarises suffixes which may be generally encountered together with notes relating to selected affixes.

-all takes a hyphen when suffixed to form a noun. Exception is *overall*. *Over-all* is the normal adverbial form.

be-all	end-all	over-all
be-all and end-all	free-for-all	overall
carry-all	hold-all	save-all
cure-all	Jack-of-all-trades	you-all
do-all	know-all	

SUFFIXES

-away

When used as a separate word *away* is normally an adverb (e.g. *to throw away*). Where conjoined, it may form a noun (*he is a bit of a tearaway*), an adjective (*a throwaway item*) or, what used to be known as an adjectival noun but better referred to as a compound noun (*a foldaway*). Note *give-away* product (two consecutive vowels). The hyphenated suffix is normally an adjective: *a hide-away dugout*.

The following includes those terms where the adverb (a separate) word (e.g. *to give away, to run away*) may be confused with the suffixed term and/or the hyphenated version comprising a noun (a) or adjectival noun (e.g. *a giveaway*).

breakaway	give-away product	straightaway
fade-away	going-away outfit	take-away *or* takeaway
faraway	hide-away *or* hideaway	tearaway
foldaway *or* fold-away	home-and-away	throwaway
getaway	runaway	walk-away *or* walkaway
giveaway	towaway	wash-away

-back

back is found in many terms and compound words. Most terms comprising two words are phrasal verbs (e.g. *to play back*), but conjoined words are nouns (e.g. *a playback*). A few nouns use the hyphenated form. Some are optional (e.g. *fallback* or *fall-back*). The following shows those nouns which are hyphenated.

blowback *or* blow-back	hump-back	pull-back
buy-back	humpback bridge	razor-back
carry-back	hunchback	rusty-back
centre back *or* centre-back	knock-back	splash-back
diamond-back	ladder-back	swart-back
fallback *or* fall-back	laid-back	swayback *or* sway-back
fastback	leather-back	swing-back
hark-back	olive-back	turnback *or* turn-back
hog's-back	pass-back	write-back

-by

As a suffix, *-by* is largely used to form a noun. In addition there is the adjective *sell-by (date)*. The verbs are not hyphenated (*to lay by, to pass by*).

fly-by	lay-by	stander-by
fly-by-night	passer-by	swing-by

The compass bearings relating to north and south are *not* hyphenated: *north by east/west; south by east/west*. Those relating to east and west *are* hyphenated: *east-by-north/south; west-by-north/south*.

-down

Nouns are mostly conjoined (e.g. a *splashdown, lockdown*). Two separate words are phrasal verbs (e.g. *to splash down*). Adjectival forms (e.g. *slimmed-down*) and some nouns are hyphenated. These are shown.

backing-down	rubdown	top-down
broken-down	rundown *or* run-down	torn-down
draw-down	showdown	turn-down
dressing-down	sit-down	up and down *or*
knock-down	slimmed-down	up-and-down
let-down	slow-down	upside down *or*
mark-down	splash-down	upside-down
paste-down	sponge-down	watered-down
round-down	thumbs-down	

-fold

Preferably not hyphenated: e.g. *twofold, tenfold* etc. (Note, however, *two-handed, four-legged* etc.)

-free

Hyphenate.

E.g. *ice-free, tax-free* etc.

Exception: *handsfree* (noun or adjective, e.g. handsfree set for the mobile phone)

-in

Hyphenated for nouns, e.g. *cave-in, fill-in*, etc.

-less

This affix is only hyphenated after 'll': wall-less. Single 'l' is not hyphenated, e.g. *heelless, recoilless*, etc. Exception *tail-less*, although *tailless* may be encountered.

All other words conjoined (e.g. *aimless, fearless*).

-like

There are few rules for forming compound words with the suffix 'like'. When the stem word ends in 'l', a hyphen is used: *bell-like, spaniel-like*. Some texts suggest that those with animal connections are not hyphenated: *crablike, catlike, lionlike*. But there are many exceptions: *lamb-like, ostrich-like*. The same vagueness applies to the human touch: *king-like, queen-like, man-like*, but *princelike, ladylike*. Where the term begins with un– as in *ungodlike, unladylike*, a hyphen does not precede *'like'*, even though the original form was hyphenated. Thus we have *unladylike, unqueenlike*. '-like' words may be formed from many nouns. If your spell-checker reacts to the

SUFFIXES

compound form, then hyphenate it.

-ness
This affix is never hyphenated. It is used to form a noun from an adjective for example: strict – strictness. Words ending in 'y' change form: *happy – happiness*.

-off
Phrasal verbs are not hyphenated (e.g. *to write off*). These are not shown. Nouns and adjectives are normally hyphenated (e.g. *a write-off, a written-off car*). A few adverbial phrases are not hyphenated (e.g. *he was badly off*).

badly-off *or* badly off	mid-off	show-off
(*but* better off)	on-and-off	shut-off
blast-off	one-off	spin-off
blow-off	on-off	split-off
brush-off	part-off	stand-off
cast-off	pay-off	stop-off
cut-off	play-off	take-off
face-off	push-off	taking-off
falling-off	put-off	teeing-off
fall-off	rake-off	tee-off
hand-off	rip-off	telling-off
hands-off	run-off	ticking-off
jumping-off site	sawed-off	tip-off
jump-off	sawn-off	trade-off
kick-off	sell-off	turn-off
lay-off	send-off	well off *or* well-off
lift-off	set-off	write-off

-on
Separate words from phrasal verbs (e.g. *to add on*). These are not shown. Hyphenated terms are nouns (e.g. *hanger-on*), or adjectival phrase (e.g. *unbuilt-on land*) and/or adverb (e.g. *end-on*).

add-on	odds-on	spot-on
bolt-on	off-and-on *or* off and on	spray-on
carry-on	pull-on	try-on
clip-on	right-on *or* right on	turn-on
come-on	roll-on	unbuilt-on
end-on	roll-on-roll-off	unsmiled-on
hands-on	run-on	wait-on
hanger-on	side-on	walker-on
have-on	slip-on	walk-on
knock-on		

-out
Phrasal verbs comprise separate words (e.g. *to bail out*). These are not shown. Adverbial phrases (e.g. *they went all out to win*) are separate words. These are shown. Nouns and adjectival phrases are normally hyphenated (e.g. *a hand-out, an all-out strike*). However, there are one or two exceptions (e.g. *lookout*), and rather surprisingly (two consecutive vowels), *takeout*.

all-out	far-out	push-out
bail-out	fit-out	read-out
bug-out	fitting-out	rig-out
burn-out	fold-out	sell-out
buy-out	freeze-out	shake-out
call-out	get-out	share-out
carry-out	grey-out	shoot-out
check-out	hand-out	shut-out
chucker-out	hang-out	spun-out
clapped-out	hole-out	stake-out
clean-out	lead-out	stressed-out
clear-out	long-drawn-out	takeout
cop-out	lookout	try-out
count-out	not-out	walk-out
cut-out	opt-out	washed-out
dim-out	pay-out	wash-out
down-and-out	played-out	watch-out
drop-out	pour-out	way-out
fade-out	print-out	white-out
fall-out	pull-out	work-out
		worn-out

-over
Phrasal verbs comprise separate words (e.g. *cross over*). These not shown. Adjectives are hyphenated or conjoined (e.g. *all-over paint, takeover bid*). Adverbs are conjoined (e.g. *moreover*). Nouns may be hyphenated or conjoined (e.g. *a push-over* or *pushover*, *a takeover*).

all-over	makeover	switch-over
crossover	moreover	takeover
cut-over	once-over	tick-over
flash-over	out-over	turnover
flyover	Passover	twice over
going-over	pullover	under-and-over
handover	pushover *or* push-over	up-and-over
hangover	roll-over	up-over
holdover	slip-over	walk-over
leftover	spillover	work-over
limited-over	stopover	wrapover

-up
The notes applying to *–over* also apply to this suffix.

all-up	mixed-up	smash-up
all-up service	mix-up	speed-up
back-up	mock-up	stand-up
back-up file	mop-up	start-up
blow-up	muck-up	step-up
brew-up	paid-up	stick-up
build-up	paste-up	stitch-up
built-up	patch-up	stuck-up
buttoned-up	picker-up	take-up
call-up	pick-me-up	tarted-up
check-up	pick-up	tie-up
cover-up	pick-up head	tip-up
get-up	pin-up	ton-up
get-up-and-go	pop-up	topping-up
hard-up	press-up	top-up
hold-up	punch-up	top-up loan
hook-up	push-up	toss-up
hyped-up	put-up	totting-up
jumped-up	put-up job	turn-up
jump-up	roll-up	turn-up for the books
knees-up	roll-up fund	two-up
knocker-up	round-up	used-up
lay-up	runners-up	wake-up
let-up	runner-up	warmed-up
lighting-up	run-up	warm-up
lighting-up time	set-up	washed-up
line-up	shake-up	washing-up
link-up	shape-up	wash-up
lock-up	slap-up	well-set-up
make-up	slip-up	wind-up
mark-up	slow-up	write-up
mess-up		

-wise
Conjoined: e.g. *clockwise, coastwise, leastwise, streetwise*. Exceptions: *penny-wise, worldly-wise*.

14
Hyphenated and Conjoined Words

The following list covers terms comprising separate words (e.g. *air freight*); conjoined words (e.g. *airmail*); hyphenated words (e.g. *air-mechanic*). Terms are sorted in this order (most sorting routines ignore hyphens). For reasons of space the predominant category for each word is omitted and only the exceptions (where applicable) are given. By way of example, there are about a dozen everyday terms employing 'air' as one of two or more separate words, just over fifty conjoined words commencing with 'air', and almost seventy hyphenated terms. The latter, comprising the most numerous group, are therefore not given: it can thus be assumed that the term '*air-intake*' is hyphenated.

> % all separate words. Exceptions given
> ‡ all conjoined. Exceptions given
> – all hyphenated. Exceptions given.

Verbs are not normally hyphenated (e.g. *to fade out*) and are not given. It should also be noted that dictionaries may vary in their use of hyphenation. Spell-checkers do not normally respond to hyphenated words and would not detect *air-terminal* (instead of *air terminal*) or *air-base* (instead of *airbase*).

The previous comments concerning dictionaries particularly apply here and where the Collins and Oxford use the conjoined form more frequently than Chambers.

- A -	after-effect	air terminal
able-bodied	after-life	airbase
A-bomb	age-bracket	airborne
about-face	agent-general	aircraft
above-board	age-old	aircraftman
above-mentioned	à go-go	airfield
above-named	aide-de-camp	airflow
absent-minded	AIDS-related	airfoil
accident-prone	air: –	airframe
account-book	air ambulance	airlift
across-the-board	air bag	airline
add-on	air force	airliner
adjutant-general	air gun	airlock
ad-lib	air letter	airmail
ad-man	air rifle	airman
aero-engine	air scout	airmanship
Afro: –	air support	airplane
after-dinner	air taxi	airport

HYPHENATED AND CONJOINED WORDS

airship
airsick
airspace
airspeed
airstrip
airtight
airtime
airwave
airway
airworthy
air-vice-marshal
aircraft-carrier
airy-fairy
alarm: –
Alice-in-Wonderland
all- (See Prefixes)
alms-house
also-ran
altar: –
ambassador-at-large
analogue-to-digital
angel: –
Anglo: –
Anglo-American
animal-worship
ante-mortem
anti- (See Prefixes)
apple: –
armour-plate
arm-rest
arms-length
arrow-head
Ascension-day
Attorney-General
audio: –
auto: –
avant-garde
awe-inspiring
awe-stricken

- B -
baby: –
back- (See Prefixes)
badly-off
bad-tempered

bald-eagle
bald-faced
ball: –
ball and socket
ball lightning
ballet-dancer
ballot-box
ballot-paper
ballot-rigging
balls-up
bank: –
bank: %
bankroll
bankrupt
barbed-wire
bar-bell
barber-shop
bar-b-q
bar-chart
bar-code
bare-knuckled
bargain: –
barley-sugar
barrel-organ
base: ‡
base coin
base fee
base jumper
base metal
base rate
base-burner
base-court
base-level
base-line
base-load
basket-maker
bath-house
bathing: –
bathing beauty
bathing belle
baton-charge
battle-axe
bay-window
beach-ball
be-all and end-all

beam-end
bed-and-breakfast
bed: ‡
bed-bath
bed-closet
bed-jacket
bed-linen
bed-plate
bed-rest
bed-settee
bed-sheet
bed-sitter
bed-table
bed-wetting
bed-worthy
beech-oil
beef-tea
bee-moth
beer: –
beer belly
beetle-browed
before-mentioned
beggar-my-neighbour
bell: –
bell end
bellpush
belly: –
below-the-line
belt-tightening
between-decks
Bible: –
big-time
bilge: –
bill-broker
billiard: –
bin-liner
bird: –
bird of prey
bird strike
birdbath
birdcage
birdcall
birdlike
birdman
birds of a feather

183

A HANDBOOK FOR WRITERS OF ENGLISH

birdseed
birdsong
birdwatcher
bird's-eye view
bird's-foot
birthday-suit
birth-rate
bit-map
bi-weekly
bi-yearly
black-and-blue
black-and-tan
blind-alley
blind-drunk
blindman's-buff
blind-side
bloody-minded
blotting-pad
blow-by-blow
blow-dry
blow-up
blow-valve
blue-chip
blue-collar
blue-green
board-game
boarding: %
boarding-house or
boarding house
boarding-school or
boarding school
boat: –
boatman
boat people
boatrace
body-bag
body-builder
bog: –
bog down
boiling-point
bold-faced
bomb-disposal
bone: –
bone china
bone marrow grafting

bonehead
boneless
boneshaker
booby-prize
boogie-woogie
boo-hoo
book: –
book club
book out
book price
book sale
book through
book trade
book value
bookbinder
bookcase
booked-up
booking: –
bookkeeper
bookmaker
bookmark
bookrest
bookseller
bookshelf
bookshop
bookstall
bookstand
bookstore
bookworm
booze-up
born-again
bottle: –
bottle bank
bottle neck
bottleneck
bottom-heavy
bottom-up
boulder-clay
bow-legged
bowling: –
bow-wave
bow-window
box: –
box file
box junction

box number
box profits
boxroom
boxwood
boy-meets-girl
brain: %
brainbox
braincase
brainchild
brainpower
brains trust
brainstorm
brainwashing
brain-dead
brain-teaser
brain-wave
branch: –
brand-new
brazen-faced
bread-and-butter
break-even
breakfast-room
breakfast-table
break-out
break-up
breast-feed
breathing-space
breeding-ground
brew-up
bric-à-brac
bride: ‡
bride-chamber
bride-price
bride's-cake
bride's-maid (or
bridesmaid)
bridge-builder
bridle: –
brief-case
bright-eyed
brim-full
broad: ‡
broad bean
broad daylight
broken: –

184

HYPHENATED AND CONJOINED WORDS

broken home
brother-in-law
brush-off
bubble: –
bubble and squeak
bubble bath
buck-rabbit
building-block
build-up
built-in
bull: –
bulldog
bulldoze
bumble-bee
bunny-girl
burial-ground
burning-point
burn-out
burying-ground
bus-conductor
bus-fare
bush-baby
bushy-tailed
butter: –
buy-back
buy-in
buy-out
by- (See Prefixes)
by-and-by
by-corner
bye-bye
bye-law

- C -

cable-car
cab-rank
cacao-bean
call-box
call-up
camera-ready copy
candle-holder
cannonball
cannon-shot
can-opener
captain-general

carbon-copy
car-coat
card-holder
card-table
card-vote
carriage-free
carriage-paid
carry-all
carry-on
car-sickness
cart-horse
cartridge-paper
carve-up
carving-knife
car-wash
case-law
cash-and-carry
cash-book
cash-box
cash-credit
cashew-nuts
cash-register
casting-vote
cast-iron
castle-building
castor-oil
castor-oil plant
cat-and-mouse
cat-burglar
catch-phrase
cat-flap
cathode-ray
cat-o-nine-tails
cave-dweller
cave-in
CD-ROM
cease-fire
cedar-nut
centre-forward
centre-half
centre-rail
cha-cha-cha
chain-smoke
chargé-d'affaires
charge-hand

chart-buster
chat-line
check-in
checkbook (US)
checking-room
check-up
cheque book *but*
cheque-book journalism
chewing-gum
chicken-hearted
chicken-livered
child-resistant
chimney-sweep
chock-a-block
chock-full
chopping-block
chopping-board
Christmas-tide/time
chucker-out
church-parade
cigar-shaped
cinema-goer
clapped-out
class-conscious
clean-cut
clean-living
clean-shaven
clean-up
clear-cut
clear-headed
clear-out
clear-sighted
cliff-face
climb-down
climbing-frame
clip-on
clock-radio
close-down
close-in
close-knit
close-up
clothes-horse
clothes-line
clothes-peg
cloud-cuckoo-land

club-foot
coach-horse
co-agency
co-agent
coal-black
coal-box
coal-fired
coast-to-coast
co-author
Coca-Cola
cocoa: –
cocoanut
coconut: –
code-breaker
code-name
co-dependant
co-dependency
co-dependent
cod-fishing
cod-liver oil
co- (See Prefixes)
co-driver
coffee-maker
coin-operated
cold-blooded
cold: %
cold-blooded
cold-drawn
cold-hearted
cold-rolled
cold-shoulder
cold-weld
colonel-in-chief
come-and-go
commander-in-chief
common-law
communion-cloth
company sergeant-major
computer-aided design
concert-goer
conning-tower
con-rod
conscience-stricken
conveyor-belt
cooling-off period

co-op
co-operate
co-opt
co-ordinate
co-pilot
copper: –
copper nickel
copperhead
copperplate
coppersmith
copperworks
copy-edit
coral-reef
cork-tipped
corn: ‡
corn-beef
corn-cake
corn-chandler
corn-cracker
corn-cure
corn-cutter
corn-dealer
corn-fed
corn-merchant
corn-spirit
cost-accounting
co-star
cost-benefit analysis
cost-effective
co-tenancy
cotton-gin
counter- (See Prefixes)
country-and-western
country-dancing
court-martial
cover-up
cow-dung
crash-proof
cream-bun
crease-resistant
crêpe-de-chine
crêpe-soled
criss-cross
cross- (See Prefixes)
cross-and-pile

crossing-sweeper
country: %
countrywide
country-and-western
country-dancing
country-folk
country-house
country-rock
country-seat
crown-wheel
crystal-clear
crystal-gazer
cuckoo-spit
cul-de-sac
cupboard-love
curly-headed
currant: –
custom-built
customs-house
cut-and-thrust
cut-price

- D -
daddy-long-legs
dairy-farm
daisy-chain
damp-course
damp-proof
dance: –
darning-needle
data-processing
date-palm
date-stamp
daughter-in-law
Davy-lamp
day: –
day by day
day care centre
day centre
day of action
day off
day room
day trip
daybreak
daydream

HYPHENATED AND CONJOINED WORDS

daylight
daylight robbery
Daylight Saving Time
daylong
daystar
daytime
D-day
dead-end
dead-eye
deaf-and-dumb
death: –
death certificate
death penalty
death row
death squad
death wish
deathlike
deathwatch
deck: –
deck officer
deckchair
deckhouse
deep-freeze
de-ice
delivery-man
demi- (See Prefixes)
depth-charge
devil: –
dew-drop
diamond: –
diamond jubilee
diamond snake
diamond wedding
die-cast
dilly-dally
ding-dong
dining: –
direct-grant school
director-general
dirt-cheap
discount-broker
dish-cloth
dishwater
ditch-water
divan-bed

diving: –
D-notice
dock-labourer
dog-collar
dog's-body
dog-tired
dogtooth
do-it-yourself
doll's-house
donkey-man
Doomsday-book
dot-matrix printer
double: –
double act
double axel
double back
double bassoon
double bed
double bill
double bluff
double chin
double concerto
double cream
double dagger
double doors
double Dutch
double exposure
double fault
double feature
double figures
double first
double knit
double negative
double or quits
double play
double pneumonia
double spread
double standard
double star
double time
double top
double up
double vision
double wedding
double whammy

dove-house
Dow-Jones average
down- (See Prefixes)
down-to-earth
draft-dodger
drag-parachute
drag-queen
drag-racing
drawing-paper
draw-leaf table
dray-horse
dress-circle
dressing-gown
dress-rehearsal
drift: –
drill-hole
drink-drive
drinking-up time
drink-money
drip-dry
drip-feed
driving: –
driving licence
driving seat
driving test
drop: –
drophead coupé
drug-addict
dry: %
dry-cell
dry-clean
dry-dock
dry-eyed
dry-fly
dry-goods
dry-iced
dry-nurse
dry-point
dry-rot
dry-shod
dry-stone
dry-stove
dry-wash
dual-control
dumb-waiter

A HANDBOOK FOR WRITERS OF ENGLISH

dung-cart
dung-fly
dust: –
dust bag
Dust Bowl
dust cover
dustbin
dustcart
dustman
dustproof
dustsheet
duty-free
duty-paid
dwelling-house
dyed-in-the-wool

- E -
each-way
eagle: –
early-Victorian
early-warning
ear-piercing
earth: –
earth science
earthbound
ear-trumpet
East-ender
easy-going
eating-apple
echo-sounder
eco- (See Prefixes)
egg: –
egg custard
egg white
eggcup
egghead
eggnog
eggshell
eggwash
ego-trip
eider-duck
ejector-seat
elbow-grease
electro: &
electro-optic

eleven-plus
e-mail
Ember-day
emery-paper
empire-builder
empty-handed
end-on
end-product
end-user
engine: –
environmentally-friendly
epoch-making
errand-boy
Euro: ‡
Euro-American
Euro-dollars
Euro-MP
Euro-Parliament
Euro-passport
Euro-sceptic
even-handed
evening-dress
evil: –
ex-directory
exercise-book
ex-libris
ex-serviceman
extra- (See Prefixes)
eye: –
eye bank
eye contact
eye for an eye
eye lotion
eye muscle
eye socket
eye to eye
eye up
eyeball to eyeball
eyebright
eyebrow
eyeglass
eyehook
eyelash
eyeless

eyelet
eyelet-hole
eyelid
eyeliner
eyeshade
eyeshadow
eyesight
eyesore
eyestrain

- F -
face: –
face down
face out
face pack
face powder
face the music
face to face
face-to-face
face value
faceworker
fact-finding
factory-gate sale
fade: –
fail-safe
faint-hearted
fair: –
fair comment
fair enough
fair play
fair trade
fairground
fairway
fair-and-square
fairyland
fairylike
fairytale
fairy-godmother
faith-healer
fall-out
fancy-free
far (See Prefixes)
farm-hand
far-reaching
fast-talking

HYPHENATED AND CONJOINED WORDS

fast-track
father-figure
father-in-law
fatigue-dress
fault-finding
feather: –
featherweight
feature-length
feeble-minded
feed-pipe
feel-good
fellow: –
fellowship
felt-tip(ped) pen
ferro: ‡
ferro-manganese
ferro-molybdenum
ferro-nickel
ferry-boat
ferry-house
fiddle-bow
fifth-generation
fifty-fifty
fifty-pence
fig-leaf
fig-tree
file-cutter
file-fish
file-leader
fill-in
fill-in flash
film-strip
filter-bed
filter-paper
filter-tip
fine-draw
fine-spoken
fine-spun
fine-tooth(ed) comb
fine-tune
finger-painting
finger-pointer
Finno-Ugric
fir-cone
fire-and-brimstone

fire: –
fire blanket
fire brigade
fire bucket
fire door
fire drill
fire engine
fire escape
fire extinguisher
fire hose
fire sale
fire station
fire up
firearm
fireball
firebox
firebrand
firebrick
firecracker
firefloat
firefly
fireguard
firelight
firelighter
firelock
fireman
firemark
firepan
fireplace
firepot
fireproof
firescreen
fireside
firestone
firethorn
fireweed
firewood
firework
first: –
first cousin
first degree burn/
 murder
first floor
first gear
First Lady

first lieutenant
first light
first name
first night
first offender
first past the post
first person
first principles
first reading
first refusal
first storey
first strike
first thing
first water
First World
fir-tree
fish: –
fish cake
fish eagle
fish eaters
fish stick
fishball
fishburger
fisherman
fisheye
fishing-tackle
fishmonger
fishskin
fishskin disease
fishwife
fishing: –
fitting-out
five-a-side
five-day week
fixed-interest
flag: –
flagship
flagstaff
flagstone
flame-thrower
flat-footed
flea-bite
flesh: –
flesh wound
fleurs-de-lys

189

flexi-cover
flip-side
flip-top
flower: –
flower child
flower power
flowerpot
fly-by-night
fly: –
fly front
fly line
fly powder
fly rail
fly rod
fly swat
fly whisk
flycatcher
flyleaf
flyover
flypaper
flytrap
flyway
flyweight
flywheel
f-number
fog-bank
folk: –
folk hero
folk music
folk rock
folklore
follow-on
foot: ‡
foot brake
foot fault
foot-bath
foot-candle
foot-dragging
foot-in-the mouth
foot-passenger
foot-patrol
foot-pump
foot-soldier
foot-stall
foot-tapping

foot-ton
foot-warmer
foot-and-mouth
force-feed
force majeure
fore- (See Prefixes)
fore-and-aft
forest: –
fork-lift truck
fork-tailed
fortune-teller
foster: –
foul-mouthed
foundation-stone
fountain-pen
four-by-four
four-footed
four-foot way
four: –
fourfold
fourscore
foursome
fourth dimension
fourth estate
fowl-pest
fox: –
foxberry
foxglove
foxhole
foxhound
foxtrot
frame-saw
frame-up
Franco: ‡
franking-machine
free-and-easy
free: % (adjective)
free: –
freebooter
freeborn
Freefone
freehand
freehold
freelance
freeman

freemason
freephone
Freepost
freestyle
freethinker
freeway
freewheel
freeze-dry
freezing-point
freight-car
French-Canadian
French-polish
front-bench
front: –
front door
front line
front man
front row
fruit-bat
fruit-tree
frying-pan
fry-up
fuel-injected
full: –
full blast
full brother
full cousin
full dress
full hand
full house
full marks
full moon
full nelson
full of beans
full pelt
full pitch
full sail
full score
full point
full tilt
full time
full toss
full up
fullback
fully-fashioned

HYPHENATED AND CONJOINED WORDS

fully-fledged
fund-raising

- G -
gambling-house
game-chicken
game-dealer
gaming-table
gang-rape
gaol-bird
gas: –
gas burner
gas chamber
gas cooker
gas engine
gas escape
gas fire
gas fitter
gas fixture
gas furnace
gas heater
gas helmet
gas jar
gas jet
gas lamp
gas leak
gas main
gas mantle
gas mask
gas meter
gas oil
gas oven
gas pipe
gas plant
gas poker
gas ring
gas shell
gas station
gas stove
gas tank
gas tap
gasbag
gasholder
gaslight
gaslit

gate-keeper
G-clef
gear: –
gear ratio
gearbox
gearchange
gearshift
gearwheel
gender-specific
general-purpose
get-rich-quick
get-up-and-go
ghost-writer
glass: –
glass eye
glass fibre
glass paper
glass wool
glasshouse
glassware
glassworker
globe-trotter
glue-sniffing
go-between
go-cart
God-almighty
god-forsaken
go-getter
going-away kit
gold: –
gold card
gold certificate
gold disc
gold dust
goldfield
goldfinch
goldfish
goldsmith
goldstone
golden: %
goldenrod
golden-crested
good: –
good afternoon
good faith

good for anything
good for you
Good Friday
good gracious
good heavens
good offices
good sense
good turn
goodnight
goodtime
goodwill
goose: –
goose bumps
goose step
gooseberry
gooseberry-wine
gooseflesh
gossip-monger
governing-body
governor-general
Grace-and-Favour
grass-cutter
gravel-pit
gravel-voiced
great-aunt
Greco-Roman
green-keeper
grey-coat
grief-stricken
gripe-water
ground-beetle
ground-to-air
group-captain
growing-pains
grown-up
G-string
guest-house

- H -
habit-forming
hack-saw
hail-storm
hair-brained
hair-brush
hair-raising

A HANDBOOK FOR WRITERS OF ENGLISH

hair's-breadth	hang-glider	hardnosed
hair-splitting	hang-up	hardparts
half-a-dozen	hansom-cab	hardshell
half: –	happy-go-lucky	hardship
half back	harbour-dues	hardtop
half board	hard-and-fast	hardware
half nelson	hard: –	hardwood
half past eight	hard bop	hare-and-hounds
halfpace	hard by	hare-brained
halfpenny	hard card	harness-maker
halfway	hard case	harvest: –
halfwit	hard cash	has-been
ham-fisted	hard cheese	have-a-go
hand: ‡	hard coal	have-nots
hand and foot	hard copy	hawk: ‡
hand ball	hard core	hawk-beaked
hand grenade	hard court	hawk-eyed
hand in glove	hard currency	hawk-moth
hand line	hard disk	H-bomb
hand over fist	hard edge	head-on
hand puppet	hard facts	head-to-head
hand to mouth	hard feelings	hearing-aid
hand-ball	hard hat	hearing-impaired
hand-barrow	hard hit	heart-failure
hand-basket	hard labour	heart-free
hand-feeding	hard landing	hearth-rug
hand-glass	hard left	heart-to-heart
hand-held	hard line	Heath(-)Robinson
hand-in	hard luck	heaven-born:
hand-in-hand	hard of hearing	heavy-duty
hand-knitted	hard pad	heavy-handed
hand-loom	hard right	hedging-bill
hand-lotion	hard rock	heir-apparent
hand-me-down	hard roe	hell: –
hand-mill	hard rubber	he-man
hand-out	hard sauce	hemp-seed
hand-painted	hard sell	hem-stitch
hand-picked	hard shoulder	hen: –
hand-post	hardboard	henpecked
hand-press	hardface	hero-worship
hand-screw	harddisk	herring-bone: ‡
hand-sewn	hardgrass	hide-and-seek
hand-to-hand	hardhead	high: –
hand-to-mouth	hardline	high admiral
hands-free	hardmouthed	high altar

HYPHENATED AND CONJOINED WORDS

high and dry
high and mighty
high bailiff
High Church
high command
High Commissioner
high court
high explosive
high fidelity
high frequency
high gear
High German
high horse
high jinks
high jump
high life
high living
high mass
high noon
high point
high priest
high profile
high relief
high school
high seas
high season
high sheriff
high society
high spirits
high spot
high street
high table
high tea
high technology
high tide
high time
high treason
high water
high wire
highball
highbrow
highjack
highland
highlight
highlighter

highly: –
highroad
highway
highwayman
hill-billy
hire-purchase
hit-and-run
hitch-hike
hi-tec
hit-or-miss
hit-parade
hog's-back
hold-all
hold-up
hole-in-the-wall
holier-than-thou
holly-oak
home: %
homebound
homebuyer
homecraft
homeland
homeless
homemaker
homeowner
homesick
homespun
homestead
homeward
homework
home-bred
home-brew
home-coming
home-croft
home-defence
home-farm
home-fire
home-grown
home-keeping
home-life
home-made
home-produced
home-ruler
home-signal
home-straight

home-stretch
home-thrust
home-town
home-truth
homeward-bound
homo: ‡
Homo sapiens
honey: –
honey creeper
honey fungus
honeybun
honeycomb
honeydew melon
honeymoon
honeypot
honeysuckle
hop-vine/bine
horse: –
horse artillery
horse box
horse brass
horse chestnut
horse fair
Horse Guards
horse latitudes
horse mackerel
horse mushroom
horse mussel
horse race
horse sense
horse soldier
horseback
horsecar
horsefeathers
horseflesh
horsefly
horsehair
horsehide
horselaugh
horseman
horsemeat
horseplay
horsepower
horseradish
horseshoe

A HANDBOOK FOR WRITERS OF ENGLISH

horsetail
horsewhip
horse-and-buggy
hot-air balloon
hot-tempered
hot-water bottle
house-breaking
house: ‡
house agent
house arrest
house call
house guest
house lights
house martin
house physician
house plant
house sparrow
house surgeon
house-breaker
house-dog
house-father
house-mother
house-party
house-proud
house-to-house
house-trained
house-warming
house-to-house
how-do-you-do
howdy-do
hub-cap
humble-pie
hunger-strike
hunting: –
hurdle-race
hurricane-lamp
hymn-book

- I -
ice: %
iceball
iceberg
iceblink
icebound
icebox

icebreaker
icecap
icefield
icepack
ice-action
ice-belt
ice-blue
ice-cold
ice-cream soda
ice-free
ice-ledge
ice-skate
ill- (See Prefixes)
in-between
-in-chief
index-finger
index-linked
Indo: –
in-fighting
in-flight
ink-blot
in-law
in-patient
input-output analysis
in-situ
internal-combustion engine
intra-articular
in- (See Prefixes)
iron: –
Iron Age
Iron Cross
Iron Curtain
iron horse
iron lung
iron maiden
iron ore
iron pyrites
ironing-board
ironmaster
ironmonger
ironsmith
ironstone
ironware
ironwood

ironwork
ivory-black
ivory-palm

- J -
Jack-in-the-box
jail-bird
jerry-builder
jet: –
jet boat
jet engine
jetfoil
jetliner
jetplane
jetsam
jetstream
jewel-case
jewel-house
Jew's-harp
jib: –
joint: –
joint account
joint resolution
joint venture
joint will
joint-stock bank
joy-ride
Judas-kiss
judgement-day
ju-jitsu
juke-box
jump-jet
junior-(weight): ‡
junk-shop: ‡
jury-box

- K -
kerb-crawler
key-ring: ‡
kick-off
kidney: –
kiln-dried
kind-hearted
king: –
king of beasts

HYPHENATED AND CONJOINED WORDS

king of the castle
king penguin
kingfisher
kingmaker
kingpost
kiss-and-tell
kitchen: –
kitchen unit
kitchenware
kite-flying
kite-mark
knee: –
knee sock
kneecap
kneehole
knife: –
knight: –
knitting: –
knock-down
knock-on effect
Ku-Klux Klan

– L –
labour: –
lady-in-waiting
lady-killer
ladylike
laissez-faire
lake-dweller
lamp: –
lampholder
lamplight
lamplighter
lamppost
lampshade
lance-corporal
land: –
land grant
land office
Land Registry
landfall
landfill
landform
landholder
landlady

landless
landlord
landmark
landmass
landowner
landscape
landslide
landslip
landwind
landing: –
larger-than-life
last-ditch
last-gasp
last-minute
lattice-work
laughing-gas
laughing-stock
launching-pad
laundry-maid
law: –
law agent
law centre
lawsuit
lawyer
lawn tennis
lawnmower
lawn-party
lawn-sprinkler
lay-by
layer-cake
lay-off
lead-free
leaf: –
leafbud
leaflike
lean-to
leap-frog
lease-lend
leather: –
leathergoods
left-bank: ‡
Left Bank
left guard
left tackle
left wheel

left wing
leg: –
leg break
leg bye
leg side
leg slip
leg spin
leg spinner
leg warmers
legwear
legwork
lemon-grass
lend-lease
let-down
letter: –
letter quality
letterbox
letterhead
level: –
level best
liberty-boat
Lib.-Lab.
lie-in
lieutenant: –
life-and-death
life: –
life annuity
life assurance
life expectancy
Life Guards
life insurance
life peer
life sciences
life sentence
life story
lifebelt
lifeboat
lifebuoy
lifeguard
lifelong
lifespan
lifestyle
lifetime
life-support system
lift-boy

light: –
light bulb
light engine
light horse
light industry
light infantry
light literature
light meter
light music
light opera
light railway
light up
light welterweight
lighter-than-air
lighthouse
lighting-up
lighting-up time
lightning-conductor
lightship
lightweight
like-minded
lime-green
lime-tree
lime-twig
lime-wood
limited-liability company
limited-over
line: –
line drawing
line feed
line judge
line up
lineman
line drawing
line feed
line judge
line up
link-up
linseed: –
lionlike
lion-hearted
lip: –
lip brush
lip liner

listening-in
litter-bug
litter-lout
live-bait: ‡
live birth
live cartridge
live circuit
live shell
lived-in
livestock
livery-servant
living-room
loan: –
loan collection
loan shark
loan translation
loan word
lobster-pot
lock-keeper
lock-nut
lock-down
lock-up
locum-tenancy
log: –
log cabin
log in
log out
log tables
long: %
longboat
longbow
longhand
longhorn
longhouse
longship
longshoreman
longsuffering
longwearing
long-ago
long-chain
long-dated
long-distance
long-drawn-out
long-eared
long-faced

long-haired
long-haul
long-legged
long-life
long-line
long-lived
long-measure
long-range
long-sighted
long-standing
long-stay
long-tail
long-term
long-time
long-wave (adj.)
long-winded
look-alike
looking-glass
loose-cut
loose-leaf
Lord Justice-General
lotus-eater
love: –
love affair
love game
love life
lovebird
lovebite
lovelock
lovemaking
lovesick
loving-kindness
low: –
Low Church
low comedy
low frequency
low gear
Low German
low life
low mass
low profile
low technology
low tide
low water
lowland

HYPHENATED AND CONJOINED WORDS

lowlight
lozenge-shaped
lucky-dip
luggage-van
lumber-yard
lump-sugar
luncheon-bar
lynch-law
lynx-eyed

- M -
mace-bearer
machine: –
machine gun
machine-gunner
machine code
machine language
machine tool
macro- (See Prefixes)
magneto: –
mail: ‡
mail drop
mail order
mail-boat
mail-car
mail-coach
mail-order
mail-plane
mail-train
maintenance-man
major-general
make-believe
make-do
make-or-break
make-peace
malt: –
malt liquor
malt tea
malt vinegar
malt whisky
man-hours
manic-depressive
man-of-war
man-servant
mansion-house

man-sized
man-years
many-sided
map-pin
map-reading
mark-down
market: –
market cross
market economy
market forces
market garden
market gardener
market leader
market profile
market research
market share
market square
mark-up
marriage: –
marriage bureau
marriage guidance
marriage partner
marsh-gas
Mason-Dixon Line
mass-energy equation
mass: %
mass(-)production
mass-bell
mass-book
mass-energy equivalence
mass-marketing
mass-produced
master: –
master-at-arms
master of ...
master page
mastermind
masterpiece
mastersinger
masterstroke
masterwork
match-maker
match-play
matter-of-fact

means-test
measuring-tape
meat-eater
medico: –
medium: –
meeting-house
melting-point
melt-water
memory-resident
men-of-war
merry-go-round
mess-tin
mess-up
mezzo-soprano
micro- (See Prefixes)
middle: %
middlebrow
middleman
middlemost
middleweight
middle-age
middle-bracket
middle-class
middle-distance
Middle-Eastern
middle-income
middle-of-the-road
mid- (See Prefixes)
midi- (See Prefixes)
mile-post
milk: –
milk chocolate
milk of ...
milk round
milk stout
milkfish
milkmaid
milkman
mill: –
millboard
milldam
millpond
millrace
millstone
millstone-grit

millwright
mince-pie
mind-altering
mind: –
mine: –
minefield
minesweeper
mini- (See Prefixes)
minute: –
minute steak
minuteman
mirror: –
mirror symmetry
mirrorwise
mischief-maker
mixed-ability
mock-up
money: –
money belt
money clip
money supply
moneybags
moneylender
monkey: –
moon: ‡
moon daisy
moon-eyed
moon-faced
moon-fish
moon-flower
moon-god
moon-madness
moon-stricken
mooring-mast
morning: %
morning-after pill
morning-glory
morning-gown
morning-prayer
morning-room
mortice-lock
moss: –
moss green
moss stitch
mossback

mossland
mossplant
moth-eaten
mother-in-law
mother-to-be
motor: –
motor car
motor caravan
motor generator
motor home
motor neurone
motorail
motorcycle combination
motorcyclist
motorway
mounting-block
mourning: –
mouse-colour: ‡
muck-rake
multi- (See Prefixes)
music-holder
mussel-shell
mustard-oil
mutton-suet
mystery-man

- N -

nail: –
nail gun
nail polish
nail punch
nail set
nail varnish
name-calling
name-plate
nanny-goat
narrow-boat
narrow-gauge
narrow-minded
nature-cure
near: –
Near East
near gale
near miss
nearside

neck-bone
neo- (See Prefixes)
net-fishing
never-ending
new: %
newborn
newcomer
newfangled
New-Age
new-blown
new-fallen
new-fledged
new-found
new-laid
new-made
new-mown
newly-qualified
news: ‡
news agency
news conference
news fiction
news magazine
news-sheet
news-stand
news-theatre
news-value
news-vendor
news-writer
newly-wed
night: –
night air
night duty
night fighter
night nurse
night out
night safe
night school
night shift
nightbird
nightcap
nightclass
nightclothes
nightclub
nightdress
nightgear

HYPHENATED AND CONJOINED WORDS

nightgown
nighthawk
nightjar
nightlife
nightlong
nightmare
nightpiece
nightrider
nightshade
nightshirt
nightspot
nightwear
nig-nog
nine-hole
noble-minded
no- (See Prefixes)
non- (See Prefixes)
north-country
north-east
nose-cone
Notre-Dame
nuclear-free zone
nuclear-powered
nut-wrench

- O -
oak-tree
object-lesson
obtuse-angled
obtuse-angular
ocean-going
odd-job
odds-on
off- (See Prefixes)
office-boy
office-girl
oil: –
oil(-)field
oil immersion
oil length
oil of ...
oil paint
oil painting
oil platform
oil rig

oil shale
oil slick
oil well
oilcan
oilcloth
oilfield
oilman
oilskin
oilstone
old: –
old age
old girl
old-age pension
O-level
on-board
once-for-all
once-over
one-man band
one-sided
on-going
on-the-job training
open: –
open access
open adoption
open book
open cheque
open circuit
open court
open day
open door
open economy
open fire
open harmony
open house
open letter
open market
open marriage
open mind
open prison
open question
open sandwich
open score
open sea
open season
open secret

open sentence
open shop
open side
open skies
open system
open verdict
opening time
open-and-shut
opera-glasses
orange-blossom
orange-peel
order-book
organ-builder
ostrich-egg
otter-hunting
out-and-out
out- (See Prefixes)
out-of-the-way
out-of-work
outward-bound
over- (See Prefixes)
oxy-acetylene
oyster-bed: ‡
ozone-friendly

- P -
pace-bowler
pack: –
pack ice
packsheet
packing: –
paddle-boat
paddy-field
page-boy
pain-killer
paint-box
palette-knife
pall-bearer
pall-mall
palm: –
palm court
palmhouse
Pan: –
panty-hose
paper: –

paper money
paper profits
paper tape
paper tape reader
paper tiger
paperback
paperboard
paperless
paperware
paperwork
park-and-ride
parking lot
parking meter
parking-place
parking-ticket
parliament-house
parrot: –
partition-wall
part: –
part of speech
partridge-wood
party: –
party line
party machine
party man
party plan
party politics
party sales
party spirit
party wall
pass-book
passe-partout
passer-by
pasture-land
patent-rights
patrol-wagon
pattern: –
pay-as-you-earn
pay: –
paymaster
payroll
payslip
peace: –
peacemaker
peacetime

pea-green
pearl: –
pearl barley
pearly king/queen
pear-shaped
pea-soup
pea-stone
pea-straw
peat: –
pebble-stone
pedal: –
peep-hole
pen-and-ink
pencil-case
pen-friend
penny-farthing
penny-pinching
pen-pusher
pepper: –
pepper-and-salt
pepper
pepper tree
peppercorn
peppermill
peppermint
percussion: –
photo: ‡
photo call
photo opportunity
photo-ageing
photo-emission
photo-engraving
photo-etching
photo-finish
photo-process
photo-relief
piano: –
piano roll
pianoforte
picket-duty
pick-pocket
picture: –
picture postcard
piece: –
piecemeal

pieds-à-terre
pie-eyed
pier-head
pigeon: –
pigeon's milk
pigeonhole
pig: ‡
pig swill
pigfeed
pig-eyed
pig-faced
pig-fish
pig-iron
pig-lead
pig-lily
pig-rat
pike-perch
pile-driver
pile-up
pile-worm
pill-box
pillion-rider
pillow-fight
pilot: –
pilot burner
pilot engine
pilot jet
pilot lamp
pilot light
pilot officer
pilot project
pilot scheme
pince-nez
pincer-movement
pin: –
pine: –
pine cone
pine kernel
pine marten
pine needle
pine tar
pine tree
pineapple
pinewood
ping-pong

HYPHENATED AND CONJOINED WORDS

pipe: –
pipe dream
pipe fitting
pipe major
pipe organ
pipeclay
pipefish
pipeline
pitch: –
pit-coal
plain-cook
plain-spoken
plane-polarised
plane-tree
plate: –
plate glass
plate rack
play-acting
player-piano
plea-bargaining
pleasure-giving
plough-iron
plug-in
plum-cake
plus-twos/fours
pocket-handkerchief
point-blank
point-duty
point-of-sale
point-to-point
poison-ivy
poison-oak
poker-faced
police: –
police dog
police force
police inspector
police office
police officer
police state
police station
police trap
policeman
policewoman
polishing-paste

politico-economic
polka-dot
poll-tax
pop-up
portrait-gallery
post- (See Prefixes)
pot-belly
pot-roast
pot-sick
poultry-farm
pound-foolish
poverty-stricken
powdering-room
power-amp
preaching-cross
pre- (See Prefixes)
present-day
preserving-pan
press-button
press-gang
press-up
pressure-cook
pre-stressed
pre-war
price-cutting
price-earnings ratio
price-fixing
printing: –
printing paper
print-out
pro-chancellor
procurator-fiscal
profit-orientated
profit-sharing
profit-taker
pro (see Prefixes)
pro-life
proof-correcting
proof-mark
provost-marshal
psalm-book
psalm-tune
pseudo: –
pub-crawl
public-domain

public-relations
public-school
public-spirited
pudding: –
pug-faced
pull: –
pullover
pulse-rate
pump-room
punch-bag
puppet-show
puppy-dog
puppy-fat
purse-seine
purse-strings
push: –
pushover
pushrod
put: –
putting-green
putting-stone
putty-coloured
putty-faced
putty-knife
putty-powder
put-up
puzzle: –
pye-dog
pyro: –

- Q -
quarter: –
quarter past
quarter to
quarterback
quarterdeck
quarterlight
quartermaster
quartermaster-general
quartz-crystal
quasi: –
queen: –
queen bee
queen mother
queer-basher

201

A HANDBOOK FOR WRITERS OF ENGLISH

question-mark
question-master
queue-jumping
quick: –
quick fire
quick time
quicklime
quicksand
quicksilver
quickstep
quickthorn
quicktrick
quill-pen
quotation-mark

- R -
rabbet-joint
rabbit-hole
raccoon-dog
radar-gun
radial-ply tyre
radio: ‡
radio altimeter
radio amateur
radio astronomy
radio beacon
radio communication
radio compass
radio frequency
radio galaxy
radio ham
radio microphone
radio spectrum
radio star
radio station
radio telescope
radio wave
radio-actinium
radio-frequency heating
radio-gramophone
radio-isotope
radio-strontium
radio-telegraphy
radio-therapy
radio-thorium

rag
rags-to-riches
rail: –
railbus
railcard
railhead
railman
railroad
railway: –
railway station
rainbow-coloured
rain: –
rainbow trout
rainbow-chaser
rainbow-coloured
rainbow-tinted
raincoat
raindrop
rained off
rainfall
rainforest
rainmaker
rainproof
rainstorm
raintight
rainwater
rainwear
rake-off
rally-cross
rapid-fire
rat: –
razor: –
reading-book: ‡
read-only
ready: –
ready-to-wear
receiving-house: ‡
record-player
re-count
re- (See Prefixes)
refreshment-room
Registrar-General
relay-race
rent-a-crowd
rent-collector

restaurant-car
rest: –
rest stop
resting-place
Rh-negative
ribbon-development
rib: –
rice: –
ridge-pole
riding: –
riff-raff
rifle-shot
right: –
right-about face
right-mindedness
rig-out
ring: –
ring fort
ring main
ring network
ring road
ring spanner
ring up
ringbone
ringing tone
ringleader
ringmaster
ringside
ringtail
ringway
ringworm
rip-off
rip-saw
risk-money
river: –
river basin
river blindness
river novel
riverbank
rivercraft
riverfront
riverside
road: –
road hump
road manager

HYPHENATED AND CONJOINED WORDS

road pricing
road sign
roadblock
roadhouse
roadrunner
roadshow
roadside
roadway
roadworks
roast-beef
robe-maker
rock: –
rock bottom
rock cake
rock candy
rock crystal
rock drill
rock garden
rock lobster
rock melon
rock music
rock pigeon
rock plant
rock rose
rock salt
rock snake
rock tripe
rock wool
rockfish
rocksteady
rockwater
rockweed
rockwork
rocking: –
rock-'n'-roll
rocket: %
rocket-launcher
role-play
roll-call
roller: –
rolling-pin
rolling-stock
roll-neck
roll-on
roll-on-roll-off (RoRo)

roll-top
roll-up
roly-poly
romper-suit
rood: –
roof: –
roof garden
rooftop
rooftree
room: –
room service
rope: –
rope stitch
rope trick
roper-in
ropeway
ropework
ropeworks
ro-ro ship
rose: –
rose geranium
rose laurel
rose oil
rosebay
rosebowl
rosebud
rosebush
rosefinch
rosefish
rosehip
rosemary
rosewater
rosewood
rosewood-oil
rosy-cheeked
rouge-et-noir
rough: –
rough-and-ready
rough cut
rough diamond
rough grazing
rough house
rough justice
roughcast
roughneck

rough-and-ready
rough-and-tumble
round: –
round about
round dozen
round game
round off
round on
round tower
round up
roundabout
roundhand
Roundhead
roundhouse
rounding error
roundworm
route-march
rowan-berry
rowan-tree
rowing-boat
row-port
rubber-stamp
rubbish-heap
rubble-stone
rule-of-thumb
rum-punch
run-down
run-in
runner-bean
runner(s)-up
run-off
run-of-the-mill
rush-grown
rust-coloured
rustic-work
rust-proof

- S -
Sabbath-day
sabre: –
saddle-shaped
sad-eyed
safe: –
safe house
safe light

safe period	sand grouse	school book
safe seat	sand lance	school doctor
safe sex	sand leek	school house
safeguard	sand lizard	school nurse
safety: %	sand martin	school ship
safetyman	sand mole	school term
safety-catch	sand pipe	school year
safety-deposit	sand plough	school-age
sail-maker	sand sole	school-bred
sale-catalogue	sand trap	school-friend
salmon-fisher	sand wasp	school-inspector
salmon-pink	sandbag	school-leaver
saloon-keeper	sandbank	school-mate
salt: –	sandblasting	school-trained
salt bath	sandbox	scissors-and-paste
salt cake	sandboy	scissor-tooth
salt dome	sandcastle	scorched-earth policy
salt eel	sandfly	scoring-board
salt flat	sandglass	scrag-end
salt lake	sandheap	scrap-man
salt marsh	sandhill	scrap-metal merchant
salt pan	sandiver	screech-owl
salt pit	sandpaper	screen-wiper
salt spoon	sandpiper	screw-up
salt spring	sandpit	scribbling-book
saltbox	sandpump	scrubbing-brush
saltbush	sandshoe	scullery-maid
saltcellar	sandspout	scythe-stone
saltchuck	sandstone	sea: %
saltfish	sandstorm	seabank
saltpetre	sandsucker	seabed
saltwater	sandwich	seabird
saltworks	sandworm	seaboard
sand: –	sapphire-quartz	seaborne
sand bar	saucer-eyed	seacoast
sand bath	savanna-forest	seacock
sand bed	savoir-faire	seacraft
sand blow	saw-frame	seadrome
sand break	scalping-knife	seafarer
sand bunker	scarlet-bean	seafaring
sand dab	scene-of-crime (adj.)	seafolk
sand eel	school: ‡	seafood
sand flea	school age	seafowl
sand grain	school bell	seafront
sand grass	school board	seagull

204

HYPHENATED AND CONJOINED WORDS

seahawk	seal rookery	sheep station
seahog	sealed-beam	sheep tick
seahorse	searing-iron	sheep's sorrel
seahound	seat-of-the-pants	sheep's-foot
seakale	second-class: ‡	sheep's-head
sealine	second-to-none	sheepcote
seaman	secretary-general	sheepdog
seamark	seed-coat: ‡	sheepfold
seaplane	seek-no-further	sheepshank
seaport	self- (See Prefixes)	sheepshearer
seaquake	sell-by date	sheepskin
seascape	selling-price	sheeptrack
seashell	sell-out	sheet: –
seashore	semi- (See Prefixes)	sheet film
seasick	senate-house	shell: –
seaside	send-off	shell bean
seaward	Serbo-Croatian	shell mound
seawater	sergeant-at-arms	shell ornament
seaway	sergeant: –	shell out
seaweed	serpent-eater	shell parrot
seawoman	serpent-lizard: ‡	shell star
seaworm	servant-maid	shell suit
sea-bathing	session-clerk	shelldrake
sea-beaten	session-house	shellduck
sea-blue	set-aside	shellfire
sea-born	set-down	shellfish
sea-fight	se-tenant	shellproof
sea-fire	set-to	shellshock
sea-fisher	set-up	shellwork
sea-fishing	seven-a-side	ship: ‡
sea-going	seven-day	ship('s) boy
sea-green	Seventh-day Adventists	ship canal
sea-island	sewage-farm	ship carpenter
sea-like	sewing-machine	ship chandler
sea-pig	sex: –	ship fever
sea-rocket	shadow-boxing	ship letter
sea-roving	shaft-horse	ship money
sea-wolf	shaggy-dog story	ship railway
sea-worn	shape-up	ship water
sealing-wax	share-capital	ship-breaker
seal: –	share-out	ship-holder
sealskin	sharp: –	ship-of-the-line
sealwax	shaving-brush	ship-owner
seal off	she-devil	ship-rigged
seal ring	sheep: –	shock-absorber

shoot-out
shop-floor
shop-lifter
short: –
short circuit
short cut
short fuse
short hundredweight
short leg
short list
short measure
short metre
short odds
short order
short rib
short sale
short score
short sea
short selling
short sheep
short shrift
short slip
short story
short tennis
short time
short ton
short track
shortarm
shortbread
shortcake
shortcoming
shortfall
shorthand
shortstop
shortsword
shoulder-high
shove-halfpenny
shrill-voiced
shrink-resistant
sick-fallen
side-on
siege-artillery
sight-read
signal-to-noise ratio
sign-painter

simple-minded
singing-bird
single: –
single cream
single figures
single file
single house
single parent
single soldier
single tax
single transferable vote
singletree
sister-in-law
sit-in
sitter-in
sitting-room
six-footer
six-pack
sixth-form college
skating-rink
ski-jump
skin-deep
skin-diver
skipping-rope
skirting-board
sky: ‡
sky marshal
sky pilot
sky sign
sky troops
sky wave
sky-blue
sky-bred
sky-diving
sky-high
sky-jumping
sky-surfing
sky-writing
slave-driver
sloop-of-war
slop: –
slow-up
small: %
smallholder
smallpox

small-arm
small-bore
small-coal
small-hand
small-minded
small-screen
small-time
small-tooth comb
small-town
smash-and-grab
smear-dab
smelting-furnace
smelting-house
smoke: –
smoke abatement
smoke alarm
smoke detector
smoke helmet
smoke signal
smoke test
smoke tunnel
smokeboard
smokehouse
smokeproof
smokescreen
smokestack
smoketight
smooth: –
snack-bar
snail-paced
snake-oil
snake-pit
snow-hole
snuff: –
snuff mill
snuff movie
snuff spoon
snuff video
snuffbox
so-and-so
sober-minded
soda-siphon
soft-billed: ‡
Solicitor-General
solid-state

HYPHENATED AND CONJOINED WORDS

son-in-law
soul-confirming: ‡
soul mate
soul music
soul sister
sound-carrier
south-west
space-age
space-heating
spare-time
speaking-voice
spear-point
speed-cop
speed-up
sperm-whale
spin-bowler
spin-doctor
spin-dried
spin-dryer
spine-chiller
spin-off
split-level house
split-screen
spoon-feeding
spot-check
spot-welder
spray-on
spray-paint
spread-eagle
spring-clean
spring-loaded
spun-out
squadron-leader
square: %
squarehead
square-bashing
square-built
square-cut
square-dance
square-lipped
square-rigger
square-sail
square-shouldered
square-toed
staff-system

staff-tree
stage-manage
stage-struck
stamping-ground
stand-alone
standard-bearer
stand-by
stand-in
stand-off
stand-up
star: ‡
star billing
star fruit
star grass
star map
star sapphire
star shell
star sign
star trap
star wars
star wheel
star-apple
star-bright
star-crossed
star-gaze
star-shaped
star-spangled
star-studded
stark-naked
starry-eyed
state-aided
state-of-the-art
station-manager
station-master
steady-state theory
steam-driven
steam-roller
steel: –
steel band
steel drum
steel erector
steel pan
steel plate
steel wool
steelman

steelworker
step: %
stepbrother
stepchild
stepdancer
stepfather
stepladder
stepmother
stepping-stone
stepwise
step-cut
step-daughter
step-down
step-in
step-parent
step-parenting
step-sister
step-son
step-up
stiff-necked
still-life
stock-farmer
Stone-Age
stone: %
Stone(-)Age loach
stonecast
stonecutter
stonefish
stonefly
stonemason
stones-cast
stonewaller
stoneware
stonewashed
stonework
stone-age
stone-blind
stone-breaker
stone-broke
stone-cold
stone-coloured
stone-crazy
stone-dead
stone-deaf

stone-hard
stone-lily
stone-still
stop-and-search
stop-consonant
stop-loss
stop-press
straight-cut
strato-cumulus
street-level
stretcher-bearer
strip-poker
strong-minded
sub- (See Prefixes)
sugar-coated
sugar-cube
summit-level
sun: ‡
Sun Belt
sun bittern
sun bonnet
sun dance
sun deck
sun lounge
sun parlo(u)r
sun protection factor
sun room
sun visor
sun worship
sun-blind
sun-clad
sun-dried
sun-god
super- (See Prefixes)
sure-enough
sure-fire
surface-to-air
surf-bathing
swaddling-clothes
swans-down
swan: –
sweat-shirt
sweep-net
sweet: %
sweetbread

sweetcorn
sweetfish
sweetheart
sweetie-pie
sweet-and-sour
sweet-briar
sweet-savoured
sweet-scented
sweet-talk
sweet-tempered
sweet-toothed
sweet-water
swell-headed
swell-mob
swimming-pool
swing: –
swinging-post
swingtail aircraft
switch-over
sword: –
system-built

- T -
table: –
table football
table game
table knife
table licence
table linen
table manners
table money
table napkin
table salt
table tennis
table water
table wine
tablecloth
tablespoon
tablespoonful
tabletop
tableware
tag-end
tail: –
tail wind
tailback

tailboard
tailgate
taillie
tailpiece
tailpipe
tailplane
tailrace
tailspin
tailwheel
tailor-made
take-down
take-home pay
take-in
take-off
take-up
talent-spotter
talk-in
tally-system
tap-dance
tape-recording
tar-paper
task-force
tax-collector
tax-deductible
tax-exempt
tax-free
taxi-driver
tax-payer
T-bone
tea-cosy
tea-drinker
team-mate
tear-jerker
tee-off
telephone-tapping
telling-off
tender-hearted
tennis-ball
ten-pounder
ten-score
terror-struck
test-ban treaty
test-bed
test-drive
test-tube baby

HYPHENATED AND CONJOINED WORDS

tête-à-tête
text-editor
theatre-goer
thick-and-thin
thick: –
thickskin
thickset
think-tank
third-class
thought-reader
thousand-pound
thousand-year
three-colour
three-day event
three-dimensional
three: –
three-four time
three cheers
three deep
three quarters
threefold
threepence
threescore
three-line whip
thunder: –
thunderbolt
thunderclap
thundercloud
thunderflash
thunderstorm
thunderstruck
thunder-and-lightning
tick-over
tide-gauge
tie: –
tie beam
tie clip
tie line
tieback
tiepin
tight-fisted
tile-stone
timber: –
timber hitch
timberline

timberyard
time: %
timecard
timed-release
timeframe
timekeeper
timepiece
timescale
timetable
time-bill
time-consuming
time-expired
time-honoured
time-lapse
time-release
time-saving
time-share
time-thrust
title-holder
T-junction
tobacco-pouch
toffee-apple
toilet-table
toll-free
tone-deaf
tongue-and-groove
tongue-in-cheek
tongue-tied
ton-up
tooth-picker
toothpick
top: –
top brass
top dead centre
top dog
top drawer
top gear
top hat
top secret
top table
top the bill
top up
topcoat
topfull
topless

topline
topmaker
topman
topmast
topmost
topping-up
topsail
topside
topsoil
topspin
totting-up
touch-and-go
town-dweller
trade-off
traffic-lights
traffic-manager
trail-blazer
train-spotter
tram-stop
transit-trade
travel-sick
trawl-line
treasure-trove
trellis-work
trench-coat
trestle-table
trickle-charge
trigger-happy
tri-jet
trolley-car
troop-ship
trouser: –
truck: –
true: –
true blue
true time
true-love knot
trump-card
trumped-up
trumpet-flower
trunk-call
trunk-road
trust-house
T-shirt
tug-of-war

tumbler-drier
tuna-fish
tuning-fork
turbine-pump
turbo-generator
turning-point
turnpike-road
turn-screw
turn-up
turtle-soup
tusk-shell
tutti-frutti
tut-tut
'tween-deck
twelve-tone
twin: –
twin bed
twin town
twinset
two-by-four: ‡
two-dimensional
type-bar: ‡
type-body

- U -
U-bend
U-boat
U-shaped
ultra- (See Prefixes)
un-[country]
unbuilt-on
uncalled-for
unco-ordinated
under- (See Prefixes)
unheard-of
unlived-in
unslept-in
untalked-of
unthought-of
up- (See Prefixes)
up-and-coming
up-and-down
upper-bracket
upper-case
upside-down

up-till
user-friendly

- V -
vacuum-clean
vacuum-packed
vampire-bat
vaulting-horse
velvet: –
vice- (See Prefixes)
vine-leaf
violin-bow
visiting-card
V-neck
vol-au-vent
V-shape

- W -
wage-earner
wage-push inflation
wages-fund theory
wagon-lits
waist-deep
waiting: –
walkie-talkie
walking: –
walk-on
walk-over
warm-blooded
war-proof: ‡
wash-and-wear
washed-up
washing: –
water: %
waterborne
watercolour
watercourse
watercraft
watercress
watered-down
waterfall
waterfowl
waterfront
waterglass
waterhen

watering
watering: –
waterlily
waterline
waterlogged
watermark
watermelon
waterproof
watershed
waterspout
watertight
waterway
waterweed
water-bearing
water-borne
water-bound
water-breather
water-carriage
water-carrier
water-cooled
water-diviner
water-heater
water-jet
water-parting
water-repellent
water-resistant
water-ski
water-softener
water-soluble
water-spaniel
water-sprinkle
water-worn
watt-hour
wax-proofed
weak: –
weak point
weak side
weak spot
weasel-faced
weather: %
weatherboard
weathercock
weatherman
weatherproof
weather-beaten

HYPHENATED AND CONJOINED WORDS

weather-bitten
weather-bound
weather-driven
weather-wise
weather-worn
web-toed
weigh-in
weight-lifter
well: –
well and good
well and truly
well curb
well deck
well drain
well hole
well in
well met
well off
well preserved
wellbeing
wellhead
wellhouse
wellspring
wet-and-dry paper
whale-fishing
wheel-clamp
whip-round
whistle-stop
white: %
whitebait
whitebass
whitefly
whitehead
whitepot
whitesmith
whitethroat
whitewall
whiteware
whitewash
whitewing
whitewood
white-bearded
white-bellied
white-billed
white-breasted

white-collar
white-crested
white-crowned
white-eye
white-face
white-footed mouse
white-fronted
white-haired
white-handed
white-headed
white-heart
white-hot
white-listed
white-livered
white-out
white-slave traffic
white-supremacist
white-tailed
white-tie
white-water
white-winged
whole: –
whole blood
whole cloth
whole milk
whole note
whole number
whole step
whole-tone scale
wholefood
wholegrain
wholemeal
wholesale
wholestitch
wholewheat
wicket-keeper
wide: –
wide awake
wide boy
wide of the mark
wide open
wide receiver
wide screen
wideawake
widebody

widescreen
widespread
Wild-West Show
wind-chill factor
window-dressing
window-shop
windscreen-wiper
wind-up
(to) wind up
wine: %
wineberry
wineglass
winepress
wine-berry
wine-bibber
wine-coloured
wine-cooler
wine-grower
wine-stone
wine-tasting
winter-clad
woman: –
woman: ‡
woman-born
woman-hater
woman-suffrage
wonder-struck
wool: –
wool ball
wool card
wool clip
wool comb
wool mill
wool oil
wool shears
wool staple
woolfat
woolman
woolpack
woolsack
woolshed
woolsorter
woolwork
woollen mill
woollen-draper

211

woollyback
woollybutt
woolly-haired
woolly-hand crab
woolly-headed
woolly-minded
word-association: ‡
word: –
word for word
word memory
word of honour
word order
word picture
wordbreak
wordgame
wordplay
wordsmith
working: %
working-beam
working-class

working-day
working-over
world: –
world power
World Series
World War
worldscale
worldwide
world-without-end
worldly: –
worm-eaten
worn-out
worst-case
write-back: –
writing: –
wrought-iron

- X -

X-factor
X-rated

X-ray

- Y -

yacht-club
Yankee-Doodle
yard-arm
year-end
year-on-year
year-round
yellow: –
yes-man
Y-fronts
you-know-what
young-offenders institution

- Z -

Z-DNA
zero: –
zip-fastener

15
UK English vs US English

A colleague recently remarked that he did not think it important to draw attention to differences between UK or US English – 'we all understand each other'. In this TV-age he is right, of course. But many may feel this to be a one-way process. American terminology is no longer entering by the back door. Terms such as 'N.Y. lockdown' impact immediately on the screen. US spellings are now widely acceptable. There is hardly an –ise word that we cannot use –ize. We return to that. Nevertheless, it is interesting to observe some of the differences that still remain, in part if not in whole.

Use of words

There are many words used differently or which take on a different meaning in American. A few do exist only in the one language. Examples of different words in UK English and US English respectively are *flat – apartment; taxi – cab* (also used in UK English); *railway – railroad; autumn – fall*. A *high-riser* is certainly not a term in general use in UK English, but neither is *block of flats* in US English. Useful lists are given in Swan (1991), Bickerton (1998) and Etherington (1999). It should, however, be noted that most UK speakers know the meanings of the American equivalents due to high exposure to American films on TV and at the cinema.

American grammar

Sufficient examples may be found for a whole book on UK versus US English usage and grammar. There are several books covering this subject. Not least is the situation enriched by the broad variety of dialects found in each country.

There are many differences in grammar related to colloquial language. For example, the use of 'have' is more limited in US English:

I have got a seat reserved at the restaurant (UK).
I got a seat reserved at the restaurant (US).

Note the perfect participle of *get* used in US English: *She has gotten a place at university*. The term *gotten* is only found in the UK in the expression *ill-gotten gains* (plural).

Compound words

There is a tendency in US English to conjoin terms which, currently, are written as two words in English, occasionally hyphenated:

213

UK English   US English
non-profit   *nonprofit*
non-scientific   *nonscientific*
per cent   *percent* (less frequently *per cent*)
pre-exist   *preexist*
trade mark   *trademark*

Spelling, US vs. UK

Outside of the UK, many word-processors use the US word-base or lexicon. It is probably differences between UK English and US English spelling that will concern many authors. However, it may be said that many spellings using *z* in US texts are rapidly becoming acceptable in UK texts (e.g. *utilize*). Examples of different UK – US spellings include:

aluminium (UK) – *aluminum* (US); *cheque* – *check*; *grey* – *gray*; *specialities* – *specialties*; *tyre* – *tire*. The spelling '*programme*' is '*program*' in US English. In UK English, we refer to a *TV-programme*, but a computer *program*. US English uses the shorter version in both instances.

There are a number of generalisations which readily distinguish between UK and US English.

-able Nouns ending in *e* in adjective form often drop the *e* in American.

ageing (UK) – *aging* (US)
size – sizeable (UK) – *sizable* (US)
unshakeable (UK) – *unshakable* (US)

-ae The *ae* in words derived from Latin and Greek such as *gynaecology* is often written as *e* (*gynecology*) in American. Also *encyclopaedia* (UK) – *encyclopedia* (US).

-ce *ce* is normally *se* in American. Examples: *license, defense*. However, note *fence* in both countries.

-l English often doubles the *l*, but some exceptions may be encountered in both English and American:

annul – annulled (UK and US, due to the stress being on the final syllable)
cancel – cancelled (UK) – *canceled* (US)
council – councillor (UK) – *councilor* (US)
counsel – counsellor (UK and US) – *counselor* (US)
enrol – enrolment (UK and US) – *enroll – enrollment* (US)
instal – installment (UK and US) – *install – installment* (US)
rebel – rebelled (UK and US, cp. *annul - annulled*)

UK ENGLISH vs US ENGLISH

skill – skilful (UK) – *skillful* (US)
travel – traveller (UK) – *traveler* (US)
wool – woollen, (UK) – *woolen* (US)

-ge American normally drops the *e*:
judge – judgement (UK) – *judgment* (UK and US)

-ise Modern (UK) English dictionaries now give the –ise and –ize spellings for virtually every word using these affixes. A few retain –ise in both languages (concise, coastwise). Apart from 'capsize' or other words ending in -size, I have not found any more which only use –ize in both languages. Even 'standardize' and 'agonize' may employ –ise.

-ou A few English words using *ou* are found using just *o* in American:
mould (UK) – *mold* (US)

-our Virtually all English words ending in *our* use *or* in American: *behaviour – behavior; colour – color; favour – favor; harbour – harbor; honour – honor; labour – labor*

-re Many English words ending in *re* are Americanised in the US: *centre – center; metre – meter.*

-yse Retains the 's' form in UK English. The US form is mostly 'z': UK analyse – US analyze, and so forth.

There are a number of other words which differ in spelling: *plough* (UK) – *plow* (US), *manoeuvre* (UK) – *maneuver (U*S). *Whilst* is still fairly common in English, although perhaps somewhat antiquated. It does not appear in the Encarta (US) Dictionary. Finally, we may find alternative spellings in both languages: *enquire – inquire.*

A useful summary of English and American terminology is to be found in Bickerton A. (1998) *American English – English American.* Here you will be not only be enlightened about such things as a 'banknote' (UK) being called a 'bill' in the US, but whereas the English say 'loo, toilet, or WC', the Americans – in all their modesty – say 'bathroom', or more colloquially, 'john'. At public places in the US the term 'restroom' is used. It's the same in any language really!

An early draft of this book included all the variants of US and UK spellings, but as the spell-checker will pick these up, there is no requirement for a comprehensive list.

16
Nations of the World

Reports, research papers and similar, frequently require to refer to the *official* title of a country. My experience is that the official titles are not always familiar. The following is compiled on the basis of information from the Norwegian Foreign Ministry in January 2002.

A. Official names

AFGHANISTAN: The Islamic State of Afghanistan
ALBANIA: The Republic of Albania
ALGERIA: The People's Democratic Republic of Algeria
ANDORRA: The Principality of Andorra
ANGOLA: The Republic of Angola
ANTIGUA AND BARBUDA: Antigua and Barbuda
ARGENTINA: The Argentine Republic
ARMENIA: The Republic of Armenia
AUSTRALIA: Commonwealth of Australia
AUSTRIA: The Republic of Austria
AZERBAIJAN: The Azerbaijani Republic
BAHAMAS: The Commonwealth of the Bahamas
BAHRAIN: The State of Bahrain
BANGLADESH: The People's Republic of Bangladesh
BARBADOS: Barbados
BELARUS (WHITE RUSSIA): The Republic of Belarus
BELGIUM: The Kingdom of Belgium
BELIZE: Belize
BENIN: The Republic of Benin
BHUTAN: The Kingdom of Bhutan
BOLIVIA: The Republic of Bolivia
BOSNIA-HERZEGOVINA: Bosnia and Herzegovina
BOTSWANA: The Republic of Botswana
BRAZIL: The Federative Republic of Brazil
BRUNEI: Brunei
BULGARIA: The Republic of Bulgaria
BURKINA FASO: Burkina Faso. (Previously Upper Volta)
BURUNDI: The Republic of Burundi
CAMBODIA: The Kingdom of Cambodia
CAMEROON: The Republic of Cameroon
CANADA: Canada
CAPE VERDE: The Republic of Cape Verde
CENTRAL AFRICAN REPUBLIC: The Central African Republic
CHAD: The Republic of Chad
CHILE: The Republic of Chile
CHINA: The People's Republic of China
COLOMBIA: The Republic of Colombia
COMOROS (The): The Islamic Federal Republic of the Comoros
CONGO: Democratic Republic of the Congo (The). (Previously Zaïre)
CONGO: The Republic of the Congo
COSTA RICA: The Republic of Costa Rica
CROATIA: The Republic of Croatia

THE NATIONS OF THE WORLD

CUBA: The Republic of Cuba
CYPRUS: Republic of Cyprus
CZECH REPUBLIC (The): Czech Republic (The)
DENMARK: The Kingdom of Denmark
DJIBOUTI: The Republic of Djibouti
DOMINICA: The Commonwealth of Dominica
DOMINICAN REPUBLIC (The): Dominican Republic (The)
EAST TIMOR: The Democratic Republic of East Timor
ECUADOR: The Republic of Ecuador
EGYPT: The Arab Republic of Egypt
EL SALVADOR: The Republic of El Salvador
EQUATORIAL GUINEA: The Republic of Equatorial Guinea
ERITREA: The State of Eritrea
ESTONIA: The Republic of Estonia
ETHIOPIA: The Federal Democratic Republic of Ethiopia
FIJI: The Republic of Fiji
FINLAND: The Republic of Finland
FRANCE: The French Republic
GABON: The Republic of the Gambia
GEORGIA: The Republic of Georgia
GERMANY: The Federal Republic of Germany
GHANA: The Republic of Ghana
GREECE: The Hellenic Republic
GRENADA: Grenada
GUATEMALA: The Republic of Guatemala
GUINEA: The Republic of Guinea
GUINEA-BISSAU: The Republic of Guinea-Bissau
GUYANA: The Co-operative Republic of Guyana
HAITI: The Republic of Haiti
HONDURAS: The Republic of Honduras
HUNGARY: The Republic of Hungary
ICELAND: The Republic of Iceland
INDIA: The Republic of India
INDONESIA: The Republic of Indonesia
IRAN: The Islamic Republic of Iran
IRAQ: The Republic of Iraq
IRELAND: Ireland. (Occ. The Irish Republic)
ISRAEL: The State of Israel
ITALY: The Italian Republic
IVORY COAST (The): The Republic of Côte d'Ivoire
JAMAICA: Jamaica
JAPAN: Japan
JORDAN: The Hashemite Kingdom of Jordan
KAZAKHSTAN: The Republic of Kazakhstan
KENYA: The Republic of Kenya
KIRGISTAN: The Kyrghyz Republic
KIRIBATI: Republic of Kiribati
KUWAIT: The State of Kuwait
LAOS: Lao People's Democratic Republic (The)
LATVIA: The Republic of Latvia
LEBANON: The Lebanese Republic
LESOTHO: The Kingdom of Lesotho
LIBERIA: The Republic of Liberia
LIBYA: The Socialist People's Libyan Arab Republic
LIECHTENSTEIN: The Principality of Liechtenstein
LITHUANIA: The Republic of Lithuania
LUXEMBOURG: The Grand Duchy of Luxembourg
MACEDONIA: The former Yugoslav Republic of Macedonia
MADAGASCAR: The Republic of Madagascar
MALAWI: The Republic of Malawi
MALAYSIA: Malaysia
MALDIVES (The): The Republic of Maldives
MALI: The Republic of Mali
MALTA: The Republic of Malta

MARSHALL ISLANDS (The): The Republic of the Marshall Islands
MAURITANIA: The Islamic Republic of Mauritania
MAURITIUS: The Republic of Mauritius
MEXICO: The United Mexican States
MICRONESIA: the Federated States of Micronesia
MOLDOVA: Republic of Moldova (The)
MONACO: The Principality of Monaco
MONGOLIA: Mongolia
MOROCCO: The Kingdom of Morocco
MOZAMBIQUE: The Republic of Mozambique
MYANMAR: the Union of Myanmar. (Previously Burma)
NAMIBIA: The Republic of Namibia
NAURU: The Republic of Nauru
NEPAL: The Kingdom of Nepal
NETHERLANDS: The Kingdom of the Netherlands
NEW ZEALAND: New Zealand
NICARAGUA: The Republic of Nicaragua
NIGER: The Republic of the Niger
NIGERIA: The Federal Republic of Nigeria
NORTH KOREA: The Democratic People's Republic of Korea
NORWAY: The Kingdom of Norway
OMAN: The Sultanate of Oman
PAKISTAN: The Islamic Republic of Pakistan
PANAMA: The Republic of Panama
PAPUA NEW GUINEA: Papua New Guinea
PARAGUAY: The Republic of Paraguay
PERU: The Republic of Peru
PHILIPPINES (The): (The) Philippines
POLAND: The Republic of Poland
PORTUGAL: The Portuguese Republic
QATAR: The State of Qatar
RUMANIA: Romania/Rumania
RUSSIA: Russian Federation (The)
RWANDA: The Rwandese Republic
SAINT CHRISTOPHER AND NEVIS: Saint Christopher and Nevis (The Federation of)
SAINT LUCIA: Saint Lucia
SAINT VINCENT AND THE GRENADINES: Saint Vincent and the Grenadines
SAN MARINO: The Republic of San Marino
SÃO TOMÉ AND PRÍNCIPE: The Democratic Republic of Sao Tome and Principe
SAUDI ARABIA: The Kingdom of Saudi Arabia
SENEGAL: The Republic of Senegal
SEYCHELLES: The Republic of Seychelles
SIERRA LEONE: The Republic of Sierra Leone
SINGAPORE: The Republic of Singapore
SLOVAKIA: The Slovak Republic
SLOVENIA: The Republic of Slovenia
SOLOMON ISLANDS: Solomon Islands
SOMALIA: The Somali Democratic Republic
SOUTH AFRICA: The Republic of South Africa
SOUTH KOREA: Republic of Korea (The)
SPAIN: The Kingdom of Spain
SRI LANKA: The Democratic Socialist Republic of Sri Lanka
SUDAN (The): The Republic of the Sudan
SURINAME: The Republic of Suriname
SWAZILAND: The Kingdom of

Swaziland
SWEDEN: The Kingdom of Sweden
SWITZERLAND: The Swiss Confederation
SYRIA: Syrian Arab Republic (The)
TAJIKISTAN: The Republic of Tajikistan
TANZANIA: United Republic of Tanzania (The)
THAILAND: The Kingdom of Thailand
TOGO: The Republic of Togo
TONGA: The Kingdom of Tonga
TRINIDAD AND TOBAGO: The Republic of Trinidad and Tobago
TUNISIA: The Republic of Tunisia
TURKEY: The Republic of Turkey
TURKMENISTAN: Turkmenistan
TUVALU: Tuvalu
U.A.E. (The): United Arab Emirates (The)
UGANDA: The Republic of Uganda
UKRAINE: Ukraine
UNITED KINGDOM (The): United Kingdom of Great Britain and Northern Ireland (The)
URUGUAY: The Eastern Republic of Uruguay
USA: United States of America (The)
UZBEKISTAN: The Republic of Uzbekistan
VANUATU: The Republic of Vanuatu
VATICAN (The): Vatican City State (The)/Holy See
VENEZUELA: The Republic of Venezuela
VIETNAM: The Socialist Republic of Viet Nam
WEST-SAMOA: The Independent State of Western Samoa
WHITE RUSSIA: The Republic of Byelorussia
YEMEN (The): The Republic of Yemen
YUGOSLAVIA: The Federal Republic of Yugoslavia Serbia and Montenegro
ZAMBIA: The Republic of Zambia
ZIMBABWE: The Republic of Zimbabwe

B. CIS (USSR)

The former Soviet Union (USSR) comprised 15 republics and ceased to exist in 1991. Twelve Autonomous Soviet Socialist Republics (ASSR) along with Russia (Socialist Federal Soviet Republic, SFSR), subsequently agreed to form the Commonwealth of Independent States (CIS).

The abbreviation FSU is frequently used for *Former Soviet Union*. However, it should be noted that the Baltic states (Estonia, Latvia and Lithuania) did not become members of the CIS and in official documents it is not politically correct to refer to these as FSU countries. The term *Baltic states* should be used.

Membership states (Soviet Socialist Republics – SSR) in The Commonwealth of Independent States (CIS)

Armenia	Kazakhstan	Turkmenistan
Azerbaijan	Kyrgyzstan	Ukraine
Belarus	Moldova	Uzbekistan
Georgia	Tajikistan	

Autonomous Soviet Socialist Republics (ASSR) by S.S.R.

Russia (SFSR)
Bashkiriya, (Bashkir ASSR)
Buryatiya, (Buryat ASSR)
Checheno-Ingushetiya, (Chechen-Ingush ASSR)
Chuvashiya, (Chuvash ASSR)
Dagestan, (Dagestan ASSR)
Kabardino-Balkariya, (Kabardino-Balkar ASSR)
Kalmykiya, (Kalmyk ASSR)
Karelia, (Karelian ASSR)
Komi, (Komi ASSR)
Mari, (Mari ASSR)
Mordoviya, (Mordvinian ASSR)
Severnaya Ossetiya, (Severo-Ossetian ASSR)
Tatarstan, (Tatar ASSR)
Tuva, (Tuvinian ASSR)
Udmurtiya, (Udmurt ASSR)
Yakutiya, (Yakut ASSR)

Georgian SSR
Abkhaziya, (Abkhaz ASSR)
Adzhariya, (Adzhar ASSR)

Azerbaijan SSR
Nakhichevan, (Nakhichevan ASSR)

Uzbek SSR
Karakalpakiya, (Karakalpak ASSR)

C. The USA

The United States of America comprise 54 States. The two-letter postal abbreviations are also encountered in a variety circumstances and are given here.

State	Postal code	State	Postal code
Alabama	AL	Maryland	MD
Alaska	AK	Massachusetts	MA
Arizona	AZ	Michigan	MI
Arkansas	AR	Minnesota	MN
California	CA	Mississippi	MS
Colorado	CO	Missouri	MO
Connecticut	CT	Montana	MT
Delaware	DE	Nebraska	NE
District of Columbia	DC	Nevada	NV
Florida	FL	New Hampshire	NH
Georgia	GA	New Jersey	NJ
Guam	GU	New Mexico	NM
Hawaii	HI	New York	NY
Idaho	ID	North Carolina	NC
Illinois	IL	North Dakota	ND
Indiana	IN	Ohio	OH
Iowa	IA	Oklahoma	OK
Kansas	KS	Oregon	OR
Kentucky	KY	Pennsylvania	PA
Louisiana	LA	Puerto Rico	PR
Maine	ME	Rhode Island	RI

THE NATIONS OF THE WORLD

State	Postal code	State	Postal code
South Carolina	SC	Virgin Islands	VI
South Dakota	SD	Virginia	VA
Tennessee	TN	Washington	WA
Texas	TX	West Virginia	WV
Utah	UT	Wisconsin	WI
Vermont	VT	Wyoming	WY

D. Other

A distinction is made between **Great Britain** or **Britain** (England, Scotland and Wales) and **The United Kingdom** (England, Scotland, Wales and Northern Ireland). However, the latter is also occasionally referred to as Great Britain. The **British Isles** includes the whole of Ireland (Northern Ireland and Eire).

The **Scandinavian peninsula** comprises Norway and Sweden; **Scandinavia** usually refers to Norway, Sweden and Denmark, but will frequently include Finland, Iceland and occasionally The Færoe islands. The **Nordic countries** (occasionally referred to as Norden) comprise Norway, Sweden, Denmark, Finland and Iceland are closely linked through the Nordic Council of Ministers.

17
Foreign Terms and Phrases

Omne ignotum pro magnifico[1]

Latin was compulsory in grammar schools in England well into the 1950s. By the school it was considered necessary as a sign of quality, standing and education: by the average pupil it was considered a bloody waste of time. Pupil power seems to have been exerted in the late 1960s and early 1970s and Latin largely became a 'free choice' subject. Not so French!
Many dictionaries, especially of the pre-war era, normally contained a supplement with Latin terms, although I am not aware of any such general dictionary today containing these gems of wisdom. It may scarcely be denied that the occasional foreign term adds a little colour to the text even though we have a sneaking feeling that the author was not quite as familiar with French as he would have us believe. Do not let your manuscript become tainted with use and over-use of foreign terms – it may all too soon be misunderstood as being *langage des halles*.[2]

Foreign terms and phrases are *normally placed in italics* except where these have now become standard usage not (et al., ad infinitum, etc.). The following includes a variety of expressions, including many Latin terms encountered in law.[3]

a posteriori	by induction; from the effect to the cause *(Lat.)*
a priori	by deduction; from the cause to the effect *(Lat.)*
à couvert	under cover *(Fr.)*
à la mode	according to fashion *(Fr.)*
à point	precisely to the point *(Fr.)*
à tout prix	at any price *(Fr.)*
à votre santé	to your health *(Fr.)*
ab initio	from the beginning *(Lat.)*
ad infinitum	to infinity *(Lat.)*
ad literum	to the letter *(Lat.)*
ad referendum	for further consideration *(Lat.)*
anno domini	in the year of our Lord *(Lat.)*
argumentum ad judicium	an appeal to common sense *(Lat.)*
bon vivant	one who lives well *(Fr.)*

---

1 That which is unknown is thought to be magnificent!
2 Language of the fish market!
3 A comprehensive overview of Latin legal terms is to be found in *Osborn's Concise Dictionary of Law*, Sweet and Maxwell, London.

FOREIGN TERMS AND PHRASES

bona fide	in good faith *(Lat.)*
c'est à dire	that is to say *(Fr.)*
caveat emptor	let the buyer beware *(Lat.)*
certiorari	order a record from a lower court for presentation in a higher court *(Lat.)*
circa	about *(Lat.)*
cogito, ergo sum	I think, therefore I am *(Lat.)*
comme il faut	as it should be *(Fr.)*
compos mentis	of sane mind *(Lat.)*
conseil d'état	Privy council *(Fr.)*
coram	in the presence of *(Lat.)*
corpus delecti	the material evidence of the offence *(Lat.)*
coup de grace	the finishing stroke *(Fr.)*
Das Beste ist gut genug	The best is good enough *(Ger.)*
de facto	in fact *(Lat.)*
de jure	by right *(Lat.)*
de rigeur	by custom *(Fr.)*
Dei gratia	by the grace of God *(Lat.)*
démenti	official denial *(Fr.)*
dies iræ	Day of Judgement *(Lat.)*
Dieu et mon droit	God and my right *(Fr.)*
dramatis personæ	characters represented *(Lat.)*
editio princeps	original edition *(Lat.)*
ex æquo	by right *(Lat.)*
ex curia	out of court *(Lat.)*
ex officio	by virtue of his office; as his position allows *(Lat.)*
ex post facto	after the event *(Lat.)*
exempli gratia	by way of example *(Lat.)*
fait accompli	something completed *(Fr.)*
faux pas	a false step/wrong move *(Fr.)*
genes de guerre	soldiers *(Fr.)*
gens d'église	people of the church *(Fr.)*
gens de condition	people of rank *(Fr.)*
gens de lettres	people of letters/literary people *(Fr.)*
habeas corpus	a writ to oppose detention of a person *(Lat.)*
hoc loco	in this place *(Lat.)*
hors de saison	out of season *(Fr.)*
ibidem	in the same place *(Lat.)*
id est	that is *(Lat.)*
impasse	an insoluble problem *(Fr.)*
imprimatur	let it be printed *(Lat.)*
in curia	in the court *(Lat.)*
in extenso	in its entirety *(Lat.)*
in loco parentis	in the place of a parent *(Lat.)*

in memoriam	in memory of *(Lat.)*
in nominee	in the name of *(Lat.)*
in puris naturalibus	stark naked *(Lat.)*
in reum natura	in the nature of things *(Lat.)*
in situ	in its original situation *(Lat.)*
in statu quo	in its original state *(Lat.)*
in toto	entirely *(Lat.)*
inter alia	among other matters *(Lat.)*
ipso facto	by the fact itself *(Lat.)*
ipso jure	by the law itself *(Lat.)*
jour de fête	festival *(Fr.)*
Juge de paix	Justice of the peace *(Fr.)*
jure divino	by divine law *(Lat.)*
jure humano	by human law *(Lat.)*
lapsus calami	a slip of the pen *(Lat.)*
lapsus linguæ	a slip of the tongue *(Lat.)*
lapsus memoriæ	a slip of the memory *(Lat.)*
Le roi et l'état	The King and The State *(Fr.)*
lex non scripta	the common law *(Lat.)*
lex terræ	the law of the land *(Lat.)*
loco citato	in the place quoted *(Lat.)*
mal à propos	ill-timed *(Fr.)*
mala fide	in bad faith *(Lat.)*
manu propria	with one's own hand *(Lat.)*
me judice	as I judge it *(Lat.)*
meo periculo	at my own risk *(Lat.)*
modo et forma	in manner and form *(Lat.)*
modo præscripto	in the manner prescribed *(Lat.)*
modus operandi	the manner of working *(Lat.)*
mon ami	my friend *(Fr.)*
Mon Dieu!	My God! *(Fr.)*
more suo	after his own manner *(Lat.)*
mos pro lege	custom for law *(Lat.)*
mot à mot	word for word *(Fr.)*
mot juste	the correct word *(Fr.)*
mots d'usage	common expressions *(Fr.)*
né *(m.)*, née *(fem.)*	born *(Lat.)*
necessitas non habat legem	necessity has no law *(Lat.)*
Nicht wahr?	Is that not so? *(Ger.)*
nihil ad rem	nothing to the purpose *(Lat.)*
nom du guerre	an assumed name *(Fr.)*
non compos	mentis of unsound mind *(Lat.)*
non sequitur	it does not follow *(Lat.)*
nota bene	mark well *(Lat.)*
nouveau riche	the new rich *(Fr.)*

FOREIGN TERMS AND PHRASES

nulli secundus	second to none *(Lat.)*
nunc aut nunquam	now or never *(Lat.)*
omnia vincit amor	love conquers all *(Lat.)*
omnia vincit labor	work conquers all *(Lat.)*
onus probandi	the weight of the proof *(Lat.)*
pace tua	by your leave *(Lat.)*
pacta conventa	on the agreed terms *(Lat.)*
pas dans le train	not up to date *(Fr.)*
passe-partout	a master key *(Fr.)*
passez-moi ce mot-là	excuse the expression *(Fr.)*
pax vobiscum	peace be with you *(Lat.)*
peccavi	I acknowledge the error *(Lat.)*
pendent lite	pending the litigation *(Lat.)*
per contra	on the contrary *(Lat.)*
per diem	by the day *(Lat.)*
per se	by itself *(Lat.)*
pièce bien faite	something well done *(Fr.)*
pièce de résistance	(Prev. used for food – the main joint at meals) *(Fr.)*
pleno jure	by full authority *(Lat.)*
pluries	on several occasions *(Lat.)*
poco à poco	little by little *(It.)*
post meridian	after noon *(Lat.)*
post mortem	after death *(Lat.)*
pour ainsi dire	so to say *(Fr.)*
præmontius, præmunitus	forewarned, forearmed *(Lat.)*
primus inter pares	first among equals *(Lat.)*
pro et con	for and against *(Lat.)*
pro patria	for our country *(Lat.)*
pro rata	at the same rate; in proportion *(Lat.)*
pro tanto	as far as it goes *(Lat.)*
pro tempore	for the time being *(Lat.)*
probatum est	thus proved *(Lat.)*
projet de loi	a legislative bill *(Fr.)*
proximo	next month *(Lat.)*
pur et simple	purely and simply *(Fr.)*
quand même	all the same *(Fr.)*
quantum sufficit	as much as is required *(Lat.)*
quantum volueris	as much as you please *(Lat.)*
quo warranto?	by what warrant (legal writ)? *(Lat.)*
quoad hoc	to this extent *(Lat.)*
quondam	former *(Lat.)*
raison d'état	by reason of state *(Fr.)*
raison d'être	by reason of being *(Fr.)*
regium donum	a royal grant/decree *(Lat.)*

rente viagère	an annuity *(Fr.)*
repetatur	let it be repeated *(Lat.)*
répondez, s'il vous plait	Please reply (RSVP or R.S.V.P.) *(Fr.)*
res judicata	the case is already determined *(Lat.)*
ruse de guerre	a strategem *(Fr.)*
s'il vois plait	if you please *(Fr.)*
salus populi suprema est lex	the supreme law is the welfare of the people *(Lat.)*
salvo jure	saving the right *(Lat.)*
salvo pudore	without offence to modesty *(Lat.)*
sang-froid	indifference *(Lat.)*
savoir faire	with tact *(Fr.)*
savoir vivre	with good manners *(Fr.)*
secunda artum	according to the rule *(Lat.)*
seriatim	in a series *(Lat.)*
sic passim	so everywhere *(Lat.)*
simel et simul	once and at the same time *(Lat.)*
sine die	without a day being appointed/indefinitely *(Lat.)*
sine quâ non	that which is indispensable *(Lat.)*
soit dit entre nous	between ourselves *(Fr.)*
sous tous les rapports	in all respects *(Fr.)*
stet	let it stand *(Lat.)*
sub judice	under consideration *(Lat.)*
sub pœna	under a penalty *(Lat.)*
sub silentio	in silence *(Lat.)*
sufficit	it is enough *(Lat.)*
sumendus	to be taken *(Lat.)*
suppressio veri	suppression of truth *(Lat.)*
talis pater, qualis filius	like father, like son *(Lat.)*
tant bien que mal	it is the same to us *(Fr.)*
tant mieux	so much the better *(Fr.)*
tant pis	so much the worse *(Fr.)*
telle vie, telle fin	as they live, so they die *(Fr.)*
terminus ad quem	the goal *(Lat.)*
tête-à-tête	confidential conversation *(Fr.)*
tiers Ètat	The Third Estate *(Fr.)*
totidem verbis	in so many words *(Lat.)*
toties quoties	as often as *(Lat.)*
tour-à-fait	altogether; quite *(Fr.)*
tout bien ou rien	all or nothing *(Fr.)*
tout ensemble	the general effect *(Fr.)*
touts frais faits	all costs paid *(Fr.)*
tutte quanti	et cetera *(It.)*
ubi sutra	where above mentioned *(Lat.)*

una vôce	unanimously; with one voice *(Lat.)*
unum et idem	one and the same *(Lat.)*
ut infra	as below *(Lat.)*
ut supra	as above stated *(Lat.)*
vaille que valle	at all events *(Fr.)*
valiorum notae	notes of various authors *(Lat.)*
variæ lections	various readings *(Lat.)*
vendre en gros et en detail	wholesaler and retailer *(Fr.)*
verba volant, scripta manent	words fly, the written word remains *(Lat.)*
via media	the middle course *(Lat.)*
vice	in place of *(Lat.)*
vide ut supra	see preceeding statement *(Lat.)*
vis-à-vis	opposite; as opposed to *(Fr.)*
voilà tout	that's all *(Fr.)*
vulgo	popularly *(Lat.)*
Wie gewonnen, so zerrinnen	Easy come, easy go *(Ger.)*
Zumbeispiel	For example *(Ger.)*

Quod scripsi, scripsi[4]

---

4 What I have written, I have written.

18
Proof Correction

In 1976, The British Standards Institute published guidelines for *Copy preparation and proof correction* (BS 5261:2:1976). This has been widely reproduced and may be found for example, in *Writers' & Artists' Yearbook*. This was compiled at a time when typesetting was undertaken by the printer and thorough checking of the proof was required by the author. Text requiring to be corrected had to be indicated by marks in both the text and in the margin. This 'double' indication was necessary as the printed proof was frequently single-spaced using a small font. However, the apparent complication of the proof-marks required often resulted in further confusion and many authors did not correctly indicate the changes that the typesetter was required to make.

Today, the PC enables the author to undertake his many of his own corrections. Even when a colleague is asked to 'glance through this when you get a moment', the 'comments' feature on the word-processor seems to be the most productive method of correction. There is no longer a need to be fully acquainted with all the BSI proofing marks.

Nevertheless, there are times when proofing has to be undertaken manually. The following indicates the most common corrections required. These follow BSI standards except that I only use the marginal mark where absolutely essential.

A. Proof marks

General

1. Leave text unchanged. Grammar satisfactory; speling a disaster! ✓
2. The reported date of his death in 1963 needs to be checked. ?

Deletion, insertion and substitution

Note: The oblique dash / is used to indicate deletion of alphanumeric characters and punctuation signs. A line with vertical tails (to give an extended 'H') is placed through text to be deleted. An 'insert' sign (similar to the Greek 8) is used for characters of text to be inserted. The oblique dash is also used in the marginal marks to show the end of a correction mark. This is particularly important where two or more such marks shown in the same margin.

Where there is insufficient space to enter the actual correction, this may be shown in the margin. If there are two such corrections on a single line, these may be given in the left and right margins respectively. Where shown in the same margin, separate the marks with the oblique dash [/].

PROOF CORRECTION

3. Insert the missing character. If text has to be inserted, reference should be made as follows and the missing text written at the bottom of the page for example. Delete a character and close up. Delete several characters or text.
4. Substitute a character or substitute several words.
5. Change this word to *italics*. Use capitals for the uk. Capital first letter in <u>united</u> <u>nations</u>, rest lower case.
6. Heading. The heading should be changed bold type. It could be bold type italics. (This text) should not be in italics.
7. Change the (CAPITAL) letters to lower case.
8. The period is occasionally forgotten Note that periods and colons to be inserted or removed are ringed commas and semi-colons are not!
9. Here, we substitute the period with a colon/ Occasionally desirable with short associated sentences.
10. It may be necessary to insert 'single' or "double" quotation marks. Marginal marks (example) if necessary.
11. An oblique dash between hishers has been omitted.
12. Semi colon needs a hyphen!

Positioning and spacing

13. Paragraphing is important.
    The run on is indicated by the preceding line. The start of a new paragraph is indicated accordingly.
14. Words transposed are using this mark.
15. This line to be indented.
16. This indented line should be left flush.
17. Close up unnecessary spaces especially after a period. (Only a single space required.) A space maybe required elsewhere.
18. Reduce space between paragraph using this mark.
19. This is a new paragraph. The following sign is used to mark an increases space between paragraphs.
20. This is the new paragraph.

A HANDBOOK FOR WRITERS OF ENGLISH

Other proofing marks

There are almost sixty different proofing marks recommended by BSI. There are another thirty marks given in part 3 of this BSI publication, published separately, which relate to mathematical proof correction (BS 5261:3:1989). This is for the specialist and not covered here.

In any proofing, the marks should be clear. Of course, we nearly always find that when a proof is returned from the printer some corrections still have to be made. In that case you are advised to follow the BSI standards and the corrections clearly shown in the margins.

19
Internet Addresses

A. International addresses

The following list shows the major national addresses on the Internet.

address	country	address	country
.at	Austria	.kr	South Korea
.au	Australia	.li	Liechtenstein
.ba	Bosnia, Herz.	.lt	Lithuania
.be	Belgium	.lu	Luxembourg
.bg	Bulgaria	.lv	Latvia
.ca	Canada	.ly	Lybia
.cc	Cocos Islands	.ma	Morocco
.cn	China	.mc	Monaco
.cs	Czechoslovakia	.mt	Malta
.cy	Cyprus	.mx	Mexico
.cz	Czech Republic	.my	Malaysia
.de	Germany	.nl	Netherlands
.dk	Denmark	.no	Norway
.ee	Estonia	.nz	New Zealand
.eg	Egypt	.ph	Philippines
.es	Spain	.pk	Pakistan
.fi	Finland	.pl	Poland
.fo	Faeroe Islands	.pt	Portugal
.fr	France	.py	Paraguay
.gb	Great Britain	.ro	Romania
.gl	Greenland	.ru	Russian Federation
.gr	Greece	.sa	Saudi Arabia
.hk	Hong Kong	.se	Sweden
.hr	Croatia	.sg	Singapore
.hu	Hungary	.si	Slovenia
.ie	Ireland	.sk	Slovak Republic
.il	Israel	.tn	Tunisia
.in	India	.tw	Taiwan
.iq	Iraq	.ua	Ukraine
.ir	Iran	.uk	United Kingdom
.is	Iceland	.us	USA
.it	Italy	.ve	Venezuela
.jm	Jamaica	.vg	U.S. Virgin Islands
.jo	Jordan	.vi	British Virgin Islands
.jp	Japan		

International

.co.uk
.com
.edu
.gov
.net
.org

B. Hyperlinks

When writing an email address or the name of a website (www.....), it is probable that the hyperlink will be automatically activated as the default setting. Frequently this means that the address will appear in blue and underlined, e.g. john@jgtaylor.com What this means is that when the cursor is placed on the address, it changes such that by clicking on the address, your PC will automatically connect to the address or website, assuming you are connected to the Internet. You may not want this. Under 'Tools' in your word-processor you will find 'Hyperlink' and where you can activate/ deactivate the link.

C. Information on the Internet

General information

Unquestionably, the Internet is an unrivalled source of information. When we search for information a search engine checks out sources of information. You may have noticed that a search on Yahoo, for example, will provide different results to another site. There are a number of search engines which link to others, thus broadening the field. For research purposes, **www.twics.com/takakuwa/search/** will enable you to locate the major search engines in most countries. The Internet is constantly changing, but try these for information:

www.askjeeves.com; **www.just35.com**; **www.infoplease.com**; **www.dogpile.com**, and one of the best, **www.goggle.com** (not to be confused with google.com).

Dictionaries and glossaries

You no longer need to purchase an electronic dictionary. Try **www.xrefer.com** As their site says, '*xrefer contains encyclopedias, dictionaries, thesauri & books of quotations from the world's leading publishers. All cross-referenced, all in one place – providing you with a single source for reliable factual information.*' I have found this to be indispensable. Another superb site: **www.yourdictionary.com** with 1800 dictionaries in 230 languages. Here are dozens of lists of acronyms, synonyms and so forth. This site is real fun – and educational! You can supplement this via a link to **www.britannica.com** where you may not only utilise the Merriam-Webster Dictionary and Thesaurus, but gain access to millions of articles. Another link goes to **www foreignword.com** where you can translate between several foreign languages. This site also has links to many other useful sites for people working with languages and translators. Of course, you do not need to use the links – just go direct to your chosen www site. You may find that you want to register these under 'Favourites'.

An excellent site for new words: **www.worldwidewords.org** – and asking about them is **www.quinion.com/words** Michael Quinion is an authority. His site will lead you to many others (use *Other words sites*), one of which is exceptionally useful – **www.zilker.net**, covering 1700 glossaries listed by subject and compiled by Frank Dietz. Almost 1000 of these are in English (the others are in German). Here, you will find Education Measurement Terms, London Slang (and Rhyming slang), Telecom Terms, Cargo Acronyms, Rubber Glossary, Cricket Dictionary and a whole range of more 'standard' dictionaries, lists and glossaries.

Other useful sites

Grammar is well covered under **www.englishplus.com** and then link to the 'grammar slammar'.

What is that acronym? Try **www.acronymfinder.com**

If you need to include a map in your article look at **www.expedia.com** Select 'Site Map', then 'Maps', and 'Find a Map'.

20
References

I must admit to being something of a bibliophile regarding dictionaries. There are a number of superb dictionaries published in the 1920s and 1930s and which may be purchased for a song, often at flea markets or boot sales! One of these, The *King's English Dictionary,* British Books Limited, 1927, is inscribed by my grandmother to her daughter (my mother): *'To Read, mark, learn, and inwardly digest.'*

Another gem is *Nuttall's Standard Dictionary of the English Language. Based upon the Labours of the most Eminent Lexicographers.* Warne & Co. 1929. This contains the following definition:

> GAY: in bright spirits; lively; mirthful; showy; devoted to pleasure; inflamed or merry with liquor.

Times have changed! (– or perhaps not!!). Nevertheless, these publications frequently contain appendixes of material and information seldom encountered. The latter publication contains, among other things:

- Phrases, Proverbs, Maxims, Quotations and Mottoes from the Latin and other languages
- Greek, Latin and Geographical Names and their pronunciation
- Etymology of place names
- Group terms
- Esperanto
- Forms of address
- Traffic signs!

The first-mentioned dictionary contains similar material plus:

- Pseudonyms and Pen-Names. (Did you know that Maxim Gorki's real name was Alexei Maximovitch Pyeshkov?)
- Glossary of terms used in Aviation and Motoring (empennage = tail plane)
- Glossary of Scottish words and phrases
- Not least – an atlas, in full colour.

The following comprises more modern dictionaries and handbooks. I have added comments where appropriate in order to inform the more curious reader of the nature of certain publications. Further, I have listed those electronic dictionaries and thesauri available on the market. These are becoming virtually indispensable. At least selecting one of these will ensure a degree of consistency in spelling, hyphenation, etc.

REFERENCES

A. Dictionaries and handbooks

[*A number of major dictionaries which have been consulted are not included in this list.*]

Aitchison, James (1994), *The Cassell Guide to Written English*. London: Cassell.
Amis, Kingsley (1997), *The King's English. A Guide to Modern Usage*. London: HarperCollins. [Excellent reading, entertaining.]
Baugh, Sue L. (1991), *Essentials of English Grammar*. London: Guild Publishing.
Better Word Power. Oxford: OUP.
Bickerton, Anthea (1998), *American English – English American*. London: Abson Books.
Bowden, John (1997), *Writing a Report*. Oxford: How To Books.
Burt, Angela (2000), *The A to Z of Correct English*. Oxford: How To Books.
Burchfield, R.W. (ed.), *New Fowler's Modern English Usage*. Oxford, OUP.
Butcher J. (1992), *Copy-Editing for Editors, Authors and Publishers*. Cambridge: CUP.
Carey, G. V. (1976), *Mind the Stop. A Brief Guide to Punctuation with a Note on Proof-correction*. Harmandsworth: Penguin. [First published 1939. Very enjoyable reading.]
Chalker, S., and Weiner, E. (1994), *The Oxford Dictionary of English Grammar*. London: BCA.
Chambers Good punctuation Guide (1996). Edinburgh: Chambers.
Chambers Dictionary of Spelling and Word Division (1995). Edinburgh: Chambers.
Collins Cobuild English Guides, 1. Prepositions (1994). London: HarperCollins.
Collins English Spelling Dictionary (1993), London: HarperCollins. [Hyphenation guide.]
Concise Family Medical Handbook (1981), London: HarperCollins.
Cutts, Martin (1995), *The Plain English Guide*. Oxford: OUP.
Delahunty A., Weiner E.S. (1995), *The Oxford Guide to English Usage*. Oxford: OUP.
Devlin. J. A. (1961), *Dictionary of Synonyms and Antonyms*. New York: Popular Library Inc.
Dictionary of English Usage (1995). London: Brockhampton Press.
Dictionary of Philosophy (1979). London: Pan Books.
Encarta World English Dictionary (2000). Microsoft. [Also CD version. Probably the most comprehensive US dictionary with excellent computer dictionary.]
English Dictionary (1969). London: Penguin.
Etherington, Mike (1999), *The Best of British. The American's Guide to Speaking English*. Basingstoke: Effingpot Productions Ltd.
Field, M. (2000), *Improving Your Spelling*. Oxford: How To Books.

Field, M. (2000), *Polish up your Punctuation and Grammar*. Oxford: How To Books.
Fowler, H.W. (1994), *A Dictionary of Modern English Usage*. London: Wordsworth.
Grubb, P. and Reah, D. (1998), *Writing a Textbook*. Oxford: How To Books.
Gould, William (1991), *Harrap's English Punctuation and Hyphenation*. London: Harrap.
Greenbaum, S. (2000), *The Oxford Reference Grammar*. Oxford: OUP.
Hart's Rules for Compositors and Readers at the University Press, Oxford (1893) [39th edn 2000.] Oxford: OUP.
Hilton C., Hyder, M. (1992), *Getting to Grips with Punctuation and Grammar*. London: BPP (Letts Educational) Ltd.
King, Graham (2000), *Punctuation*. Glasgow: HarperCollins.
Kipfer, Barbara Ann (1993), *21st Century Manual of Style*. New York: Philip Lief Group.
Knowles E. & Elliot J. (1998), *The Oxford Dictionary of New Words*. Oxford: OUP.
Lang, L. B. (1994), *Letter Writing*. (Collins Pocket Reference). Glasgow: HarperCollins.
Langenscheidt's Pocket Merriam-Webster. Guide to Punctuation (1995). Mass USA: Merriam-Webster.
Lewis, N. (ed.) (1961), *Roget's Thesaurus in Dictionary Form*. New York: Berkeley Publ. Corp.
Longman Language Activator (1993). London: Longman.
Oxford Dictionary of Abbreviations (1998). Oxford: OUP.
Page, G. Terry (1991), *The Book of Spelling Rules*. Edinburgh: Harrap.
Partridge, Eric (1973), *Usage and Abusage. A Guide to Good English*. Harmandsworth: Penguin.
Partridge, Eric (1953), *You have a point there*. London: Routledge. [The ultimate in punctuation, somewhat overwhelming.]
Penguin Dictionary of [Various titles: *Computers, Economics, English idioms, Literary terms and Literary theory, Psychology*. Several good reference books are published by Penguin.
Phythian, B. A. (1985), *Correct English* ('Teach Yourself Series'). London: Hodder & Stoughton.
Phythian, B. A. (1980), *English Grammar* ('Teach Yourself Series'). London: Hodder & Stoughton.
Ritter, R. M. (ed.) (2000), *The Oxford Dictionary for Writers and Editors*. Oxford: OUP. [Superb handbook and reference.]
Roget's International Thesaurus (1963), London: Collins. [There are many versions of this standard reference in different forms, such as the Penguin version. This is the classic version. If buying a 'dictionary version', check to see if antonyms are referred to.]
Roget's Thesaurus (1953). Harmandsworth: Penguin.

REFERENCES

Rutherford, L., Bone, S. (eds) (1996), *Osborn's Concise Law Dictionary*. London: Sweet & Maxwell. 8th edn.
Speake, Jennifer (ed.) (2000), *The Oxford Dictionary of Foreign Words and Phrases*. Oxford: OUP.
Swan, Michael (1991), *Practical English Usage*. Oxford: OUP.
Swan, Michael (1992), *Oxford Pocket Basic English Usage*. Oxford: OUP.
The Compete handy reference: Dictionary, Thesaurus, Guide to English Usage (1997). London: Chancellor Press.
The Concise Oxford Dictionary (1951). Oxford: Clarendon Press.
The Economist Style Guide (2000). London: Profile Books Ltd.
The New American Roget's College Thesaurus in Dictionary Form (1958). New York: Signet Books. [Certainly republished since, but an excellent version.]
The New Shorter Oxford English Dictionary (1993). Oxford: OUP. [2 vols.]. [The ultimate in dictionaries, but many of the latest words missing. See below.]
The Oxford Dictionary of New Words (1998). Oxford: OUP. [Excellent supplement to the above.]
The Oxford Dictionary for Writers and Editors (2000). Oxford: OUP.
The Oxford Dictionary of English Grammar (1993). Oxford: OUP.
The Oxford Reverse Dictionary (1999). Oxford: OUP. [Essentially a thesaurus, but where a variety of associated phrases and terms are given.]
The Universal Dictionary of the English language (1988). London: Wordsworth.
Todd, L. (1995), *The Cassell Guide to Punctuation*. London: Cassell.
Trask, R. L. (2000), *The Penguin Dictionary of English Grammar*. Harmandsworth: Penguin Books.
Trask, R. L. (1997), *The Penguin Guide to Punctuation*. Harmandsworth: Penguin Books.
Wiener, E. S. C. and Delahunty, A. (1994). *The Oxford Guide to English Usage*. London: BCA.
Wood, F. T., Flavell, R. H., and Flavell, L. M. (1981). *The Macmillan Dictionary of Current English Usage*. London: Macmillan.
Writers' & Artists' Yearbook. London: A&C Black. [Annually.]
Youngson, Robert M., (1992), *Collins Dictionary of Medicine*. Glasgow: HarperCollins. [Nearly all the medical words not found in the spell-checker. The Oxford publication is very similar.]

[As this book does not cover grammar, only a few basic references are included. Use the power search on amazon.com and search for authors Quirk R., and Greenbaum S. for some of the major grammar texts.]

B. Electronic dictionaries

Electronic media are essential for professional writers. I use the following.

Except where stated these are CD-ROM. Some of these were free with PC magazines. Keep your eyes open!

Cambridge International Dictionary of English on CD-ROM. [Comprehensive with UK and US pronunciation. Good advanced-search function, but I had problems in installing it on one PC.]

Cassell's Concise Dictionary and Thesaurus. London, Cassell. [Unique feature that one can use definition key-words to find a single word: e.g. 'skull + brain' gave 7 matches of which 'phrenology' was the one I was looking for.]

Chambers Dictionary [UK] (1997), Larousse plc. [Comprehensive, user-friendly.]

CLUE [International two-way dictionaries on diskettes. Comprehensive but basic.]

Collins Cobuild Lexicon (2001). UK, HarperCollins (Lingea Lexicon). [Replaces the three following items.]

Collins Cobuild on CD-ROM. (1994), UK, Harper-Collins. [Dictionary, Thesaurus, Word bank, phrases etc.]

Collins Cobuild. English Collocations (1994), UK, Harper-Collins. [2.6 million examples of word usage.]

Collins Electronic Dictionary and Thesaurus. (1995), UK, Harper-Collins. [Excellent, also many useful abbreviations.]

Encarta World English Dictionary, Thesaurus and Computer Dictionary. Microsoft.

Euterpe. (1998), Stuttgart, TRADOS GmbH. [European Parliament Data Base.]

Harrap's Multilingual Dictionary. [Superb 12-language e-dictionary including all major European languages plus Chinese and Japanese! Now 'out-of-print' but can be obtained at PC markets for a song! I paid $5.]

IBM World Book [includes IBM World Book Dictionary.]

Longman Dictionary of Contemporary English, London, Pearson Education Ltd.

Merriam-Webster Dictionary [US] (1994-5), US, Zane Publishing. [US. Vers. 2.11]

New Oxford English Dictionary (2000), UK, Oxford University Press.

Oxford English Dictionary on CD ROM. (1995), UK, Oxford University Press. [Probably the most expensive CD you will ever buy, but a wealth of material – 600,000 words.]

Oxford Thesaurus. (1993), UK, Oxford University Press. [Comprehensive.]

Penguin Hutchinson Reference Library. [Includes The Longman Dictionary of English Language.]

Random House Electronic Dictionary. [US] (1995), NY, Random House.

Stedman's/25 Medical Word List. WordPerfect UK. [Diskettes. Contains WordPerfect 5.2 Word list together with several thousand medical terms. Windows version available.]

The American Heritage Talking Dictionary. [Very comprehensive.]

Webster's New Word Dictionary and Thesaurus. [Excellent, US.]

C. Encyclopædia

Who does not have need of an encyclopædia? I manage with the following CD ROMS. If you need a map, then check those in the encyclopædia. The quality varies and may be better than some CD atlases.

Encyclopædia Britannica. [The best! Can be expensive.[1]]
IBM World Book (and Encyclopaedia). [Previous year's edition often available in January/February as 'give-away' in PC journals.][2]
Microsoft Encarta Encyclopedia. [My version is '98, but later available. See note above.]
Websters World Encyclopedia. [Also available in PC journals. See note above.]

Other encyclopædia are often available as CD ROM 'give-ways' in PC magazines. Keep your eyes open!

D. Statistics

Many authors require to quote some statistical facts, but it is amazing how many do not know what the *standard deviation* is, for example. If you really are at the basic level (admit it!), then the following is ideal:

Gwilliam, Peter (1988). *Basic Statistic* (Penguin 'Self-starter' series). Harmandsworth: Penguin.

If you require an absolute basic understanding of statistical formulae, how to understand, interpret and even use them, then one of the following:

Porkess, Roger (1988). *Dictionary of Statistics.* Harmandsworth: Penguin. [Not just a dictionary. Many examples will explain how the standard deviation, regression coefficient. etc., are calculated.]
Robson, Colin (1983). *Experiment, Design and Statistics in Psychology.* Harmandsworth: Penguin. [Don't worry about the title, it applies to any discipline.]
Swinscow, T. D. V. (1983). *Statistics at Square One.* London: British Medical Association. [Originally a series of lectures – for doctors I assume, but ideal for anyone.]
Rowntree, Derek (1981). *Statistics without tears. Harmandsworth:* Penguin. [A good introduction.]
Spiegel, Murray R. (1972). *Statistics* (Schaum's Outline Series). New York: Mcgraw-Hill. [Excellent, comprehensive, many examples, inexpensive.]

---

1   Latest version available for $50 from Global Microsystems Inc. on glomicro@aol.com
2   I have acquired several through *PC Advisor* – available in many European countries.

E. General references

There is an increasing number of books on the market for the writer, both for professional and general purposes, particularly for non-English authors, for example, *Letter Writing*, in Collins Pocket Reference series (Collins 1994). This contains a useful list of abbreviations.

Phrasal verbs have become an 'in' subject and there is now a variety of books available. Check up on Amazon.com or Barnesandnoble.com.

A popular sales gimmick by data journals, often in December or January, is to supply encyclopaedic and other reference works on the accompanying CD – often the outgoing editions for the previous year, but a bargain at about $10 for the monthly magazine. Other gems on CDs from this source include full versions of word-processors, spread sheets, atlases and so forth. Even if you are not a subscriber to any of these journals, keep an eye open on your local newsagent's shelves.

F. British Standards Institution Publications

BSI has published a number of pamphlets, one of which, *Copy preparation and proof correction*, has been widely reproduced. However, those concerned with documents which have to comply with specific BSI standards will find the following useful:

BS 1629:1989 *Recommendations for references to published materials*

BS 4148:1985 *Specification for abbreviation of title words and titles of publications*

BS 5261-1:2000 *Copy preparation and proof correction. Part 1: Design and layout of documents*

BS 5261-2:2000 *Copy preparation and proof correction. Part 2: Specification for typographic requirements, marks for copy preparation and proof correction, proofing procedure*

BS 5261-3:2000 *Copy preparation and proof correction. Part 3: Specification marks for mathematical copy preparation and mathematical proof correction and their use*

BS 5605:1990 *Recommendations for citing and referencing published material*

BS 5848:1980 *Numbering of divisions and subdivisions in written documents (point-numbering)*

Appendix

It was not my intention that you should struggle through this book. I hope that you realised that it was a reference guide! Language is living, rules are flexible (there to be broken) and times change as the following (modified) from the Internet explains:

> The European Union Commissioners have announced that agreement has been reached to adopt ENGLISH as the preferred language for European communications, rather than GERMAN, which was the other possibility.
>
> As part of the negotiations, the British government conceded that English spelling had some room for improvement and has accepted a five-year phased plan for what will be known as EuroEnglish (Euro € for short).
>
> In the first year, 's' will be used instead of the soft 'c'. Sertainly, sivil servants will resieve this news with joy. Also, the hard 'c' will be replaced with 'k'. Not only will this klear up konfusion, but typewriters kan have one letter less.
>
> There will be growing publik enthusiasm in the sekond year, when the troublesome 'ph' will be replaced by 'f'. This will make words like 'fotograf' 20 per sent shorter. Confusion between 'ir' and 'er' will be standardised. In the therd year, publik akseptanse of the new spelling kan be expekted to reach the stage where more komplikated changes are possible.
>
> Guvernments will enkurage the removal of double letters, which have always ben a deterent to akurate speling. Also, al wil agre that the horible mes of silent 'e's in the languag is disgrasful, and they would go. Where 'our' is pronounced as 'or' (as in 'your'), the u will no longer be rekwird
>
> By the forth year, peopl wil be reseptiv to steps such as replasing 'th' by 'z', and 'w' by 'v'. Trublsum 'er' will be standardizd to 'ur' and 'ai' to just 'a'. ('ear' will now bekum 'er'). As for 'tion' the natral speling of 'shon' will be used.
>
> During ze fifz year, ze unesesary 'o' kan be dropd from vords kontaning 'ou', and similar changes vud of kors be aplid to uzur kombinashons of leturs.
>
> After zis fifz yer, ve vil hav a reli sensibl riten styl. Kapital letr E vil be riten as €. € vrivun vil find it ezi tu understand ech uzur. Zer vil be

no mor trubls or difikultis. Ze drem vil finali hav kum tru!

Of kors, yor speling cheker ma not be abl to korekt evry inakurasi but riters vil be abl to expres zemselvs freli wizout ani inhibishon. Publish and be damd.

Mi publisher ses that i am alredi!

(A kopi of zis tekst is avalibl in gurman, rushan and sevrl uzur langwigis.)